P9-EFI-583

THE LAST OF THE TRIBE

The Epic Quest to Save a Lone Man in the Amazon

Monte Reel

SCRIBNER
New York London Toronto Sydney

SCRIBNER
A Division of Simon & Schuster, Inc.
1230 Avenue of the Americas
New York, NY 10020

First Scribner hardcover edition June 2010

DESIGNED BY ERICH HOBBING

Manufactured in the United States of America

1 3 5 7 9 10 8 6 4 2

Library of Congress Control Number: 20090370974

ISBN 978-1-4165-9474-1
ISBN 978-1-4165-9716-2 (ebook)

Photographs are courtesy of Altair Algayer, pp. 2, 32, 144, 154, 212; Fred Pacifico Alves, pp. 16, 34, 48, 64, 84, 195, 222; Vincent Carelli/Vídeo Nas Aldeias, pp. 104, 132; Sydney Possuelo, p. 178; and Orlando Possuelo, p. 196.

To my family

"We need the tonic of wildness. . . . At the same time that we are earnest to explore and learn all things, we require that all things be mysterious and unexplorable, that land and sea be indefinitely wild, unsurveyed, and unfathomed by us because unfathomable."

—Henry David Thoreau, *Walden*

Contents

PANAMA
VENEZUELA
GUYANA
SURINAME
FRENCH GUIANA
Roraima
Amapá
COLOMBIA
Equator
ECUADOR
Amazonas
Pará
BRAZIL
Ceará
Rio Grande do Norte
Maranhão
Piauí
Paraíba
Pernambuco
PERU
Acre
Rondônia
Mato Grosso
Tocamins
Alagoas
Sergipe
Bahia
BOLIVIA
Brasília
Minas Gerais
Mato Grosso do Sur
Espírito Santo
São Paulo
PARAGUAY
Rio de Janeiro
PACIFIC OCEAN
CHILE
Tropic of Capricorn
Paraná
Santa Catarina
Rio Grande do Sur
ATLANTIC OCEAN
URUGUAY
ARGENTINA
0
1000 Miles
0
1000 Km

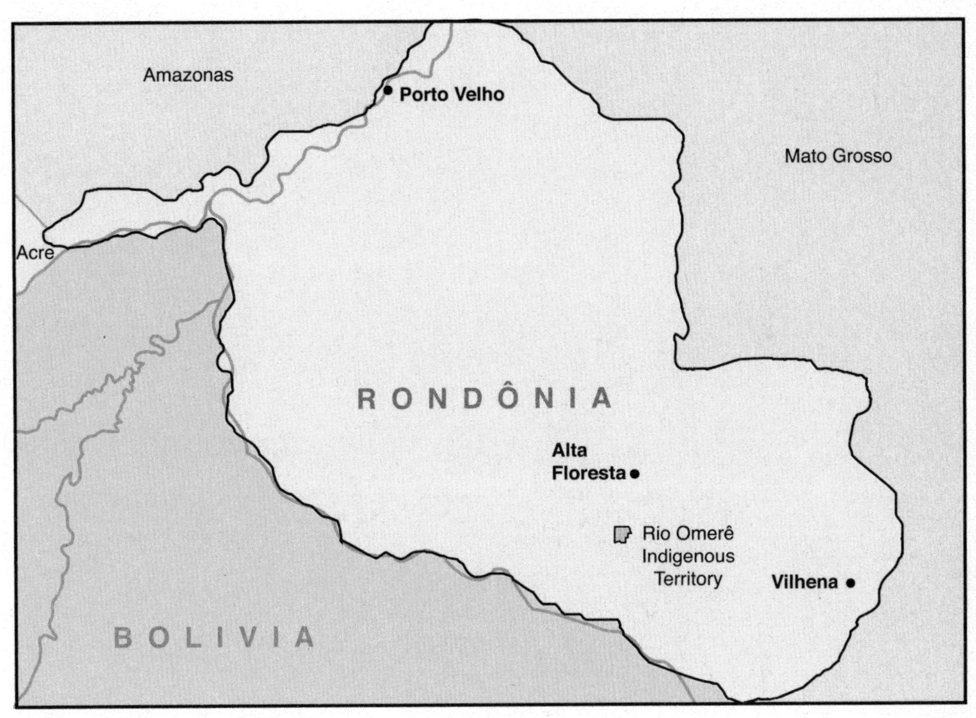
Amazonas
Porto Velho
Mato Grosso
Acre
RONDÔNIA
Alta Floresta
Rio Omerê Indigenous Territory
Vilhena
BOLIVIA

THE LAST OF THE TRIBE

Prologue

Behind a ragged green curtain of fern and palm fronds, a dry twig snapped unseen. It was an unnatural noise, a sharp note amid the softer sounds that hung in the air: the warble of antbirds, the leafy flutter of insect wings, a solitary man's respirations.

He was squatting in a contemplative pose. His elbow was resting on his leg, his chin was propped on the bend of his wrist. But he jumped to an expectant crouch upon hearing the twig crack.

Someone was approaching, trying to catch him by surprise. Through the leaves he saw figures dressed in colorful clothing. One of them whistled, trilling the note.

The watcher slipped around the corner of his hut and ducked inside to grab his weapon. With bow in hand, he peered through a slit in the sloppy lattice of palm thatch that formed his wall.

The approaching figures babbled in a foreign tongue. He notched an arrow into his bowstring. He extended the arrow's sharply fluted tip through the wall and took aim.

The men outside spoke softly among themselves. He watched them, and they watched him. When the men noticed the arrowhead protruding from the hut, they lowered their voices. After several minutes, they approached slowly with their palms held upward. When he moved the arrow, they danced backward. They seemed to trust him as little as he trusted them.

He stood frozen inside the hut, surrounded and outnumbered. Should he lay down his bow and step outside, preserving the prospect of peace? Or should he declare war?

For two hours he barely moved, paralyzed within the pause that separates drawing an arrow back, and letting it go.

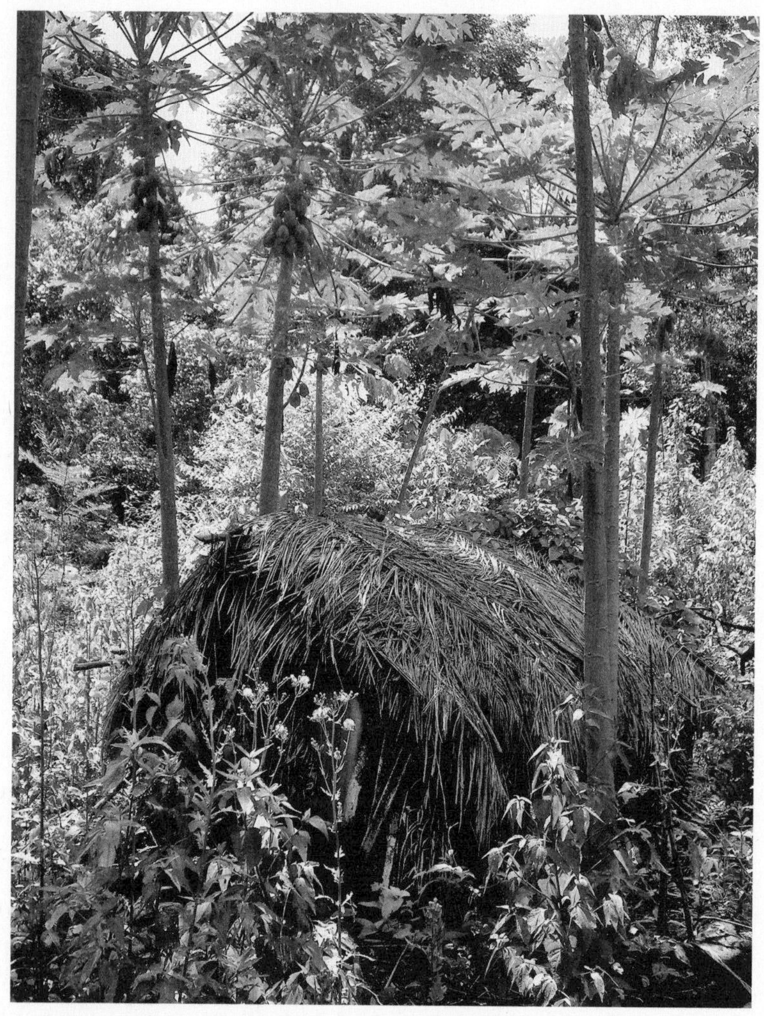

From what they could see,
he lived all alone in a tiny thatched hut.

CHAPTER ONE

The Hut

It began with a rumor, a scrap of conversation picked up by a health worker delivering antimalarial medicine in the scattered villages of southern Amazonia. In the middle of 1996, he stopped at a lumberyard in Brazil's Guaporé River Valley, near the Bolivian border. Loggers there spoke of a wild man who roamed the surrounding rain forest, which they occasionally ventured into in search of mahogany trees. The man was a naked savage, they said, probably an Indian. But he didn't appear to be part of any tribe. From what they could see, he lived all alone in a tiny thatched hut, with no apparent ties to another human soul.

That's where their story dead-ended. The few who claimed to have caught a blurred glimpse of the man said he was as quick and crafty as a jaguar—get near him, and he'd vanish into the forest's dappled shadows. Describing encounters with him apparently was like trying to remember an elusive dream: they were pretty sure it happened, but they couldn't quite grasp the details.

It was a flimsy splinter of jungle lore, but it stuck with the health worker when he left the lumberyard and eventually made his way to the town of Vilhena, where Brazil's federal agency in charge of Indian affairs maintained a regional outpost. He previously had met the man who ran that office, Marcelo dos Santos, while delivering medicines to one of the region's indigenous reserves.

If anyone could dismiss the rumor outright and label it a tall tale unworthy of a second thought, it was Marcelo. His job was to locate Indian tribes that remained isolated in the forest, completely cut off from the main current of Brazilian society. His small team of field agents was called the Guaporé Contact Front, one of five regional exploratory teams within the Isolated Indians Division of Brazil's National Indian Foundation, known as FUNAI. The Isolated Indians Division was less than a decade old, created just before the country ratified a new constitution in 1988. The new national charter specified that if Indians lived on a patch of rain forest, that land was theirs—not a single tree could be touched by an outsider. But a fundamental shortcoming threatened to completely undermine the document's intentions: no one knew how many tribes actually lived in Brazil's massive portion of the Amazon, or how much land they potentially could claim. So if a rancher stumbled across a previously uncontacted tribe in a part of the forest that he wanted to clear for grazing, the rancher had a natural incentive to chase the Indians off the property before the government could document their presence. The contact fronts were created to defuse the threat of clashes between settlers and tribes.

Marcelo was forty-two when he took the reins of the exploratory team in 1994, after twenty years as a field agent with FUNAI. One look at him and it was clear he didn't really fit in with the clean-cut farmers who dominated Vilhena's social circles. He cut his hair only when he felt like it, and he'd kept the blond beard that he grew in college, letting it go wherever it wanted, untrimmed. From his left earlobe dangled a loop of carved bark, a handmade earring common among members of the Nambiquara tribe he'd lived among for more than a decade. Give him a choice, and he just might walk down the street barefoot. Some of the farmers called him a hippie. A few turned the screws on the insult a little tighter: they called him a hippie who wanted to be an Indian. They weren't entirely wrong.

Marcelo's right-hand man was Altair Algayer, a twenty-three-year-old who had worked for Marcelo's predecessor. Altair had spent much of his life in or around the state of Rondônia's forests. He had a fourth-grade education and a mind like a thirsty sponge. If the truck broke down, Altair could fix it. If the team needed to build a permanent jungle encampment complete with shower and latrine, Altair could sketch the plans and build it. If they needed to be fed, he could track, shoot, and butcher a wild boar. He was lanky and lean, but as strong and durable as a packmule. Marcelo rarely went on an expedition without him.

Less than a year before, in September 1995, Marcelo and Altair had encountered two small Indian tribes that had never before been contacted peacefully by outsiders. The discoveries were hailed in the international press as the first of their kind in more than a decade in Brazil. For the Brazilian government, the experience had underscored the value of the contact fronts, and FUNAI was working to legally declare the newly demarcated territories as a single indigenous reserve. For Marcelo and Altair, the experience proved that the jungle, nearly five hundred years after outsiders began exploring its depths, was still capable of hiding mysteries.

So when the health worker arrived in Vilhena with the rumor about the spectral wild man believed to be an Indian, Marcelo paid close attention. The health worker passed along the name of a man at the lumberyard who might be able to tell him more.

Marcelo and Altair decided to pay him a visit. All they had to lose was a day or two, enough time to drive there and back.

Marcelo sat behind the wheel, steering the battered Toyota four-by-four across miles of dirt roads that were furrowed with wheel-deep ruts. Altair jostled beside him on the truck's unforgiving bench seat. The sun burned hot, and the wind rushing through the opened windows brought little relief, just dust and the throaty roar of the truck's engine. The noise was enough to turn a conversation into an exhausting shouting match, which is why they always traveled with a box full of cassette tapes, and the stereo cranked up loud.

The opening chords that blared from the dashboard speakers would have been instantly recognizable to almost any Brazilian: Jorge Ben's "País Tropical." The title of the song means "Tropical Country" in Portuguese, and it was something like an unofficial national anthem for many Brazilians, especially those of Marcelo's generation who'd gotten hooked on a back-to-the-land credo that flowered in the late 1960s. Marcelo shouted "Jorge!" as if calling out to an old friend:

I live in a tropical country,
Blessed by God and beautiful by nature.
(But oh, what beauty!)

Nature had been uncommonly generous in this riverine corner of Brazil, painting the landscapes according to a maximalist aesthetic that placed little value on restraint. This was nature in the extreme, laid on thick, without apology. The flora was irrepressible, accommodated by a rain forest that had enough room for just about anything—giant hardwood trees, ropy lianas, trembling ferns, fluorescent lichens, heavy fruits on bending limbs. The animals provided an equally gaudy display, if you had a keen enough eye to spot them behind a thousand shades of green: ocelots, toucans, tapirs, sloths, monkeys, peccaries, armadillos, caiman, and untold legions of insects that filled the forest with the hum of life. Scientists and environmental activists liked to say that between one third and one half of the world's total species—plant, animal, and microbe—could be found in the Amazon rain forest, but that was just a guess, because it was impossible to catalog them all. But even if the claim couldn't be proved, the spirit behind it rang true: there was a profusion of vitality in this region, and it was more than enough to overwhelm the most ambitious taxonomist.

Not everyone considered that a good thing. This part of Amazonia long ago had earned itself the nickname "the Green Hell" by those who likened it to a miasmal sump that didn't *brim* with life so much as *fester* with it. In the rain forest, the unremitting cycles of life and death are so tangled together that their differences quickly blur. By the time something dies, it has already started to become something else; the trunk of a dying tree is overtaken by fungi, and soon the tree becomes those fungi; the flesh of a peccary carcass instantly swarms with beetles, until beetles are all that's left. Individual distinctions grow nebulous, which can rattle the nerves of anyone who prefers a world defined by neatly ruled borders. The wilderness then becomes something that demands to be tamed and conquered, and civilization is separated from savagery.

Marcelo and Altair rejected that view. When they sang along with Jorge Ben on the truck stereo, they were singing about the forest, a place that was neither paradise nor perdition, but one they penciled in closer to heaven than hell on their private maps of the world. This overgrown domain was their *país tropical*.

But some of the landscape they drove through on the way to the lumberyard didn't fit the lyrics of the song. It wasn't tropical, and it wasn't beautiful. It was dead.

For miles on all sides, an ashen graveyard of charred stumps plotted the void where the forest recently stood. The land had been clear-cut with tractors and chains, then burned. The horizon was no longer obscured by treetops, but instead was washed out by a dirty white haze. Smoke was rising from live fires at the forest's sizzled edge, a frontier that crept a little farther from the road each day.

Every so often the slender trunk of a denuded *acuri* palm, with its armor of fire-resistant bark, stood tall among the encrusted termite mounds that blistered the burned crust of the earth. Some of the fields were littered with disorderly piles of sawed trunks, ready to be stacked onto enormous flatbed trucks. Marcelo and Altair had been passing those trucks all day; they were the same ones that had chewed up the roads for dozens of miles in every direction.

They regularly passed clusters of splintery gray shacks strewn along the roadside, fragile hovels that looked as if they'd collapse into kindling with one swift kick. The shacks housed the peasant laborers employed by the cattle ranches that were multiplying with bacterial efficiency throughout the region. Rondônia was still less than twenty years old, and in a single generation it had gone from a mostly unpopulated forest to the center of an agricultural explosion. As new roads began to fan throughout the region, this part of Amazonia was experiencing a rural migration that rivaled the conquest of the American West.

Boomtowns were popping up all over: little bursts of activity that invariably announced their presence with a roadside beer joint consisting of little more than a corrugated roof, a few plastic chairs, and an old pool table. Marcelo and Altair drove past such a bar when they approached the town of Chupinguaia on the way to the mill. A year before, the town couldn't be found on any map; the state had declared it a new municipality just a few months prior. The locals called it a "bang-bang town," one of several on the ragged fringe of Brazil's Wild West, and outsiders stopped at their own risk. Chupinguaia's population was anyone's guess—probably at least a few hundred—but it swelled on weekend nights, when the region's ranch hands hit the bars. Sunday mornings were a spectacle to behold.

Walk through the barren central square just after dawn, and you literally had to step over dozens of bedless ranch hands spread-eagled in the dirt, exactly where they'd passed out the night before. Everyone who called this place "lawless" was guilty of a slight imprecision of language: when Rondônia was granted statehood in 1981, plenty of laws went on the books; it's just that the government lacked the resources to enforce them.

That anything-goes atmosphere extended to the forest itself. Ranchers in the area had been known to fly over the trees in private planes spraying 2,4,5-trichlorophenoxyacetic acid, the internationally banned defoliant in Agent Orange. Worse, empty plastic drums of the chemical had been scavenged by at least one of the local Indian tribes, which had been using the containers to store water, unaware that the small print on the barrels warned against reuse. Frontier justice being what it was, the deeds went unpunished.

Marcelo and the other members of the Contact Front weren't cops, but when they witnessed illegal deforestation or other environmental crimes, they blew the whistle, calling federal prosecutors to complain. That didn't mean the police did anything about it. Hard evidence, such as earthmovers and chainsaws registered to a specific owner, could easily be moved before police were able to reach the areas in question. Outright denials of responsibility by landowners were so common that Marcelo had begun to invite Vincent Carelli, a former FUNAI agent with a passion for documentary film, to accompany the Contact Front on expeditions and document evidence with his video camera. Those whistle-blowing expeditions rankled a lot of ranchers and loggers. The Contact Front was quickly earning a reputation throughout Rondônia as an obstacle to progress.

Even before Marcelo and Altair decided to drive to the lumberyard to investigate the rumor of the lone Indian, some of the region's ranchers were publicly accusing the Contact Front of putting the interests of a few Indians above the overall economic health of the region. When the Contact Front had discovered those two isolated Indian tribes just months before, the ranchers who had already laid claim to those tribal lands banded together in defiance, hired a lawyer, and resolved to fight the government's demarcation of 193 square miles of land as an indigenous reserve, off-limits to development. Those ranchers had taken a clear stand. They had declared the Contact Front their enemy.

On September 3, 1995, Marcelo and Altair had made first contact with an isolated group of Kanoe Indians. The tribe had been reduced to only five survivors.

That peaceful encounter also had begun with a rumor. Before Marcelo and Altair had set out to find the Kanoe, Indian trackers believed that members of an isolated tribe lived in the area, but no one had seen them. Marcelo suspected that if a tribe was living there, its continued survival might be jeopardized by the chainsaws that were eating deeper into that tract of forest with each passing week.

Marcelo and Altair—with Vincent Carelli and his video camera following in their footsteps—explored the forest near the banks of the Omerê River. Marcelo walked in front, following a slender trail worn through the thick undergrowth. The trail appeared to be a natural inlet through the forest used by wild boar and other animals, but there was more to it than that. Some of the branches and stems flanking the path had been snapped in places that stood more than four feet off the ground. Few animals native to this forest stood that tall. More than likely, it meant that other humans had walked that trail before them.

For three days Marcelo's team had been hiking, crossing streams and following trails that led them deeper into the middle of nowhere. But on that third morning, they reached an area that had been partially burned. The ground had been reduced to soft white ash, and in the middle of that powdery residue they found the fresh imprints of bare human feet. The team twisted their shoulders out of their heavy backpacks and ventured deeper into the bush, carrying only the essentials. Altair propped a .22-guage Winchester rifle over his left shoulder. In his right hand he held a machete, which he waved in front of him in lazy arcs, clearing vines and branches to untangle the overgrown trail.

They inched through the forest with a measured vigilance, because making first contact with a tribe that is unaccustomed to visitors is risky business. Throughout Brazil's history, stories of first contacts were too often chronicles of violence and mayhem. In Rondônia in the early 1980s, the Uru-Eu-Wau-Wau Indians attacked an expedition from FUNAI with a fusillade of arrows, their barbed tips coated with poisonous curare. That was just one story of hundreds similar to it that loomed over the jungle's history like black clouds. But much of the violence wasn't started by the Indians. Wildcat miners in Rondônia, for example, had savagely beaten, robbed, and tortured Kithaulu Nambiquara Indians to get access to the gold they believed could be found on the tribe's reservation. Stories about *pistoleros* hired to clear prospective ranches of Indians were common in every bang-bang town.

"Look at this."

Marcelo stopped walking and inspected a tree. On its trunk he found one of the most common signs of Indian presence: someone had stripped the bark and hacked a wedge in the hollowed trunk to extract honey from a beehive inside. He continued up the path, then froze in his tracks and held a finger up, a signal for the others behind him to be quiet. He leaned forward, bending at the waist, listening. The others began to approach him, but he quickly turned and motioned for them to stay put.

"Wait! Back up!"

Someone was up ahead on the trail. Tentatively, Marcelo took a step forward, careful not to make too much noise in the leafy undergrowth.

There were Indians ahead, camouflaged by the foliage, but he didn't know how many. Maybe just one or two, maybe an entire tribe of a dozen or more. Maybe they were calm, or maybe they were poised in defense, with arrows notched and drawn. This was the most critical point of any first contact, the fulcrum upon which success or tragedy often teetered. Since the 1970s, 120 FUNAI workers had been killed in the Amazon, many at the hands of Indian tribes. Somehow Marcelo needed to try to let these Indians know that his team was friendly.

"Whooo!" Marcelo hooted, a sublinguistic greeting meant to get the attention of whoever was lurking at the end of the trail, something to let them know that he knew they were there. No response. He whistled.

About fifty feet ahead of them, two faces peered out from the leaves and palm fronds. A woman and a man stepped onto the path, padding toward the group. Both held bows and carried quivers of arrows.

"Amigo," Marcelo called to them.

The two Indians' faces were expressionless but wide-eyed and alert. Marcelo waved his hand, motioning for them to come ahead. He smiled warmly, trying to convey an aura of peace. The female Indian said something to the man, and they stopped on the trail. Marcelo walked slowly toward them, and the male lifted his bow slightly. The gesture didn't seem threatening, just cautious. Marcelo and the others continued to proceed at a ceremonial pace. The Indians observed them with tense stoicism, then offered Marcelo exactly what he'd been seeking: careful smiles.

Marcelo's shoulders dropped, and he chuckled.

The Indians held their hands out, palms up. Marcelo and Altair raised their hands in response and stepped forward. Each side of the encounter—the Indians and the members of the Contact Front—stood on the trail for a moment with their fingertips lightly entwined in a delicate, lingering handshake. Marcelo noticed that the hands of the male Indian, whose name they would learn was Purá, were shaking. He appeared to be in his early twenties. Purá's sister, Tiramantú, looked a couple of years older. Both wore short wooden pegs through their noses. In their earlobes and around their necks, they wore jewelry made from shells. Two-inch-thick bands fashioned from fibrous plants were tied around their upper arms. Large red feathers protruded from the tops of each of those bands, and a foot-long fringe of dried grass hung below. Each wore a two-piece hat made from deerskin and palm fibers—one piece was a tight skullcap, the other a ring-shaped brim that fitted over it. They also wore shorts fashioned from scavenged salt bags that had been left for cattle on the pasturelands bordering their patch of forest. Though the Indians had never before had extended contact with the outside world, the design of their clothing suggested they had, at one time or another, experienced glancing contact with the rubber tappers, miners, or ranch hands who had been traipsing through parts of these forests for centuries.

The two Indians took Marcelo and Altair by the hand and led them to their small village, deeper in the forest. The Indians fed them papayas and introduced them to the other three members of their tribe. Purá and Tiramantú talked in the shrill quarter tones of a sharp, chirpy language.

"Ba-tu, ba-tu," Tiramantú said, looking Marcelo in the eye before she broke up in enigmatic laughter. He smiled helplessly. He could speak the tribal language of the Nambiquara, a tribe native to the forests on the other side of the Guaporé Valley, but this language wasn't similar. He couldn't decipher a single word.

About a month later, scholars studied their language and determined that they were part of the Kanoe, a tribe that most believed had disappeared completely from the region after clashes with rubber tappers in the 1940s.

Vincent's footage of the encounter proved invaluable in contradicting local landowners who had insisted that the presence of an isolated tribe was nothing more than a fanciful myth, a romantic misconception standing in the way of agricultural development. The video prompted newspaper articles and television reports all over the world. *Time* magazine's piece was titled "An Amazon Discovery," and it quoted Sydney Possuelo, Marcelo's boss in Brasília, who explained that the Kanoe encounter was the first new discovery of an isolated tribe in Brazil in a decade. "We only make contact when the situation is dramatic," said Possuelo, who explained that the Kanoe might have been completely extinguished by the advance of land developers if the Contact Front hadn't taken action.

In the months following that initial encounter, the five Kanoe led Marcelo and Altair to another previously uncontacted tribe with a village about four miles through the jungle from theirs. That tribe was called the Akuntsu, and it had only seven surviving members. They were completely naked save for earrings, body paint from *urucum* berries, and armbands and anklets made of palm fibers. The Akuntsu and the Kanoe had been traditional enemies, but the pace of deforestation in the area had forced them to try to set aside their differences in the name of survival. In time, the explorers would learn that both of the tribes had been thinned out by pistolero raids. For decades, sweeping global forces had been converging upon the forest where they lived, ratcheting up local tensions to deadly extremes. The tribes had observed an undeclared truce in the face of a common enemy.

* * *

Since the discovery of the Kanoe and the Akuntsu, Marcelo and Altair were finding that more of the wooden gates erected at the borders of the ranches were padlocked. Some of the ranchers had gone so far as to station guards armed with machine guns at the gates. The Contact Front had earned a reputation as a nuisance to avoid.

But nothing blocked the dirt roads they followed around the ranch that sat at the entrance of the lumber mill. They drove over a rickety wooden bridge constructed with planks that were barely big enough for the Toyota's tires. One slip of the steering wheel, and they'd fall in the stream below.

The lumberyard was buzzing when they arrived. A warehouse stood in the middle of the yard, and the afternoon sun streamed through the cracks in the walls' irregularly spaced slats. The workers inside wore heavy white aprons, stained with the same airborne grit that they carried home in their lungs and throats. Forklifts ferried ten-foot sections of *peroba* trunks, some of them measuring five feet in diameter, toward an enormous conveyor saw. Using a heavy iron hook, two of the employees would position the trunks on a wheeled gurney, which fed the wood into the whirring blade of a large band saw. They sheared off the rounded edges of the trunk, squaring it down to its rosy heartwood, then slicing it into long, flat planks. The workers loaded the planks onto a lift and stacked them head-high in the yard. Like most of the wood that was trucked out of Rondônia daily, those planks could have ended up just about anywhere: as chairs in a dining room in São Paulo, or as kitchen cabinets in New York, or as coffee tables in London.

Across the road from that yard, Marcelo veered around the flatbed cargo trucks and found the building he'd been looking for: a collection of unfinished planks that had been nailed into a crude kitchen and commissary on the lumberyard's edge. Technically, the building was part of the logging mill, but the man inside wasn't officially employed by the ranch. His name was Gilson, and he'd been contracted to feed the loggers and ranch hands who worked its grounds. Essentially, Gilson was the company cook. And according to the health service worker who'd originally told Marcelo the story of the mysterious lone Indian, Gilson himself had seen the Indian's hut.

Gilson looked to be about thirty years old, with a peninsular hairline and a thick black beard trimmed with precision. He offered his visitors a seat at a plywood table in the middle of the room and he settled onto the stool across from them.

"So how did you find out about this Indian hut?" Marcelo asked.

Gilson said that the lumberyard employed men who scouted the forest for new cutting grounds, and two of those scouts told him they'd encountered an Indian. They didn't get a clear view of him, but saw him flee when they approached. Behind a nearby tree, they found bamboo arrows on the ground.

Those scouts got scared and left the area, afraid of being shot by a man who might still have been hiding nearby. But they returned the next day, and Gilson tagged along. Together they found the small thatched hut that appeared big enough for just one person.

Gilson told Marcelo and the others that he could show them the place, if they wanted to see it.

Marcelo told him that they most definitely did.

They followed Gilson to the sharply defined border between farm and jungle, and stepped into the bush. Over the next few days, they'd visit the site numerous times, searching for clues that might reveal who had built the hut and lived inside.

About a third of a mile into the forest, they came to a tree that had a wedge-shaped hole cut out of its trunk—the same type of honey cut they'd found just before they'd encountered the Kanoe. On the ground near the tree trunk, Marcelo found a bundled wig of sticky liana twine. He told the others that Indians often used that kind of twine as a sponge; they stuff it into the hole in the tree to absorb honey, then wring it out.

A few meters from that tree, they ducked under some leafy branches and emerged into a clearing big enough for a single hut. It stood about nine feet tall at the roof's peaked center, and it covered an area of about seven square feet. The walls were made of bundled palm wood, and the hut was roofed with dry, brown fronds. The leafy roof sloped down on all sides, forming eaves that ended within a couple feet of the ground. From the looks of the hut, it might have been the nest of some enormous ground-dwelling bird. The camouflaging effect of the materials was uncanny: if they hadn't been looking for it, they might have walked right by.

They ducked under the eaves and peered into a small opening in the wall before stepping inside. Gilson had been right: if more than one person had lived here, it would have been a tight fit. The dirt floor was littered with white ash from a small campfire in the corner. Judging from the coals, it hadn't burned in weeks.

The strangest part of the hut was the rectangular hole in the center of the floor. It was about three feet long, fifteen inches wide, and five and a half feet deep. It wasn't big enough to sleep in and didn't appear to be used for storage. It was unlike anything they'd ever seen in the huts of any of the other tribes in the region.

After that visit, Marcelo wasted no time preparing for a longer expedition. He believed that if the Contact Front didn't find the man soon, it was just a matter of time before someone else—maybe pistoleros hired by local land-grabbers—got to him first. He had no way of knowing how far the hunt would take them, or how consuming the mystery of the man's existence would prove.

All that the members of the Guaporé Contact Front knew for sure was that the rumor was more than a baseless fairy tale. Whoever had built the hut had recently decamped, retreating deeper into the forest. They chose to follow.

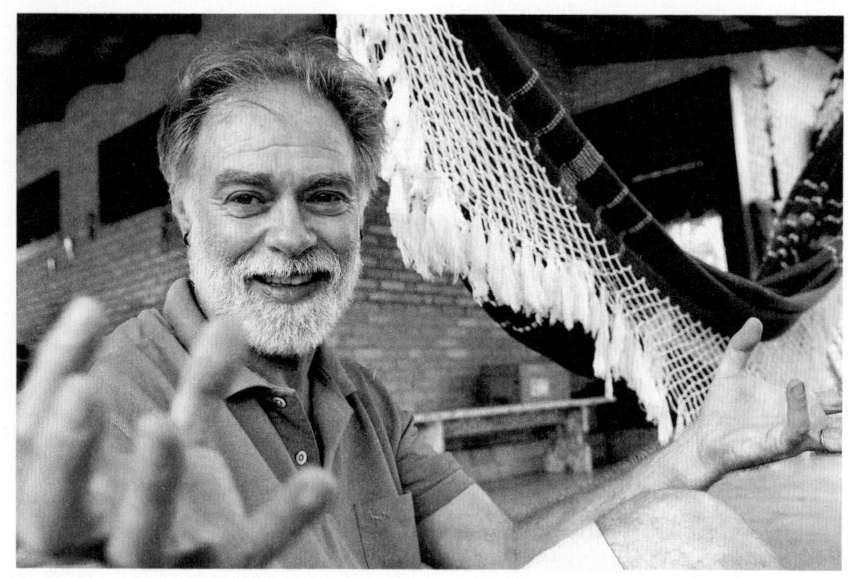

Marcelo dos Santos pictured outside his home in 2007.

CHAPTER TWO

Going Native

If Marcelo was destined to live in the forest, he was born in the wrong place. Vila Magdalena is a colorful art district that sticks out from much of the rest of São Paulo like a bright red boutonniere pinned to a drab suit. On the sidewalks, colorful galleries compete for attention with jazz bars. Marcelo's parents loved the bohemian vibe, and they raised a family in the middle of it.

When Brazil's military plotted a coup in 1964 and established a twenty-year dictatorship, his father began steeping Marcelo in the lexicon of civil disobedience. The senior Dos Santos was a painter and stage designer for the municipal theater company, and he dabbled in socialist politics. It was a dangerous hobby at a time when South America was caught in a Cold War stranglehold of dictators, dirty wars, and *desaparecidos*. In the Dos Santos household, the military government was associated with repression, confinement, unthinking conformity, inflexibility, and brutality.

Which is why it came as something of a shock when Marcelo took a government job in the summer of 1974.

He stumbled into it. Regular camping trips with his father during his youth had instilled in Marcelo a love of nature, which led him to study biology in college. But when he contemplated how he might be able to put his degree to use—working as a pharmacist or lab rat—his mood blackened. One of his friends had recently moved to Porto Velho, a town fifteen hundred miles northwest of São Paulo, to take a job with INCRA, a federal agency in charge of demarcating land. He called Marcelo and told him that the trees were huge and the forests seemed endless. In other words, it was the kind of place Marcelo loved.

Marcelo sold almost everything he owned—a rash act with which his dad, who'd taken to calling himself a Communist, couldn't convincingly argue. A few days later, he was standing outside the bus station in Porto Velho. Situated on the Rio Madeira, the city had a backwater quality to it. Diversion centered around a string of outdoor bars that sat atop the steep riverbank. Brazilian pop music wafted over the water, where beer drinkers shielded their eyes from the sun's glare to watch jumping river dolphins arc out of the muddy river.

Marcelo had figured he would ask around and someone would point him in the direction of his friend or the INCRA office. It wasn't that easy. He didn't have an address or a phone number, so he wandered the sun-baked streets, hoping to stumble across one or the other.

He found FUNAI instead.

The small office was empty and locked. But Marcelo was seduced by a notion of Indians that was based more on romance than reality: they shared all, hoarded nothing, led lives that rarely intersected with the bureaucracy of Brazil's military authority. The idea of working for the Fundação Nacional do Índio in one of its wilderness outposts captured his imagination. He set out to correct the geographical accident of his birth.

He waited outside the office, but no one showed up. He learned that the local agency head, Apoena Meirelles, was at a camp near the town of Rio Pequeno, and Marcelo went there to find him.

Apoena was a dark and wiry twenty-five-year-old with bushy hair and a mustache, a man who'd already become a legend among Amazonian explorers. He was a second-generation *sertanista,* a uniquely Brazilian profession that's part jungle explorer, part ethnologist, part government civil servant. His father, Francisco "Chico" Meirelles, had led many of Brazil's expeditions to "pacify" Indians from the 1930s to the 1960s. Chico Meirelles followed a strategy of assimilation, the idea that Indian tribes should be folded into the rest of Brazilian society, not left isolated from it. He fought against the creation of Indian reserves, believing that encouraging Indian resistance to the inexorable march of progress would only create problems. Those views still ruled Brazil's official Indian policy the day Marcelo walked in FUNAI's door and met Chico's son.

Apoena was raised among Xavante Indians to be an expert woodsman, and when he came of age, he picked up where his father left off, leading huge "peacemaking" expeditions into the bush. But like many others in his generation, Apoena was slowly veering away from his elders' strict opposition to protectionism, and had begun advocating on behalf of the Indians' sovereignty and rights to land. But he was a walking contradiction, split by the duality that tore at the institutional heart of FUNAI: he was an Indian advocate whose direct involvement in Indian affairs often seemed to do more harm than good. His expeditions, launched under the banner of Indian protection, sometimes incited violent clashes, the jungle equivalent of gang brawls, with casualties on both sides. The *Cultural Survival Newsletter* in 1980 tried to translate this grim incongruity into an explicit image: if all the Indians who'd died as a result of Apoena's peacemaking campaigns were laid out head to toe, the line of bodies would stretch for more than half a mile.

Apoena offered Marcelo a job. He started out working for meals, without salary. He'd type reports, mow the grass around the office—whatever Apoena asked him to do. But soon one of the researchers at the camp suggested that Marcelo was selling himself short, that he should try to enroll in one of the classes FUNAI had begun offering to recruit a new generation of sertanistas.

That new training program was the agency's latest attempt to try to clear an institutional reputation that had been ripped to shreds by corruption and incompetence. FUNAI was relatively new, having taken the place of a previous agency called the Indian Protection Service, which had collapsed in 1968 under a staggering record of institutional venality. A 5,115-page government inquiry had found that of the IPS's 700 employees, 134 were charged with crimes and another 38 had been hired fraudulently. Agents had massacred entire tribes using everything from dynamite to poison. Agency officials had abducted young girls to work as slaves. The former head of the agency was charged with forty-two crimes. "It's not only through the embezzlement of funds, but by the admission of sexual perversions, murders, and all other crimes listed in the penal code against Indians and their property, that one can see that the Indian Protection Service was for years a den of corruption and indiscriminate killings," Brazil's attorney general, Jader Figueiredo, told a reporter at the time.

FUNAI replaced the service shortly after the report, and the new institution wasted little time picking up right where the old one left off. In 1971, a doctor visiting the Parakanan Indian village in the northern Brazilian state of Pará found that thirty-five Indian women—and, not coincidentally, two male FUNAI agents—were infected with venereal disease. A year later, a FUNAI agent told the press that the incident in the Parakanan village wasn't an isolated one. After he resigned, he said that the agency viewed Indians only as something to exploit in almost every way imaginable, and cared not a bit about their survival. He lashed out at the government's ambitious plans to slash highways throughout Amazonia: the big development projects designed to boost the country's industrial sector were killing its natives. "I am tired of being a grave-digger of the Indians," the agent said. "I do not intend to contribute to the enrichment of economic groups at the cost of the extinction of primitive cultures."

Years later Marcelo would realize that FUNAI's attempt at renewal by recruiting new sertanistas was just another halfhearted attempt at plastering over deeply rooted problems with a public relations campaign. But in 1974, Marcelo was optimistic. He believed that if enough of the new agents were sincere, FUNAI might turn itself around. He looked into enrolling in the program and learned that he had to take a placement test to qualify. The test was in São Paulo.

Soon he was knocking on his dad's door in Vila Magdalena, explaining that he'd come back to one of the largest cities on Earth so he'd have the chance to live in the middle of nowhere.

If anyone found bare human footprints in the forests of southern Rondônia in the late 1970s, they might have belonged to Marcelo. He'd walk for miles, his bare feet collecting scars as they tripped over the rough forest floor. Carrying a bow and arrow, he would scan the treetops for game to hunt, listening for the telltale hoot of the furry spider monkeys that could be seen swinging from branch to branch, one after another, in groups of three or four. The monkeys were safe. Marcelo's aim with a bow and arrow was nothing short of pathetic.

For almost twelve years, from 1979 to 1990, Marcelo lived among the Nambiquara Indians. When he started, his job was to help organize a program that aimed to nurse the tribe back from the edge of extinction. He was hired to serve as a liaison between the Indians and federal agencies, including the national health institute responsible for providing the tribe medicines required to fight the diseases they'd been exposed to from outsiders.

As recently as the 1960s, the Nambiquara was considered one of the most primitive tribes in South America. Its members slept on the bare ground, wore no clothes, and used few tools. The French anthropologist Claude Lévi-Strauss had spent almost a year with them in the 1930s, noting that the tribe's population had diminished to five hundred from an estimated ten thousand when they were first "discovered" in 1907. In the Nambiquaras' case, measles did much of the damage. An outbreak in 1946 hit them so hard that, according to legend, they couldn't bury the dead.

Marcelo lived with a subband of the Nambiquara called the Negarote. The Negarote once numbered about three hundred, but had been reduced to a mere eighteen members by 1979. Their territory was in a transition area between rain forest and savanna, and like the rest of the forest in Rondônia and in the neighboring state of Mato Grosso, it was shrinking.

In the beginning Marcelo lived with a small family in their hut, like a foreign adoptee. The Indian jewelry he wore in his ears and around his neck wouldn't fool anyone into believing that he was one of them, but the Indians loved Marcelo like one of their own. He quickly earned a reputation within FUNAI as a rebel, and he didn't seem to care if his apparent lack of institutional loyalty rubbed his bosses the wrong way. In letters to them, he'd slam the workers that the government sent to help the tribe in times of crisis, such as the employees of a health clinic who didn't live up to Marcelo's standards during one malarial outbreak in 1983. "They think of nothing but their paychecks," he wrote to FUNAI headquarters, "and don't give a damn about the Indians."

Instead of identifying with his fellow bureaucrats, he preferred to align himself with the tribes. The romantic concepts that lured him into FUNAI didn't dissolve on contact with the Indians; they grew stronger. Instead of observing their culture at a diplomatic distance, he dove in and tried to emulate it, regardless of the fact that he wasn't fully prepared to do so.

When they ate slimy insect larvae collected by placing *buriti* palms in the dirt for forty days, he ate them too, then tried to ignore the swelling in his throat caused by an allergic reaction. For a full two years he lived completely barefoot, until his feet got so sore and battered he was forced to abandon the idea if he wanted to keep up with the other men when they hunted. After that, he wore flip-flops. Throughout his years with the Negarote, his skin was pocked with bites. Ticks latched on to his ankles and burrowed into his hair, and he'd dig them out the best he could. He suffered through malarial shivers, but all of that was part of the deal he'd made when choosing this kind of life. *If you want to be one with nature,* he discovered, *you have to let nature be one with you.*

Such zeal did wonders for his relationships with tribe members, but it came with a clear trade-off. The lifestyle, as many sertanistas before him had discovered, significantly limited his romantic prospects. As a field agent, dating a tribe member would have been an inexcusable ethical breach, and it wasn't easy to find anyone else who could tolerate his far-flung, thatched-roof lifestyle. For many FUNAI field agents, the dating pool is restricted to social workers with a penchant for fieldwork. In Marcelo's case, it was a nurse who specialized in treating the region's tribes. They eventually married during the years he worked with the Nambiquara, but the relationship ended in divorce—far from unusual among young field agents. His relationship with the tribes of the region proved more lasting.

He tried to tell his friends and family that the Indians were simply happier than the people he'd grown up among in São Paulo. Marcelo believed their happiness was unsinkable: in circumstances that would have reduced most people to tears, he never saw the Indians fall into depression. Their lack of emphasis on material acquisition, their unhurried pace, their contentment with living in the present moment—in his eyes, all of it made their relatively simple life qualitatively better than the modern analogs. It was a whopper of a generalization, and it left Marcelo vulnerable to a dismissive charge: Marcelo had fallen for the myth of the noble savage, viewing their world as some sort of Edenic throwback, a Paradise Lost. The fact that the Negarote culture—idyllic or not—was disappearing before his eyes defined his role in the tribe. He was an advocate, not a liaison.

By the time he had moved in to live among them, the Indians had already experienced years of occasional contact with the outside world. They cooked their food over their fires in aluminum pans, and they hunted with shotguns. Marcelo sometimes drove them in his Jeep to a nearby town to trade handmade arrows and necklaces for knives, axes, hoes, and shotgun shells. Traditionally, the tribe had been seminomadic, ranging over a wide territory to hunt game and follow the seasons of certain flowering fruits, which bloomed in different pockets of forest at different times. But with the new tools and weapons, they didn't need to roam as widely. They were still a long way from being sedentary, but Marcelo could see that traditions were failing. He felt a little guilty.

He tried to set an example by embracing many of the customs the tribesmen were abandoning. On hunts, while everyone else carried shotguns, Marcelo toted his bow and arrow. Instead of the ringing blast of a gun, he wanted to hear the quietly plucked note of a bowstring, the whispered hiss of the arrow, the sudden silence after contact. Of course, when he took aim at a bird in a tree, he'd almost always hear a less poetic sound: the twang of the arrow as it got stuck in a high branch. Another handmade arrow, which represented a full day of work, was lost in the unreachable heights of the forest.

The Indians regarded him as a gullible dreamer, until one day during a long hunt they ran out of shotgun shells. As they walked back to their village, they saw a group of wild boars nosing among the leaves on the path ahead. They all looked to Marcelo and to his bow and arrows.

He handed his bow to an Indian who was a far better shot. Within minutes, the hunters were trudging back to the village, hauling the heavy carcasses of two bristle-haired pigs. They feasted for days.

It marked the beginning of something of a return to tradition for the tribe. Just months before, the Xavante tribe in Mato Grosso had clashed violently with loggers, and the government began taking away their guns, leaving them at the mercy of archery skills that had turned rusty as the tribe's integration into the modern world had become more complete. The Negarote heard of the Xavantes' struggles and decided that maybe Marcelo was on to something: a return to bows and arrows might be wise. So for a year and a half, they voluntarily abandoned their firearms and started carving arrows again. The sound of arrows in the air was the sound of a victory for Marcelo: the traditional had won out over the modern.

It was short-lived.

By the early 1990s, pressure on the Negarote to sell timber on its lands to loggers had escalated to the edge of war. Logging companies were making deals with tribes throughout the region, trading food and guns for access to the mahogany that stood on their reserves. The Negarote, in part because of Marcelo's urging, refused. Another subband of Nambiquara—the Nambiquara do Campo—was recruited by loggers to pressure the Negarote to surrender its wood. Loggers and miners began hiring Indians from that tribe to serve as armed guides during incursions into Negarote territory. The idea of bows and arrows suddenly seemed quaint. The Negarote took up their guns. By 1991, two loggers and two miners had been killed during clashes, which helped spark an anti-Indian fever that swept through the towns of the Guaporé Valley. Attacks on the Indian villages became common. Death threats against non-Indians who defended the tribes—FUNAI agents such as Marcelo included—rose from whispers to shouts. Someone tried to burn down FUNAI's regional office in Vilhena.

Marcelo was horrified. The happiness he'd sworn was an inseparable part of the Indians' lives seemed a naive memory. Within months, even legislators in the U.S. Congress were talking about how illegal logging and the international timber trade had made the prospect of large-scale violence frighteningly likely. During a hearing of the Foreign Affairs Committee, one witness described Marcelo as a FUNAI agent "who has worked tirelessly to move the agency and local authorities to enforce the law." The witness added that Marcelo was forced to leave the state after years of increasingly menacing death threats.

It was true. One day in 1992, federal police had to go into the Negarote village and rescue Marcelo from a firefight between Indians and loggers. He lay down flat in the back of a police car as they sped away from the village, fearing that if anyone associated with the loggers saw him, they'd open fire.

He was shuttled to Vilhena, where the police put him on the first flight to Cuiabá, more than four hundred miles away. It would be three years before he came back to Rondônia, to take over leadership of the Guaporé Contact Front. And when he returned, he knew very well that even if traditional cultures have some powerful virtues, they're virtually powerless when facing the advance of a mechanized army of newcomers.

When the modern world comes crashing in, very little survives the collision.

In the middle of 1996, days after Gilson first showed them the mysterious hut on the edge of the logging camp, Marcelo and Altair began taking short hikes to look for signs of the Indian nearby. A narrow path led them to a second hut a little less than two miles from the first one. It was built in the same style as the first, and was roughly the same size. It also appeared to have been recently abandoned.

Those two huts suggested that the man who built them was leading a seminomadic lifestyle, living in one place and then abandoning the area when outsiders inched too close. But that assumption was nothing more than a guess, based on logic and a few leaps of imagination. He could have been an Indian who had left his tribe temporarily, scouting the forest before returning to his larger tribe. That sort of separation wasn't common among the region's tribes, but without more information they couldn't discount the possibility. To collect more evidence, Marcelo decided to launch a full expedition, hoping to find where the man had gone.

He invited Vincent Carelli to accompany the Contact Front, which in addition to Altair included a rotating cast of experienced woodsmen who helped them hack through the forest and make camp during long treks. On the first expedition, the group included just one other employee—Paulo Pereira, who'd been working for the Contact Front for several years before Marcelo had taken over. On a morning in August, the four of them gathered in the encampment that FUNAI had recently constructed halfway between the Kanoe and Akuntsu villages. The area had been officially declared an Indian reserve just days before—it was called the Rio Omerê Indigenous Territory, named after a nearby river. The months after previously isolated tribes were exposed to outside society were notoriously perilous, with tribes often losing members to new diseases or clashing with an influx of new and unknown visitors. The new camp served as a field station where health workers could stay if the tribes needed them, and where the Contact Front could monitor the reserve to make sure no one entered the land without permission.

Situated on the banks of a murmuring brook, the camp featured a pavilion-style thatched-roof hut where half a dozen people could string their hammocks for the night. The bamboo walls were draped with mosquito netting. Outside in the yard, the hum of an electric generator competed with the squawks of speckled hens and roosters that roamed through a garden sprouting with corn, pineapple, and tomato plants.

A large wooden table dominated the kitchen area, where Marcelo unrolled a poster-size satellite image of the Guaporé Valley. On the image, virgin areas of forest showed up as dark green. Partial clearings within those areas were a pale green. Pastureland and other completely deforested patches were pinkish-gray. About half of the area had already been clear-cut, according to the image. The image was the most recent one that Marcelo could get from Brazil's space agency, but it was more than a year old and already out of date. Numerous clearings they had seen on the way to the camp weren't reflected on the satellite image.

Marcelo pressed a finger to the map's lower left-hand corner to indicate their current location, as the others bent over the image and squinted. Marcelo then pinpointed the location of the huts they had found with Gilson's help, about twelve miles away. They could see the clearing of the lumberyard, as well as those of two nearby ranches—one owned by the logging company's proprietor, the other by two brothers named Hercules and Denes Dalafini. Their ranch, called the Modelo, consisted of a few cattle grazing tracts surrounded by standing rain forest. Looking at the image, it seemed clear that the Indian had most likely fled into the forest owned by the Dalafini brothers and away from the clearings on the other side of the huts.

Marcelo told the others that he guessed the Indian might have lived in the first hut for quite a while, but likely had abandoned the second hut just days after he had built it. When he and Altair visited that hut, they found seven corn plants nearby.

"He cleared the land by hand," Marcelo told them. "He planted the corn but left shortly after that, not waiting for it to grow."

Marcelo laid a sheet of tracing paper over the satellite image, and with a pencil began to create a map routing their upcoming expedition, which would take them into the Modelo's forested property. Altair consulted satellite coordinates to help Marcelo plot the dirt roads they would need to traverse to get as close as possible to the areas they sought to explore on foot.

On the way, they planned to visit some of the workers on neighboring ranches to see if the workers could tell them anything more about rumored tribes in the forest.

Altair told him that he'd already visited one of those ranches, but he wasn't able to explore the property.

"There was a guy at the gate," Altair said, "and he was guarding it with a gun."

The landowners had already learned that the Contact Front was snooping around, and they seemed determined to make the investigation as difficult as possible.

Before setting out on the expedition the next morning, the group visited the five-person Kanoe village to pick up two new members of the Contact Front: Purá and his female cousin, Owaimoro.

Marcelo believed that if the Indian was somewhere out there in the forest, two Indians who'd spent their lives surviving in the same environment might prove invaluable when searching for traces of human presence. And if the group happened to stumble upon the Indian himself, Marcelo believed that Purá and Owaimoro also might help the Contact Front communicate with him. If the encounter eventually came down to one scared Indian facing a group of unknown strangers, Marcelo figured the Contact Front could use all the diplomatic help it could get.

The group arrived at the village with an elderly translator who spoke the Kanoe language, and they waited for Purá and Owaimoro to pack for the trip.

Purá filled a wicker basket with papayas and corn, and he armed himself with dozens of bamboo arrows that he bundled together with rope. Through his nose, he wore a large feather that came from a wild turkey like the one that was clucking around his feet as he packed. The T-shirt he wore—a gift from a health service worker—was Swiss-cheesed with more than fifty holes from an attack of leaf-cutter ants.

Like the rest of her tribe, Owaimoro had the rugged build of a woman who'd spent every minute of her twenty-plus years in a forest that forced her to fend for herself. Her bare feet were calloused from regularly accompanying Purá on hunts. Her legs were short and sturdy. She wore earrings made from shells and more than a dozen necklaces of twine and shell. She almost always wore the two-piece hat of deerskin and palm. As she prepared to leave for the expedition, she brought her pet, a tufted capuchin monkey. It was her constant companion. A rope was tied around its neck and attached to a strap around Owaimoro's chest. The monkey sat on her shoulders in a constant state of curious agitation, peering this way and that, reacting to every noise with a nervous jerk of the head.

Along with the elderly Kanoe translator, they piled into the backseat of the Toyota, sitting shoulder-to-shoulder, the feathers in their armbands touching. Altair drove, Vincent rode shotgun, and Marcelo and Paulo followed them in another truck. After about two hours of driving, they reached a small clearing and parked at the side of the road. They unloaded their backpacks and baskets from the trucks and set off on foot, beginning an expedition they expected would last several days.

They walked through the forest toward the second of the huts they had found earlier. When they got close, Purá began scanning the area for clues. Clutching his bow and arrows, he stepped lightly across twigs and fallen leaves, with Owaimoro following his footsteps. Marcelo had told them all that the hut appeared to have been abandoned, but Purá wasn't convinced. He pointed out a ring about four feet off the ground around the trunk of a tree. It wasn't a honey cut, nor was it a tap mark on a *caucho* tree used to collect the gluey latex that almost all the tribes of the region used as fuel for stick torches. He told the translator that he didn't know what the purpose of the ring might be.

Nearby, what appeared at first to be a random assortment of palm fronds, low to the ground and a couple of yards off the nearest natural path, caught Marcelo's attention. The fronds had been artfully arranged to create a curtain of leaves that a man could duck behind, unseen. Purá and Owaimoro recognized it as a hunting blind, a wall of vegetation built to conceal a bow hunter waiting for wild game to approach along the narrow path. They studied the surrounding forest for traces of recent use but saw none.

When they found the hut, Purá peered at it for several moments from behind a tree. Then he walked toward it slowly, with eyes wide.

After circling the hut, Purá removed a piece of palm wood from its exterior to create an opening in the wall. He peered inside, then removed the ring brim from his hat and hung it on one of the twigs that jutted from the hut's eaves. He stepped through the small door he had created.

Thin bars of light shone through the hut's latticed roof. Purá's brown foot came down upon soft ash, leaving a broad-toed footprint and raising a tiny cloud of chalky dust. He carefully stepped around the rectangular hole in the middle of the hut. Through the opening in the wall, Marcelo handed Purá a foot-long flashlight. Purá shone it down the hole and bent at the waist to peer inside. A few sticks lay longwise over the hole, and from them hung remnants of liana fibers. Purá picked up one of the long sticks and stuck it down into the hole, banging at the hole's hard dirt walls.

Marcelo turned to the translator and said, "I don't know if this hut is for one person or two." The translator asked Purá if he had any guesses.

Purá said he had no idea.

The translator examined the fibers that hung from the sticks over the hole and theorized that it had been a firm, hammocklike sling that hung over the hole, kind of like a seat.

"He sleeps sitting," the old man guessed, "not lying down. He's half inside the hole, but not all the way."

The group stood there for a while, tossing around theories about the hut, the hole, and its occupant that were little more than wild guesses. The team had already done some research and found that in all of the literature about Indians of Rondônia, there had never been mention of a tribe that dug similar holes inside their huts. Marcelo had hoped Purá or Owaimoro might see it and offer an answer the others had overlooked, but they were equally stumped.

Eventually the group departed the clearing, searching for traces in the vegetation that might indicate where to go next. After several minutes of walking, Altair spotted some dead leaves near the trail and slowed his pace. Something didn't look right.

When he bent to investigate, he saw that the leaves covered a deep hole in the ground.

He cleared them away, uncovering a hole that was at least as deep as the one inside the hut. But this one wasn't empty. He knelt at the edge of the hole and reached deep inside—as deep as he could without falling all the way in—and yanked hard at whatever was at the bottom. Eventually he shook it loose, and he pulled up a spike made from *paxiuba,* a hard-barked palm. The tip of the spike had been carved to a sharp point. It was one of several spikes that jutted up from the bottom of the hole.

A careful search of the area revealed that several more of the holes had been camouflaged in the undergrowth.

The jungle around them was full of pitfalls.

They made camp late that afternoon by tying their hammock ropes to tree trunks. Altair smoked turtle meat over a fire, while Marcelo studied their expedition maps. They planned to continue hiking, and based on the clear signs of presence they had already found, the prospect of a face-to-face encounter suddenly had become real. Frighteningly real, in some ways. The Indian they were tracking observed customs that the Kanoe couldn't comprehend, such as digging the hole inside the hut, so the chances of Purá and Owaimoro understanding his language were slim. Based on the evidence they'd discovered so far, Marcelo believed the Indian was from an uncontacted tribe. Marcelo's previous encounter with such a tribe, the Kanoe, had been a happy one, but what if it was a fluke? Brazil's history of bloody first contacts with isolated tribes meant that the group couldn't discount the possibility that the Indian would fight if approached by enigmatic strangers.

That night they all lay in their hammocks, bone tired but unable to sleep. It wasn't the uncertainty of an encounter, however, so much as Owaimoro's monkey. The little thing wouldn't shut up. She'd tied it to a tree, and it was hopping around nonstop with a case of jangled nerves, shrieking like a siren. The more it shrieked, the more everyone else groaned.

Everyone except for Owaimoro. If the monkey was upset, he was upset for a reason. He was an extra pair of eyes and ears in a jungle full of threats. Owaimoro got up and began looking around the perimeter of their camp, following the monkey's cues. The others did the same.

Lurking in the vegetation beside their hammocks, they found what the monkey had been trying to warn them about: a snake.

Just a little snake, but it was one less thing they had to worry about.

After a few days and nights in the forest, the team's efforts to track down more clues ended in frustration. The forest was far too big to canvass. To get to the bottom of this, multiple expeditions would be necessary, on multiple plots of property.

Because the Contact Front existed under the larger umbrella of Brazil's Justice Ministry, the team members had permission to explore the region's forests, even those tracts that had been claimed by private landowners. But when Marcelo and Altair began individually touring some of the ranches in the area, the workers often demanded to see an individual warrant—a formality that forced Marcelo to waste a couple days waiting for paperwork to arrive from Porto Velho. On their way to explore a small plot of forest next to a property called the Cachoeira Ranch, the landowner even tried to block their access to a public road that skirted his property. "It was taxing," Marcelo wrote to his bosses in Brasília in September 1996, describing the incident. "Without any possibility of dialogue, I determined that we abandon the place immediately, and we left the property."

In the weeks after the first expedition, Marcelo and Altair continued to explore various tracts of forests in the region. Sometimes they took short day hikes, sometimes they camped for a night or two. During one of those early trips the two men trudged for two days along the banks of one of the dozens of tributaries that vein the forests of the Guaporé Valley, assuming that the Indian would most

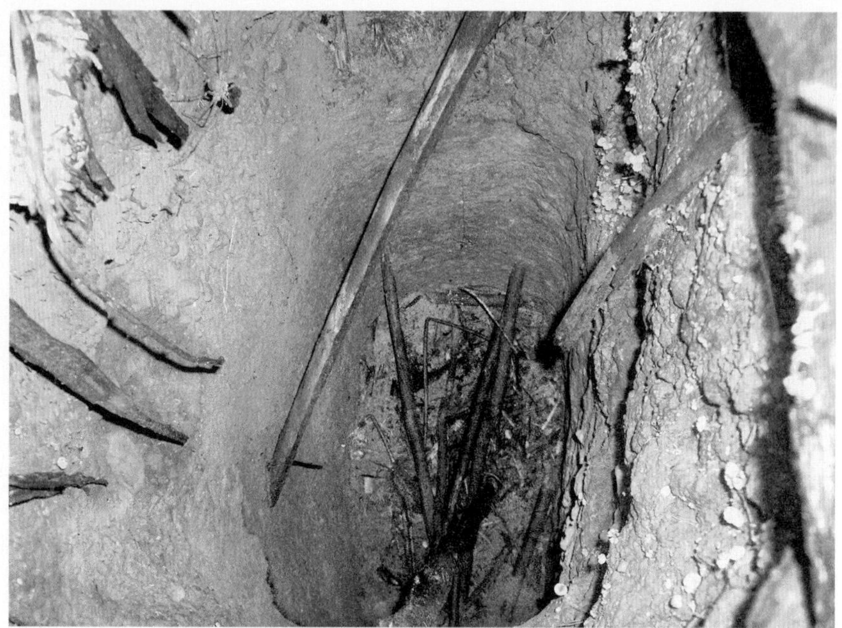

Inside the lone Indian's hut was a rectangular hole, about three feet long, fifteen inches wide, and five and a half feet deep.

Purá, a member of the Kanoe tribe, places gifts of food outside one of the Indian's huts discovered during a Contact Front expedition.

likely make his home near a water source. The stream jagged through the forest onto the Socel Ranch, a property that bordered both the logging mill property and the Dalafini brothers' tract of forest. After making camp on the first evening of the hike, Marcelo jotted down a few notes about what they'd seen.

> Clean forest, high, rich and exuberant. A lot of animal tracks, tapirs, monkeys howling, wild turkeys flying and jacus whistling. What beauty!!! We didn't see signs of indigenous presence during our hike, nor in a great muddy mire that we passed through. The weather was dry and pleasant, though it turned cold at night. We stopped to camp on the banks of the narrow river. In the morning we will go up a tributary of the left bank, which flows a little below. During the night, the cutter ants attacked, forcing us to hang our backpacks and other things from ropes.

Marcelo was in his element, and he loved it. Surrounded by thick trees on all sides, it was sometimes hard to imagine that the landscape was more than a reservoir of natural beauty. But the following morning, he and Altair discovered dozens of overgrown trails crisscrossing the forest, cut by loggers who had scouted the woods about five years before, judging by the vegetation that had tried to reestablish itself there.

Marcelo's notes from that point on in the journey lost their rhapsodic tone. It was no longer so easy to forget that the rain forests were battlegrounds and that Indian tribes weren't the only ones whose livelihoods were intricately tied to those dark green places on the map.

The Contact Front constructed this encampment in the Rio Omerê Indigenous Territory, about halfway between the villages of the Kanoe and the Akuntsu tribes.

CHAPTER THREE

A Land Without Men

Marcelo believed the Indian was living somewhere in the forest that surrounded the Modelo Ranch, owned by the Dalafini brothers. No signs or fences separated that land from the other forested properties that bordered it; the entire area appeared as a unified expanse of unbroken rain forest. But throughout the sprawling wild lands of Rondônia, invisible property lines divided the forest into individual lots of 100 hectares, or about 250 acres, each.

It was rare to find a landowner there who wanted to talk about Indians, and many looked skeptically on anyone who tried to bring up the subject. Their distrust was rooted in the region's modern history, because that history had been turned upside down, rewritten by people who looked at the world through different eyes than had Rondônia's founders.

Brazil's military government began actively encouraging people to migrate to the region in the early 1970s. The National Institute for Colonization and Agrarian Reform, called INCRA, drew the property lines for the 250-acre plots and began auctioning them at rock-bottom prices. To encourage large numbers of new settlers, the amount of land an individual could purchase was limited to 2,000 hectares, or about 5,000 acres. The government spoke of the region's purple volcanic soil as if it were a luxurious enticement, suggesting that Rondônia was perfectly suited for agricultural industry. Brazil's president in the early 1970s, General Emílio Garrastazú Médici, had launched an ambitious road-building program throughout Amazonia, which he hoped would transform the world's largest forest into economically productive territory. Public advertisements hyped "A Land Without Men, for Men Without Land." After a dirt road was cleared through the center of the Guaporé Valley, the arduous six-week journey from São Paulo or Rio de Janeiro to Porto Velho was cut to just three or four days. The government insisted that buying the forested lots was more than an economic opportunity—it was a patriotic duty. Médici warned that if Brazil didn't take advantage of the Amazon's economic potential, other countries might swoop in and seize the opportunity. *"Integrar para não entregrar"* became the government's mantra, meaning that Brazil should integrate the Amazon into its economy instead of surrendering it to someone else.

Jaime Bagattoli owned the lumberyard where the Indian's two huts were found, as well as a nearby ranch. His family had moved from Brazil's east coast to Rondônia in 1978, lured by the government's entreaties.

"You used to hear that slogan—*Integrar para não entregrar*—all the time on television," Bagattoli said. "They were really trying to do things right. It was a pilot project for agrarian reform, and it seemed well planned."

When Rondônia became a state in 1981, the military government launched an internationally financed project to pave the BR-364 highway, which pumped new life into the settlement drive. In 1980 alone, more than 70,000 people migrated to an area that had a population of only 110,000 in the most recent census, from 1970. And the road hadn't even been paved yet.

After concrete was laid in 1984, settlers kept coming from all corners of Brazil. Within a decade, more than 1 million newcomers would arrive. Most were farmers and ranchers, jumping at the chance to own property themselves instead of working as tenant laborers. "BR-364 has sparked a land rush into Rondônia unmatched in speed and ferocity by any rural migration since the settling of the nineteenth century American West," wrote Jonathan Krandall in a 1984 book about Amazonian settlement. "Nowhere else in the world are people moving into virgin territories on the scale witnessed in Rondônia."

Once they arrived, the settlers needed to clear their land if they wanted to earn any money from it. Trees were falling faster than they ever had anywhere in the world. In 1978, about 420,000 cumulative hectares of forest were cut annually in Rondônia. By 1988, that figure had jumped to 3 million hectares every year. By 1993, it was nearly 4 million. And by 1996, more than 5.2 million hectares—or 20,000 square miles—were being deforested each year in the state. By the time the Contact Front began its search for the Indian, more than half of Rondônia's forests had been leveled.

Even if farmers cleared their land, there was no guarantee of turning a profit. Amazonian soil is notoriously nutrient-poor, and Rondônia's is just slightly better than the regional average—about 10 percent of the soil in Rondônia is good for agriculture, compared to 3 percent across the Amazon as a whole, according to Michael Williams, emeritus professor of geography and environment at Oxford University. Small farmers struggled to coax crops from it, and when they did, the fledgling state's shaky commercial infrastructure made selling them difficult. Banks and the government's Amazon development agency, called SUDAM, favored ranchers over small farmers when making loans. Many of the small farmers who moved to Rondônia were forced to sell their properties. Real estate investors moved in to gobble up plots. After clear-cutting the properties, the government considered those lots "improved," allowing the investors to turn a quick profit by reselling them to other newcomers. Often those newcomers were large-scale ranchers. Eventually about 85 percent of all cleared land in Rondônia was occupied by livestock.

"At the time, the government was pressuring people to clear land—in fact, INCRA would take land back from you if you didn't clear it, saying you failed to meet your obligation of making the land productive," said Bagattoli. "But that all changed. Now they would award you a prize for not cutting trees. The government pulled us in, then they tried to push us out."

The attitude shift, he said, started around the time of Brazil's new constitution in 1988, which coincided with stricter international logging standards. But in Rondônia, those changes on paper weren't visible immediately; it took several years before anyone actually tried to enforce the new laws on a practical level. For many of the landowners, the first people they encountered who argued the letter of the law were the members of the Contact Front. Marcelo and his crew were not shy about paraphrasing Article 231 of the constitution: if

Indians live on a piece of property, no matter how or when that property was obtained, the land belongs to the Indians.

Many landowners cried foul. A group of the region's ranchers hired Odair Flauzino, an attorney from Vilhena who was a rancher himself, to serve as their de facto spokesman. He regularly spoke out against Marcelo and his crew, dismissing them as troublemakers who swept into the region, then applied a revisionist view of history to try to turn law-abiding citizens into criminals. The government had established a couple of Indian reserves in Rondônia before they auctioned the forested lots in the 1970s; therefore, all lands sold were assumed to be free of Indian presence. Years later, when the Contact Front found traces of Indian settlement on a piece of land, Flauzino argued that it meant nothing. Even if they showed him artifacts, he wasn't swayed: go to Rio de Janeiro, dig under the skyscrapers, and you might find evidence that Indians once lived there, too, he'd argue. But did that mean everyone who owned land in Rio should give up their property to a culture that didn't thrive anymore? Flauzino and his clients believed the answer was self-evident.

Flauzino cast the ranchers as practical representatives of the modern age, while the members of the Contact Front were fuzzy-headed explorers harboring lost-world fantasies. It's the kind of argument that resonates with many Amazonia residents, because there is no denying that the region—since the very beginning of its recorded history—has always attracted more than its share of dreamers deluded by their imaginations.

Francisco de Orellana, the Spanish conquistador who led the first expedition to explore the region in the 1500s, was looking for the mythical El Dorado when he set sail down what later became known as the Amazon River. According to Gaspar de Carvajal, a Dominican friar who accompanied the expedition, the explorers named the river after the all-female warriors described in Greek mythology. Carvajal—whom history would judge as a comically unreliable narrator—wrote that the members of the expedition were attacked by tall, topless women who emerged from the jungle and demanded that the sailors mate with them. He reported that this was the Amazon women's routine: they'd attack males from other tribes, forcefully mate, bear children, kill any males they birthed, and carry on as an all-female society. Carvajal wrote that the sailors dutifully satisfied the women's coital cravings, then continued on their way downriver, thankful to escape with their lives, but absolutely exhausted. Anyone who went to the area to see the natives for himself, Carvajal warned, "would go a boy and return an old man."

It read like an open invitation for the gullible and the lecherous, and it tainted Amazonian exploration from the start. Historians mocked Carvajal's account and called him an absurd fabulist. His journals weren't formally published until 1894 because no one really believed him.

Centuries later, latter-day Carvajals were still claiming that these jungles—thousands of miles from where Orellana's expedition traveled—hid mysterious and undiscovered cultures. In the 1970s, miles from the Modelo Ranch in the same Guaporé Valley, a German ethnologist and photographer named Jesco von Puttkamer discovered cave markings that featured a recurring image: a triangle marked by a deep cut from one apex to the center. The markings were similar to those that Carvajal had described on the jewelry of the Amazon women. Altair Sales, a Brazilian anthropologist, announced to the world that he believed the symbols depicted womanhood. He said that caves were decorated with masks that the women might have worn on man-raids to neighboring villages, and he said he also found a ritual mating site nearby. Shortly after the discovery, *Time* magazine reported, "Sales is convinced by the artifacts that the people who produced them were indeed Amazons. Moreover, he says, there may have once been many feminist tribes roaming all through the Brazilian jungles." Some members of the burgeoning equal rights movement in the United States picked up on the story as ammunition for their political cause, though excitement over the story quickly died down as additional hard proof failed to materialize. To the ranchers of the region, it was another example of how a little imagination could twist the flimsiest trace of "forest culture" into the wildest fantasies.

The jungle was like a Rorschach test—people often saw in it exactly what they wanted to see.

The Dalafinis' Modelo Ranch spreads across more than six square miles. A rocky driveway leads to the ranch's two main buildings:

houses built in the Mediterranean style, with white stucco walls and terra-cotta roofs. They are surrounded by pasture. White Brahman cattle graze by silvery ponds, which are scattered across the landscape like tossed coins. Egrets flit among the cows, alighting here and there, seeking insects stirred by heavy hooves. Pygmy owls maintain vigils on top of a few blunt stumps that rise like pale fossils from the earth.

Shortly after the Contact Front began roaming through the forests, Hercules and Denes Dalafini began locking their swinging wooden gates, blocking vehicular entrance to their property from the roadway. They entrusted enforcement of the makeshift blockade to a man named Milton, the head ranch hand, who lived in a white-and-green clapboard house a mile or so down the road from the main entrance. The members of the Guaporé Contact Front had tried to get past that gate, only to be turned away by Milton. If Marcelo and his crew wanted onto the property, they'd need a warrant.

When Hercules Dalafini stepped onto the porch of the ranch house one morning in September 1996, the members of the Contact Front—along with a few police officers and agents from Brazil's environmental protection agency—were standing at the bottom of the steps. They had gotten past the gate because Marcelo had already obtained a court order allowing them access to the land.

As Hercules examined the papers, Vincent asked him if he was aware that isolated Indians were rumored to live on his forested property. Hercules calmly peered down the steps at Vincent and told him he'd never heard such a thing.

Hercules' denial flatly contradicted stories the team had been picking up from ranch workers in the area. Not only had they heard rumors about Indians on the Modelo property, they'd also heard that a band of pistoleros had been hired to chase the Indians away.

In Rondônia, ranchers occasionally hired gunmen to rid their undeveloped property of Indians or squatters, sometimes with deadly results. In August 1995, the owner of a ranch outside of Corumbiara—the small town nearest the Modelo Ranch—paid a group of military police to accompany his own privately hired gunmen to clear his forested property of squatters. According to a report issued by a federal investigating commission, the pistoleros and police raided the squatter camp while the peasants slept, setting fire to their tents. In the resulting chaos, at least eleven people died. The gunmen allegedly tortured and killed some of the peasants, execution-style.

Fearing for their jobs, few of the ranch workers were willing to say anything against their employers. But Marcelo, Altair, and Vincent canvassed the region, trying to dig into rumors that pistoleros also might have tried to clear the forest around the Modelo Ranch. An armed raid against an Indian village, they believed, might explain how a single Indian might find himself alone, on the run in the jungle.

They decided to pay another visit to Gilson, the lumberyard cook who'd shown them the first hut. Vincent asked Gilson if he'd ever heard a story about pistoleros.

"I heard something about that happening at the Modelo Ranch," Gilson told him. "But not here. This is a different farm."

Gilson was just trying to protect himself, worried that he might run into trouble with his bosses if the Contact Front started interrogating them, too. He didn't volunteer any more information, but Vincent pressed him with more questions. Eventually, Gilson said he'd heard that pistoleros found Indians in the forest on the Modelo property and that they shot at a hut. "I don't know if they killed him or not, but they scared him," Gilson said.

Vincent continued to probe for details, but the cook didn't know much more than that. Gilson reminded Vincent that he was taking a risk by simply mentioning pistoleros to the Contact Front, and he fidgeted nervously. As an aside, he said that Milton, the ranch hand who normally guarded the gates to the Modelo Ranch, had visited him recently: word had spread that Gilson had been talking to the Contact Front, prompting a complaint.

That afterthought was the most interesting thing they'd heard all day. Just like his boss, Milton had told the Contact Front that he'd never heard a word about Indians on the property.

News of the Contact Front's investigation quickly spread around the region's ranches. Odair Flauzino, the lawyer who represented local landowners, dismissed the inquiries as just another round of nonsense from FUNAI, an agency he had grown to loathe after years of bitter battles.

In Flauzino's opinion, FUNAI's local office in Rondônia went off the rails sometime back in the 1980s, after João Carlos Nobre da Veiga was forced to surrender his leadership of the agency for allegedly accepting personal kickbacks. Nobre da Veiga, an army colonel who was president of FUNAI during the BR-364 construction period, had a reputation as a friend to ranchers and farmers. "He issued outright anti-Indian statements, and his allegiance to economic groups interested in Indian resources was unconcealed," wrote Marianne Schmink and Charles H. Wood in their book *Frontier Expansion in Amazonia*. David Price, an American anthropologist who had worked alongside Marcelo in the 1970s, once tried to tell Nobre da Veiga that there was a chance that an uncontacted tribe related to the Nambiquara might exist in Rondônia. According to Price, Nobre da Veiga erupted in frustration, "Good Lord, they seem to be bringing more Indians into this country all the time, just to cause problems."

That complaint was voiced so often that it had become a refrain throughout Rondônia, and Flauzino was leading the chorus. It made sense to him: if the presence of Indians meant that a forest couldn't be developed, wouldn't those who were against development want to make people believe that Indians lived in those forests? What would stop them from taking Indians from other tribes and simply planting them in the middle of lands that were slated for development?

Flauzino was among the tens of thousands of Brazilians who had flocked to Rondônia during the great land rush of 1980. When the BR-364 was paved in Vilhena a couple of years later, he and a few other landowners arranged a meeting with a military general who was visiting for a ceremonial unveiling. The landowners told the general they fully supported the paving work, but they couldn't fathom why a thousand square miles nearby were being set aside for an Indian reserve. According to Flauzino, the general told the group that the creation of the reserve was demanded by officials of the World Bank in Washington, D.C. Without the reserve, the institution wouldn't clear a loan to help pay for the road's construction. Flauzino detected a sinister international conspiracy at the heart of the story. "This area for the reserve was powerful, fertile land," Flauzino said years later. "You know how much food could be planted there?

You realize, of course, that the United States is the only superpower in the world. And do you know why they're the only superpower? It's because of their agriculture production. The United States knew all along that this region has the best potential for farmland in all of Brazil. The Americans knew. That's why they demanded that reserve be put there."

After that meeting, Flauzino came up with a plan to try to convince FUNAI to allow some of the local businessmen to go onto Indian reserves and harvest some of the mahogany that he believed was going to waste. In exchange for timber rights, the local developers said they'd pour money into things they figured the Indians could use: schools, airplane runways, a radio station, and infrastructure improvements. FUNAI nixed the proposal, and—to Flauzino's way of thinking—a great deal of economic potential simply evaporated. "It would have been a win-win situation," Flauzino recalled from his law office in Vilhena. "But it didn't happen. I tell you, if it had happened, I wouldn't be here today. I'd be in a penthouse in Copacabana."

Instead, he began representing landowners whose properties were being threatened by the alleged presence of Indian tribes. It was in that role that he first ran into the man who'd prove to be one of the biggest headaches he'd ever seen standing on two legs: Marcelo dos Santos.

It was 1986, and Marcelo was living with the Nambiquara Indians when he was told that ranch hands had been shot at with arrows while destroying an Indian village on their boss's property. As FUNAI's local representative, Marcelo decided to investigate the possibility of an isolated tribe on the property, possibly related to the Nambiquara. With a group of tribesmen, Marcelo searched the area and uncovered clay pots, grated boards used to peel manioc, and wooden cups. One of Marcelo's Nambiquara companions fell into a spiked pit. Marcelo also found a patch of bulldozed forest where banana trees, yams, sweet potatoes, tobacco, cotton, manioc, peanuts, and corn had begun sprouting through the vegetative debris. No Indians dead or alive were spotted on the land, but in two places they found .38-caliber cartridges and .20-guage shotgun shells.

The problem was that the head of FUNAI's Isolated Indians Divisions—Sydney Possuelo, who would become Marcelo's boss—had visited the area the year before and issued a report declaring it free of Indians. Possuelo had camped out in the forest and didn't spot any presence of Indians. That "negative certification" had opened the area for logging.

As soon as Marcelo began searching the forest for more evidence, Flauzino tried to stop his investigations on the ranch owner's behalf. On the same day that Marcelo and the Indians found the cartridges and shotgun shells, Flauzino flew to the ranch in a private plane and reminded him of Possuelo's report. Marcelo didn't give up, and a fierce battle between the two men was born. Sydney Possuelo returned to Rondônia to try to clear things up. Upon Possuelo's return, a crowd of ranchers gathered around the FUNAI official as he walked through the dusty streets of the town of Corumbiara. Possuelo told them that Marcelo's findings didn't necessarily conflict with his earlier report. He had simply assessed the present state of the ranch at the time of his visit based on his observations, he said.

"There's no doubt that Indians once lived there," Possuelo told the ranchers, "but not anymore."

For the next ten years, both Marcelo and Flauzino declared themselves the victors of that battle, each man convinced he was right. Marcelo told people with certainty that an Indian village had recently been destroyed there, and Flauzino kept citing Possuelo's report as proof that no Indians had been there before Marcelo's expedition. "Sydney Possuelo—this guy is a serious sertanista," Flauzino said. "And who is Marcelo dos Santos? He's someone who works under Sydney Possuelo."

In 1996 Flauzino decided to go on the offensive when FUNAI tried to reserve land for the Kanoe and the Akuntsu. He launched a public campaign to discredit FUNAI's "discoveries." He contacted Brazil's main newspapers with allegations that Marcelo had in fact planted the Indians on the land himself. Backed by an ex-FUNAI employee named Osny Ferreira, Flauzino said that Kanoe had been taken from the Cinta Larga tribe in the northern part of the state and transplanted to the Guaporé Valley.

After hearing about Flauzino's claims, Vincent visited his law office with his video camera. He didn't tell the attorney that he was a friend of Marcelo's, but wanted to hear him explain his position.

Flauzino, leaning forward in his leather desk chair, grabbed a magazine article that pictured Purá, Owaimoro, and the rest of the Kanoe dressed in the shorts they had made from salt bags. "How, how, how?" Flauzino said, pointing at the article. "How are you going to give any credence to a story about Indians, who are wearing clothes, who they say never had contact with white men?" He continued to condemn Marcelo's position by pointing out that FUNAI recently had received some funding from the World Bank for its work in the area. Marcelo, he suggested, was in the pocket of an institution that was determined to make sure that Brazil remained an underdeveloped country. He launched into one of his favorite topics: how foreign institutions, nongovernmental organizations, and environmental advocates have no right to meddle in Brazil's domestic matters. "The United States killed all of the Indians in the Northwest Territories, after crossing the Mississippi, and you know what? That allowed them to become the most powerful producing country in the world!"

Flauzino had nurtured conspiracy theories against nefarious outside influence since the day the Brazilian military general told him that the World Bank had encouraged the creation of an Indian reserve. He might have sounded like a zealot, but the argument that Brazil was being stunted by outside influence—and that the Guaporé Contact Front was simply a tool of the "green mafia"—resonated among the settlers in Rondônia. The Amazon had become an international cause célèbre. Sting and Madonna were performing concerts in its defense, and American politicians had begun questioning Brazil's stewardship of the rain forest. When then senator Al Gore said, "Contrary to what Brazilians think, the Amazon is not their property—it belongs to all of us," many in Brazil took it as a direct challenge to national sovereignty. It smacked of rank hypocrisy, to be lectured by people from a superpower built on what was once Indian-occupied forest and prairie. Teddy Roosevelt himself had once said of America's experience, "The settler and pioneer have at bottom had justice on their side; this great continent could not have been kept as nothing but a game preserve for squalid savages." After Roosevelt left office, he had had the chance to feast his eyes upon this very area of Brazil during a river expedition, and he added, "The country along this river is a fine natural cattle country, and someday it will surely see a great development." Amazonia was Brazil's frontier, and asking the country to preserve the rain forest was analogous to asking the United States a hundred years before to keep its hands off the area west of the Mississippi River. To those advocating development, Brazil's future depended on it.

Outside of Brazil, environmentalists and indigenous-rights activists may have seemed the good guys, and loggers and ranchers the bad guys, but it was more complicated within Brazil. As cities buckled under the weight of shantytown growth and violence, the idea that Brazilians shouldn't be allowed to tap into their own enormous natural resources seemed a cruel injustice. About three out of five Brazilians surveyed by the country's largest polling firm said that they distrust the activities of environmental organizations. In frontier areas such as Rondônia, the suspicions ran even hotter.

During debates over how much autonomy indigenous groups should be granted under the 1988 constitution, one of Brazil's largest newspapers—*O Estado de São Paulo*—ran a weeklong series of articles suggesting that an organization of missionaries, which was urging officials to give indigenous groups more autonomy, was part of an international conspiracy that aimed to weaken the Brazilian state by empowering indigenous tribes. The paper reported that "authenticated documents" proved that foreign interests were trying to put more of the country's resources in the hands of Indians, which would then be easily manipulated from abroad. The articles were baseless—the documents were later proved to be fraudulent and forged. But the suspicions the articles raised didn't go away.

When Flauzino and the other ranchers began questioning the Contact Front's ties to international organizations, a lot of people perceived those funding connections as a strike against the group's credibility. But even after the tribal identity of Purá and the rest of his tribe was determined through study of their language to be Kanoe, not Cinta Larga, Flauzino stuck to his story. To Flauzino and the ranchers he represented, the battle for land had grown so fierce that no amount of evidence was considered irrefutable if it came from a new generation of radicals inside FUNAI.

"I'm sure Marcelo planted those Indians there," he said.

When he heard that the Contact Front was talking about the possibility of yet another Indian—the mysterious "Indian of the Hole," as some were calling this phantasm—Flauzino geared up for another battle against what he described as another tall tale from the mouths of credulous fools.

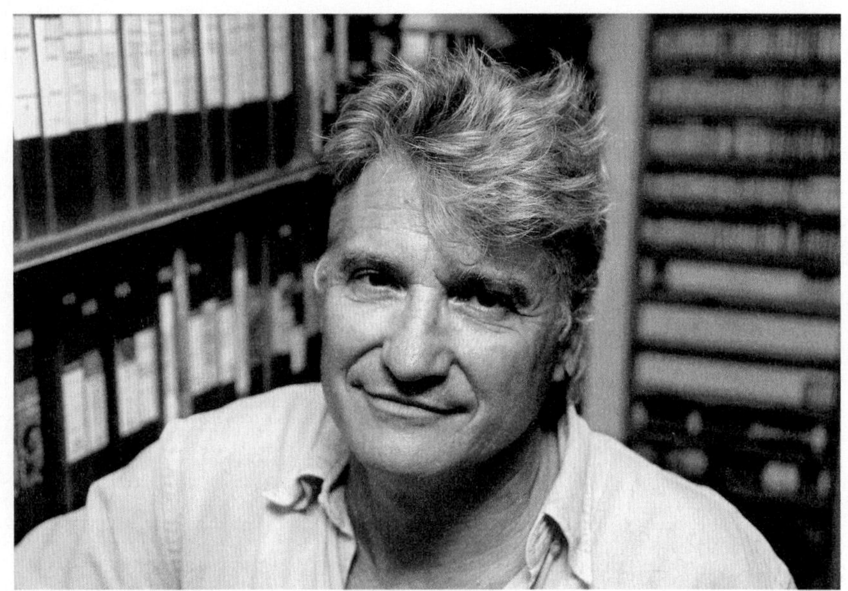

Vincent Carelli shown in his studio in 2008.

CHAPTER FOUR

The Village

The members of the Contact Front tried to talk with more ranch hands and landowners but encountered only recalcitrance and more blockades. Without the freedom to explore the forests, Marcelo was forced to embrace the side of his job he actively despised: bureaucracy. Throughout September 1996, he spent as much time in air-conditioned offices as in the jungle. But during that break from trekking, he and the other members of the Contact Front found a couple of keys that opened the investigation wider.

Marcelo traveled to Porto Velho, where the federal Justice Ministry maintained an office serving Rondônia. If the members of the Contact Front needed a warrant to search a landowner's property, it was always the same story: they had to apply for one with a federal prosecutor, wasting valuable days waiting for an uncertain response that could permanently paralyze an investigation. But a new prosecutor, Francisco Marinho, had just arrived in the Porto Velho office in June, and Marcelo recognized the newcomer's lack of connections within the state's political power structure—particularly its agricultural industry—as an opportunity.

Like most people in Rondônia, Marinho had already heard of Marcelo—specifically, he'd heard about his discoveries of the Kanoe and Akuntsu tribes. He'd also heard Odair Flauzino's public accusations that Marcelo had planted the tribes on the land. When he first read about Flauzino's conspiracy theory in a newspaper, Marinho wasn't swayed by the claim. The young prosecutor had immersed himself in the case histories of Brazilian land conflicts, carving out a specialty for himself within the federal Justice Ministry, and he knew that those kinds of unfounded allegations by ranching interests were common throughout the Amazon.

When Marcelo introduced himself and said he believed more Indians might be living in the region's forests than previously thought, Marinho's interest was piqued. He told Marcelo that he might be able to help him get around the ranchers' obstacles, but he said that any federal protections he could offer the Contact Front would come with a catch: Marinho wanted to explore the area himself first.

Marcelo jumped at the chance to give him a tour. "You can't protect what you don't understand," he told him.

That September, Marinho hiked through the forest near the newly established Rio Omerê Indigenous Territory and visited some of the surrounding ranches. On the day when he walked to the Kanoe and Akuntsu villages, he saw an enormous fire—a planned blaze set by the owner of a nearby ranch—that he estimated raged throughout at least two hundred acres of nearby forest. After that, Marinho decided that the Contact Front not only had a right to explore the jungle of the region as they wished, but he believed they also had a *duty* to do so.

From then on, Marcelo could call Marinho directly any time the Contact Front encountered another locked gate. There was no waiting: every time, Marinho instantly faxed a court order demanding that the locks come off.

Also in September, Marcelo and Vincent visited the state agency in charge of land demarcation. They discovered that a man who had surveyed the forests in the 1970s, before the government auctioned the lots, worked in that office. The Dalafini brothers and the neighboring landowners had insisted that no one had ever mentioned the possibility that Indians might have lived nearby—a claim they said was supported by the simple fact that the government would never have auctioned the forested lots in the 1970s if Indians were present. But Marcelo and Vincent believed that if the government surveyors had explored the area at the time, they might have stumbled across evidence, whether those who eventually purchased the land knew about it or not.

The surveyor's name was Luiz Claudio, and he invited Marcelo and Vincent to take a seat in front of an inclined drafting table, where he displayed a satellite image of Rondônia's forests. Claudio showed them the lands he had explored in 1977, an area that included what would become the Modelo Ranch. When Vincent asked him if he had ever suspected that Indians might have lived nearby, Claudio was matter-of-fact: his surveying team had seen tracks they believed had come from Indians in that area. Even more, one of Claudio's partners actually abandoned his explorations, fearing a confrontation with Indians he believed had entered his camp and rifled through his things as he slept.

"So what happened after that?" Vincent asked.

"Nothing," Claudio said. The government simply drew up the property lines, he said, and the lots were auctioned. As far as Claudio knew, no one within the government's land agency, INCRA, had ever known about those incidents.

Marcelo and Vincent immediately returned to Vilhena reinvigorated, eager to explore the forest more thoroughly than they ever had before. They were convinced that the ranchers' blanket denials of the possible presence of Indians in the forest were woefully ill informed at best and shamelessly deceitful at worst. Shortly after they returned home from Porto Velho, a meeting at a roadside restaurant convinced them that there was more to those denials than simple ignorance.

They had arranged to meet a man named Artur Pereira, a forty-six-year-old farmer who had worked on property abutting the Dalafinis' Modelo Ranch a few years earlier. He told them that he and a few other ranch workers had been searching for a stray bull in the forest near the border of the two property lines. They hiked over the invisible property line, a little more than a mile into the forest claimed by Hercules and Denes Dalafini, when they spotted a mud hut. The hut was surrounded by traps, and on the ground nearby they found the remains of wild animals—the carcasses of pigs and tapirs, and feathers from a variety of birds. Whoever lived there was nowhere in sight, but a fire was still smoldering outside the hut.

"We guessed it might have been either some fugitive living out there, or else an Indian," Pereira told them.

After they left the hut that afternoon, Pereira said they remained curious about what they might have seen. So they asked the police in Chupinguaia to accompany them on a return visit. But Pereira said the police they talked to didn't agree to go, and Pereira never returned to that part of the forest. But when talking to cowhands who worked on two other neighboring properties—the Expresso Bareto and the Itapratinga ranches—Pereira learned that most of them had already heard stories about uncontacted Indians living in the area. Some of them said they'd heard that a single Indian lived in that section of forest, on the run from another unknown tribe. Others suspected that the Indian had been expelled from the rest of his tribe, Pereira told them.

But Hercules Dalafini had stood on his porch, looked Vincent in the eye, and told him that he had never heard a word about Indians living in the forests around his ranch. Vincent found it hard to believe that the owners of the ranch would not have heard the same rumors, and he asked Pereira if he believed the owners of the Modelo Ranch might have had a clue about the hut he'd seen on their land.

"Yeah, at the time they did," Pereira said, nodding his head. "We actually talked with them about it. With Denes and Hercules."

Around the same time, Marcelo received another large satellite image of the area from Brazil's space agency. The image had been captured during the early months of the year, just after the rainy season. When Marcelo compared it to another satellite image from the previous July, he noticed that the newer image showed a perfect rectangle of pale pink, indicating a cleared patch of land, in the middle of the jungle on the Dalafinis' property. The same area had appeared as dark green forest in the previous image. It seemed odd that a little rectangle of land in the middle of standing forest, away from any of the previously beaten paths, would have attracted the attention of loggers. If loggers visited out-of-the-way areas like that, it was almost always for spot extractions—the cutting of one or two large and valuable hardwoods that stood among other trees that weren't worth cutting. What's more, based on the dates of the satellite images, the clearing most likely occurred during the rainy season, which runs from November through March, when the local timbering industry generally shuts down.

When planning a route for an expedition, Marcelo decided that mysterious bare patch in the middle of the forest would be a good place to start.

It was hot, and the sun burned straight overhead as Marcelo hiked into the forest on November 13. The rest of the team—Altair, Vincent, and Purá—followed in ragged single file. It was a relatively short hike to the clearing—they didn't even plan to camp for the night—but they got off to a slow start. A splinter wedged its way into Marcelo's heel, and Altair was forced to perform an impromptu surgery, prying the sliver loose with his buck knife while Marcelo clamped his jaw and grimaced. But he was back on his feet in minutes, hiking over rough terrain in his cheap plastic flip-flops, carrying a camera over his shoulder and a white plastic tube in his hand. Rolled up inside that tube were his maps and satellite images, which indicated that the group should reach the clearing in just a couple of hours.

Inside the forest, Marcelo discovered a dirt path that had been cut through the woods. The path, ribbed with tire tracks of bulldozers and other heavy equipment, led them straight to the clearing.

Stepping into the clearing was like stepping into a void. The trees had been cut, the stumps bulldozed, and everything else set on fire. The dirt was bare in some places. In others it was littered with charred timber and covered with wiry brush.

Purá, his bare feet leaving pigeon-toed tracks in the ash, noticed a stalk that was pushing up through the brush. He hacked into the brush with his machete and yanked up a rooty sprig. His blade cut easily through the brown tuber, into a soft white core. He held it up to show Vincent: it was manioc, a staple crop of Indians throughout the Amazon, often planted in gardens near their dwellings. Purá swung his machete through more brush and uncovered more manioc. Whoever bulldozed this area must have done it at least a few months earlier—enough time for the planted manioc to begin to grow back.

Across the clearing, Marcelo also had uncovered something.

He bent down and began clearing away armfuls of dead grass. Underneath was a collection of collapsed logs, which had been roughly cut to a uniform length. It was the same kind of palm wood that Indian tribes sometimes used when building longhouses. Underneath the logs, a hole had been dug deep into the ground.

Over the next couple of hours, they continued to explore the clearing, hacking through the brush. Purá found more plants, including the remnants of a small cornfield. A few scrawny stalks had started to grow again after being bulldozed.

And they found more holes. Fourteen in all, arranged in what appeared to be a semicircular pattern across the clearing. The holes themselves were rectangular and about five and a half feet deep—the same depth as the holes they had found within the two individual huts. Around these holes, they found more logs.

"You know what this was?" Marcelo said, pondering the scene and comparing it in his mind to the individual huts they'd found since that first meeting with Gilson. "This wasn't just one hut. It was an entire village."

Later that same day, before they left the Modelo Ranch for the evening, Marcelo, Altair, and Vincent decided to pay a surprise visit to Milton, the Dalafinis' head ranch hand.

It had been Milton who complained to Gilson after learning that the cook had spoken with members of the Contact Front about Indians in the area. Marcelo had spoken with him before, and Milton pleaded ignorance: he'd never heard about any Indians anywhere near the Modelo Ranch. But after spending a full day inspecting what they believed to be a destroyed Indian village and plantation, Marcelo and Vincent determined that it was time to force a confrontation.

The group found him resting on the porch of his white-and-green clapboard house. Without an invitation, Marcelo kicked off his flip-flops and made himself comfortable, taking a seat on the porch rail.

Milton looked tired. He was shirtless, dressed only in a pair of brown shorts, and he slapped at a bee buzzing around his shoulders. An old dog lazed beside him. When Vincent told him they'd been hearing more and more stories about Indians living in the area, Milton wearily said he didn't know anything. It was his stock answer for just about every question they posed to him. But then Vincent dug in: he said that some people had already told the Contact Front that Milton himself had talked to them about an Indian plantation he knew of in the forest.

"So look, your situation is getting complicated," Vincent said. "We were there in the clearing. We saw the plantations made by the Indians."

Milton took a breath, then launched into an extended oratory full of starts, stops, and contradictions. He admitted that he'd seen the clearing. He said a contractor had been hired to work there, but that he didn't know much more than that. He was just a humble ranch hand, he told them, responsible for nothing other than the herd of cattle he'd been tasked to manage.

Marcelo listened in disbelief, then turned to Vincent and accused the ranch hand of lying to them: "I think he must believe that we're kids, that we were born yesterday," Marcelo said, making sure Milton heard him loud and clear. "He went there, and he did it. He cleared the land in exactly the place the Indians had been."

Milton again pleaded his innocence, but Marcelo and Vincent didn't let him off the hook. They hammered him with questions until he admitted that contractors had made the clearing in the jungle that January, in the middle of the rainy season. Milton had gone to the area while the men were working and had seen one Indian hut still standing. But he said he didn't know anything more.

Milton explained to Vincent that he hadn't wanted to talk about the presence of an Indian on the property because he was afraid he'd be asked to go out in the forest and find the Indian—something he didn't want to do.

"I'm not hiding anything," Milton insisted. "The thing is, now you probably will want me to go after this Indian. But I have no idea where the Indian is."

"The only thing we want is a person who'll tell us the truth," Marcelo said. He and Vincent continued to press Milton for more information about the "contractors" who made the clearing in the woods. Were they hired to scare a large group of Indians off the property and to destroy their village? If so, Vincent said it would correspond to rumors they were hearing that a group of pistoleros had been hired to eliminate any trace of Indians from the forest, and that a single Indian might have survived.

But Milton had no more revelations to offer them that evening.

"Man," he said after several more minutes of fruitless interrogation, rubbing his eyes and squinting into the yard beside his house, where a couple of clucking chickens pecked in the dry, brown dirt. "My head hurts."

* * *

A few days later, the Contact Front revisited the area where they suspected the village had stood. But they found that others had arrived first.

Laborers employed by the Modelo Ranch were bulldozing the manioc and papaya that had grown up through the underbrush in the months since the area had originally been cleared. They were covering the turned ground with grass seed.

Marcelo stood in front of the bulldozer, blocking its path and demanding an explanation. The driver got off the machine and confronted Marcelo, arms akimbo, his shirt ringed with sweat around the neck and the underarms. He shrugged, and offered a casual lift of his eyebrows: he just got here, he said, and wasn't sure why he'd been asked to clear the land.

Marcelo had no patience for nonchalance. He picked up a wooden plank from the ground and held it in front of the man's face. "You're destroying an Indian village!"

Marcelo and the others refused to allow the workers to continue, but Hercules Dalafini soon arrived on the scene, saying that the members of the Contact Front had no right to be on his property. He was accompanied by a uniformed military police officer.

After explaining to the police officer that they had a court order from Porto Velho that allowed them to explore the area, Altair began showing the workers and the police officer one of the deep holes in the clearing. He explained how the individual huts they had found in other parts of the forest featured similar holes.

Vincent offered to show the officer more evidence on his video camera, which had recorded everything, but Dalafini objected. Dalafini acknowledged that the Justice Ministry had allowed members of FUNAI to explore his property, but Vincent wasn't technically employed by FUNAI. Dalafini said that meant that both Vincent and his video camera were trespassing on his property, and both should be detained.

The officer thought about it for a minute, and decided that he couldn't confiscate the camera—but he could arrest Vincent.

For the moment, that was good enough for Dalafini.

Vincent rode in a police car to Chupinguaia with a mini videocassette stuffed in his underwear, just in case the policeman changed his mind and decided to take the camera. After a couple of hours, the police released Vincent. He called Marcelo, and they hatched a plan: Vincent would stay in Chupinguaia and try to mix among the ranch hands there and figure out exactly who had cleared the area in the middle of the forest, and why. Instead of driving around that bang-bang town in a truck that advertised their affiliation—and raising suspicions of all the ranch hands who hung out there—Vincent could maintain a low profile and do a little undercover detective work.

Maybe, they figured, the fact that Vincent wasn't a FUNAI employee could work to the team's advantage.

Vincent was born in France, but like Marcelo, he'd grown up the son of an artist in São Paulo. When the two young men met in 1978, they instantly clicked.

Vincent had taken up photography as a teenager, and by the time he was twenty years old he was living in a village of Xikrin Indians in the Brazilian state of Pará. He had been drawn there by his senses: the deep reds of the genipap they spread on their skin, the air perfumed with resins, the hot pulse of the night as the tribe danced by firelight. He wanted to immerse himself completely in the tribe, but he quickly discovered that they would always view him as an outsider, a friendly foreigner who could serve as a cultural translator of the changing world around them. He helped coordinate Indian health programs and pushed for more tribal understanding from Brazil's government. After joining FUNAI in 1975, he discovered that he disagreed with his employer more often than not. He quit the agency two years later.

In 1979 he founded a nonprofit institution he called the Center for Indigenous Advocacy to fight for rights that Indians in Brazil didn't have, such as the right to an independent lawyer in disputes against the government. Then, in the mid-1980s, when VHS camcorders started hitting the market in Brazil, Vincent saw an opportunity. The cameras would allow him the chance to record and preserve the Indians' quickly disappearing cultural traditions, folklore, and tribal histories. In 1987, at age thirty-six, he began to think of himself as a photographer again, a documentarian archiving the Indians' lives with a political goal: to give them more power over their own destinies.

Vincent's passion for the work led him to spend about as much time in the forests of Amazonia as did Marcelo. Vincent's first wife—he'd eventually marry three times—was an anthropologist. She often accompanied him on trips and vice versa. Vincent's documentary style was partly shaped by their shared sensitivity about how field researchers influenced the lives of their subjects, consciously or not. One of his first discoveries was that when filming the tribespeople, he could never simply disappear into the background and allow the camera to be an invisible roving eye. In places without electricity or modern technology of any kind, the camera was conspicuous at all times, and its influence on the action it witnessed was unavoidable. He struggled with films that felt fundamentally dishonest to him. During the recording of his first film—he shot footage of the Nambiquara tribe with the help of his friend Marcelo—Vincent discovered that the Indians recognized that the images he was capturing could be manipulated. When he filmed them during a celebratory ritual, the leader of the group watched the footage and wanted a reshoot. The chief believed the film should highlight an element of ferocity in the ritual, which he believed was necessary to show the group's competence in defending its culture. Vincent let him do it, and the Nambiquara themselves became coproducers of the film. Soon, in all of his projects, Vincent was teaching Indians to operate the cameras and edit the footage themselves. The video archive he was amassing outgrew the Center for Indigenous Advocacy. Vincent founded a new nonprofit institution under the name Video in the Villages.

When he screened the films at universities and film festivals, academics regularly complained that he was polluting the purity of indigenous culture by introducing them to modern technology. Others said he was denigrating the role of females in the tribe by allowing males—the ones who acted as leaders in the tribe in almost all matters—more production control over the film. But to him, those criticisms betrayed an ignorance of actual life in most Amazonian Indian villages. Those critics were trying to look at everything through the distorting lens of what they felt the Amazon *should* be like, not what it is like, and they'd object when his images didn't match their ideals.

When academics occasionally condemned all efforts to contact isolated tribes—even those in the path of development—as "paternalistic," because they said it cast the explorers as superior protectors of a helpless race, Vincent asked them what the alternative might be. Step aside and watch the cultures get crushed? In his work as an advocate for tribes throughout Brazil, he'd repeatedly seen the effects of a hands-off approach: people died. It was inevitable that sooner or later, someone—whether it be loggers, rubber tappers, or miners—would find the Indians, and such unplanned encounters almost always went wrong, such as the time a rubber tapper infected with measles encountered the Tupari tribe in 1954, passing an infection that within a week cut the population of the two-hundred-member tribe in half. The advance of the modern world might be inevitable, but Vincent didn't believe the death of the tribes also should be assumed.

The cultures of all of the tribes Vincent was visiting had already been changing with the times for decades, ever since they had started coming into glancing contact with mainstream Brazil. He viewed his films as political tools, designed to help give the Indians a stronger voice, allowing *them* to determine how their society evolved. Through video footage, he hoped to encourage both Indians and non-Indians to see the tribes from an unaccustomed angle: not as isolated *others,* but as humans.

When Vincent began working with the Contact Front to investigate the possibility that an Indian might be on the run in the Guaporé Valley, that was the plan he hoped the team might pursue: find the Indian, make peaceful contact with him, protect him from ranchers and loggers—then let him be. Put no expectations on him, don't pretend he's beholden to those who contacted him, give him the power to steer his own course. If that was paternalistic, it seemed preferable to the alternative, which to Vincent felt like apathy, or paralysis caused by intellectual abstraction.

After his arrest at the Dalafini ranch, Vincent was quickly released. He packed his video camera in his bag, along with a small pen-size camera that could capture relatively clear images when hidden in his shirt pocket, where he had cut a tiny peephole that could be seen only if a person was looking for it. He hoped to get to the bottom of the rumors the team had been picking up in bits and pieces from the ranch hands.

Chupinguaia was an imperfect grid of pitted dirt roads, where men without shirts lingered at open-air roadside bars with bottles of Skol beer in their hands. A couple of auto shops sat on the main road, advertising their services by hanging spare tires and hubcaps out front. Stray hens occupied the main square. The best restaurant in town was tucked inside a green ranch house near the square, and its owner rented out rooms in back to anyone who needed a roof over their heads. It was the closest thing to a hotel that could be found for miles.

Vincent got a room there and settled in for a brief stay. On his first day, he spent a couple of hours walking around town, trying his best to appear like he belonged there, hoping to gauge the best places to start asking around about anyone who might have been hired to work on the Modelo Ranch during the previous rainy season. When he returned to what he started thinking of as his "hotel," for lack of a better name, he struck up a conversation with the friendly owner.

The owner had contacts all over town, and he seemed like as good a person as any to ask about the rumor that the Modelo Ranch had hired locals to clear Indians off the property. The owner tensed up slightly, which Vincent interpreted as a sign that he knew something. It turned out he didn't. But he knew someone who did, which to Vincent was just as good.

Vincent asked for an introduction, but the owner was wary. He feared that the wrong people might find out, drawing unwanted attention to his contact. But after Vincent assured him he'd be discreet, the owner relented. They didn't have to travel far for that meeting: his contact was a woman who cooked and washed dishes in the restaurant of his kitchen.

Her name was Maria Elenice. Vincent explained to her that he'd heard that some ranch hands were hired to clear land on the Modelo during the previous rainy season, and he figured they probably came from Chupinguaia. He was looking for people who might know something about it.

She was terrified. The restaurant, right there in the middle of the town, clearly wasn't the place to talk. In fact, she wasn't sure she wanted to talk at all; she'd have to think about it, she said.

The next day, Vincent tried to fish around for other sources, but his leads went nowhere. So he went to Maria Elenice's house and waited for her. He assumed the sight of a video camera would be an instant conversation-killer, so he'd hidden his camera in his shirt pocket. He planned to record her conversation, figuring that if she talked, he'd need all the proof he could get to convince local authorities to take legal action against anyone who threatened the lives of Indians.

She invited him in, and they talked for an hour in her backyard. She told him that a contractor had hired her ex-boyfriend to help clear the forested land on the Modelo property. She told Vincent that she'd even gone to the clearing site for a while to stay with her boyfriend while he worked in the forest. At the time she was told that three Indians were seen on the land, and that the first workers who had arrived in the area scared them off. All of this had happened at about the New Year, which put her memory in line with the estimate they'd heard from Milton, the Dalafinis' ranch hand.

Vincent returned to the hotel ecstatic with the discovery, but the hotel owner wasn't so thrilled. He told Vincent that someone had stopped by the restaurant asking about him. The owner said that if he cared about his safety, he should keep a low profile.

More unwelcome news came when Vincent got back to his room and replayed the tape: the grainy image of Maria Elenice was okay, but the audio was terrible. From the tape, not a word could be understood.

That night, Vincent jammed his bed against the door—just in case someone tried to burst into the room and surprise him—and decided to return to Maria Elenice the next morning.

He explained that he needed her to repeat what she had already told him so he could tape-record it. He assured her that he would never display her image and that he'd never reveal her last name.

"I didn't sleep at all last night because of this," she told him, smoking a cigarette as she sat on a bench in her yard. "I'm actually thinking about leaving town, going away. I'm nervous, nervous, nervous." She said she'd just seen the contractor who had hired her boyfriend to clear land at a nearby bar.

Vincent tried to calm her down, and she eventually decided that speaking to him more might actually take a burden off her. "It's sad, you know," she said. "Sad we got involved with this kind of thing. But staying quiet is the worst."

She went into more detail, saying that her boyfriend had actually been hired to finish the clearing process by burning the land—most of the work had been completed before he got there. The workers who did the first round of clearing had camped in the area and said they saw three Indians. Those Indians wore no clothes, she said, only a few feathers.

Vincent asked her if she knew if the workers had destroyed any Indian huts. She said they had: the wife of one of the workers who cleared the area helped him destroy a hut and set it on fire.

Maria Elenice said that the owners of the property had provided the tractors and heavy equipment to the workers. The workers had been instructed to wipe out all traces of Indians, she said, and to cover up the holes they had dug.

"Do you think they killed the Indians, or didn't they?" Vincent asked.

She said she didn't think so—the workers probably would have boasted about such a thing if they had, she said. And after initially scaring the Indians away, she said the workers later saw a single Indian. He ran away as soon as he saw them, she said.

Two days later, Vincent returned to Vilhena fired up, eager to take the tapes to the Justice Ministry and prosecute the Dalafinis for trying to wipe a possibly unique culture off the face of the Earth. But when he and Marcelo talked to the prosecutor's office, their enthusiasm was extinguished when they were told the tape wouldn't be admissible in court.

Even with the stories they were collecting and the evidence they'd found, it seemed no one was prepared to take legal action unless they proved that Indians had been killed. They couldn't prove it; they had found no bodies. Many of the regional justice officials and politicians had come to Rondônia to start ranches themselves, and they weren't likely to risk upsetting their most important constituents without indisputable evidence. When Marcelo and Vincent tried to explain their point of view to officials who grew up in a frontier environment, it was generally an exercise in futility. Even if Indians had been killed, many of the people they talked to didn't seem bothered.

But any time they needed to remind themselves that dealing with settlers wasn't a hopeless proposition, all they had to do was look to the young man who accompanied them almost everywhere they traveled. Altair Algayer had known settlers, ranchers, and loggers his whole life. Before joining their team, in fact, he'd been all three.

Altair Algayer pictured in 2008.

CHAPTER FIVE

The Accidental Environmentalist

He was just fourteen years old, but the minute he lifted his foot to step onto the westbound bus, Altair became a man.

A friend of his father's who had recently moved to Rondônia wrote about the place as if it were some kind of El Dorado. A man could find a bright and shining future there, his gold at the rainbow's end. To hear the man tell it, the past didn't matter, all slates were clean, and even the poorest tenant farmer had a fair shot at prosperity. In Rondônia, you'd be your own boss. It was every man's dream, and the government was laying it out on a silver platter: they were practically giving land away to anyone who'd promise to clear it and turn it into a productive piece of the national economy.

It was a tantalizing idea for someone such as Altair's father. Alfredo Algayer's own parents had come to Brazil as part of a wave of twentieth-century German immigrants who settled in the southeastern state of Santa Catarina. They had arrived with dreams of self-reliance, but after two generations of trying to coax prosperity out of someone else's property, their hopes got stuck in a cul-de-sac of economic dependence. No matter how hard they worked, they couldn't accumulate enough cash to buy the land they farmed.

Altair's grandfather, the patriarch who'd brought the family to Brazil in the first place, redirected his hopes heavenward. In the 1980s, American evangelical missionaries identified Brazil as the most promising territory in the world for international expansion. The rural poor rushed to dip their heads in baptismal waters, and they hungered for Pentecostal rebirth. Between 1980 and 2000, the number of Brazilians identifying themselves as evangelical Christians in the national census more than doubled, to about twenty-six million. When Altair's grandfather plunged into the movement, he wanted his grandson to join him. Altair had just exhausted the limits of his small town's school system, finishing the fourth grade, and his grandfather had recently moved to another municipality that boasted two buildings he figured would do Altair good: an evangelical church and a secondary school. Alfredo Algayer gave his eleven-year-old son a choice: you can live with Grandpa in town and continue your schooling, or you can stay here with your mother, father, and sisters and work on the farm. Altair chose to stay.

As the oldest of three children and the only boy, Altair handled a lot of the manual labor on the farm. His work helped keep the family afloat, right up until the day his father got a letter from his friend in Rondônia. The man assured Alfredo that if the family worked for just one year out there, they would have enough money to buy a plot. The man warned Alfredo not to dally: busloads of people were arriving on the BR-364 every day, snatching up any and all unclaimed acreage.

It was planting season in Santa Catarina when he got that letter, and Alfredo couldn't abandon the farm just yet. So he looked to his son. Altair had a good head on his shoulders, and those shoulders were already accustomed to carrying the workload of a full-grown man. If one overlooked the date stamped on his birth certificate, there didn't seem to be much separating Altair from the rest of the westward pioneers packing their bags and hitting the road. The boy was young, but he wasn't foolish.

So Alfredo Algayer sent his son to Rondônia to scout the area, find a patch of land, and earn a little money to give the rest of the family a cushion when they joined him the following year. His friend had promised to look after him until then.

Before Altair boarded the bus, his father handed Altair a letter to show anyone who might question why a boy was traveling across the country on his own. His father's signature at the bottom of the note said that Altair was no wayward delinquent; he was traveling on family business.

His mother also gave him something for the trip: a sack of chicken and toasted manioc flour, called *farofa*.

"Eat it on the bus," she told him. "You don't need to be buying food on the very first day."

The two-thousand-mile bus trip lasted three days and nights. All the seats were full, packed with fellow migrants pulled toward Rondônia. Most of the route was unpaved, with very little roadside scenery to entertain the eye: tin-roofed "inns" where weary travelers could hang their hammocks for the night, and service stations that siphoned gasoline out of large metal drums. Three times the road proved impassable, and each time the passengers shuffled off the bus, pulled their luggage out of the lower cargo hold, and waded across the mud to the other side of the washed-out section of roadway to wait for another bus to pick them up. The last time it happened, in the dark of night, Altair chicken-stepped through deep mud with his luggage, then returned to help elderly passengers who were struggling to carry cardboard boxes on their backs. Those boxes bulged, and Altair realized they contained all the possessions those people owned. To make this trip, they had put everything they had on the line, wading through a miry circle of hell to get to a promised land they couldn't yet imagine.

He finally arrived in the tiny town of Alta Floresta d'Oeste, a few hours' drive west of Vilhena, where his father's friend welcomed Altair into his home. Altair quickly found a job fixing engines in an auto shop. The pay wasn't much, but Altair saved it all. He bought a chainsaw, axes, and scythes—tools that his family could use to slash a future out of the overgrown forest that seemed to stretch forever beyond the borders of the town.

From the very beginning, Altair loved Rondônia. He loved it because everything was new. Back home in Santa Catarina, he had known everyone in his little village, and everyone had known him. But here people had arrived from all parts of Brazil, from exotic corners he'd never even heard of before. All had taken bold leaps of faith and landed here. The very air was perfumed with the heady spice of risk.

But almost as soon as he arrived, Altair got the feeling that the good life everyone was reaching for might not be so easily grasped.

When he began scouting around for potential plots his family might buy, he discovered that he had arrived on the scene too late. The government had already doled out almost all the titles in the surrounding region to the thousands of people who'd started rolling in four years earlier. Even when he found an owner who might be willing to make a deal for a few acres of standing forest, he couldn't sign the papers to reserve the property because he was underage. His father's friend tried to salvage the family's gamble by offering them some of his own land free of charge. He told them if they cleared it and farmed it, they could keep whatever it yielded.

The rest of the family joined Altair after the harvest in Santa Catarina. Without a house, they lived in a tent in the forest for the first month. They sawed away at the trees around them, and they used the felled timber to build a primitive cabin.

Altair spent the days working with his father, but whenever he could slip off the yoke of his responsibilities, he'd wade into the bush and drink in the scenery. He was awed by the number of surprises it held. The jungle rewarded patience. If you didn't take your time, you would overlook the best of its secrets. He'd walk without aim, admiring the hourglass swells of the trunks of *barrigudas,* or "belly trees." He'd squat by one of the swift creeks that drained the valley, cupping his hands to drink from it. He learned to spot the five-pointed prints of jaguars that could sometimes be found in the soft mud. Once during that first year he stole upon a tapir, the largest wild animal of South America, a boarlike creature that can grow to six hundred pounds. He knelt alone in the woods for hours, just watching the beast root among leaves and shoots with its questing, prehensile snout. His grandfather used to talk about the early days when he migrated to Brazil's east coast, when the Atlantic forest there was still wild with jaguars. Now Altair was the pioneer. It made him feel alive, and he kept his eyes wide wherever he walked, not wanting to miss a thing.

The things he couldn't see, however, were no less real. After one of those long days in the forest, a female mosquito alighted unseen on Altair and thrust its proboscis into his skin. A week or so later, Altair began feeling feverish. His body shook with chills, his joints ached. He looked seasick and pale.

It was Altair's first bout with malaria. Before that first year in Rondônia was over, he would shiver under its spell no fewer than eight times.

The whole family took turns battling the illness, which had accompanied the migration into Rondônia so aggressively that it had become an all-out epidemic. The most common malarial parasite in the region at that time, *Plasmodium falciparum,* also happened to be the most deadly. It stubbornly resisted most antimalarial drugs, including the chloroquine that the health centers in the nearest towns dispensed to the legions of sufferers: there was nothing anyone could do except sweat it out, which is exactly what the Algayers did, until one day—when each of his younger sisters were in the malady's throes—Altair's father decided to call it quits. Enough was enough. His dreams of providing prosperity for his family wouldn't be worth much if he had no family left. So they moved out of the jungle cabin and settled in Alta Floresta.

Altair's parents looked for jobs that would allow them to spend some time indoors, and they eventually found work for themselves in the town hall. Their two daughters got jobs as shopkeepers. But Altair wasn't ready to surrender the outdoors so easily. Unlike the rest of his family, he loved it out there in the woods. He had no interest in sitting behind a desk, so he looked around for jobs that could keep him in the forest. He soon did what most able-bodied boys of the Amazonian frontier eventually did: he became a logger.

The lumberyards had a constant demand for fresh workers, and Altair quickly found employment in a lumber mill outside of Alta Floresta. He did a little of everything. He timbered trees, cut planks, and stacked them high. If an engine broke down, he was the mechanic. When it was lunchtime, he cooked.

In 1986, his first year in the lumberyards, none of the wood stayed close to home: it was trucked to the ports of Manaus and Belém, then ferried all over the world. Unseen global forces dictated his daily routine. One day, the lumber companies would get word that demand for mahogany was surging in America and the United Kingdom, and they'd immediately explore every acre at their disposal for that bankable hardwood, *Swietenia macrophylla.* Companies sometimes cleared roads through forests to reach a single mahogany tree. When the market was flooded with that species, they'd shift to *peroba* with the same monomaniacal rapidity, forgetting all about mahogany.

By the early 1990s, environmental restrictions took a bite out of international demand, so the company that Altair worked for discovered it could make money by processing the smaller branches and limbs that previously had been ignored and selling them to Brazil's domestic market. His boss bought a six-square-mile patch of land and advertised that he'd practice sustainable harvesting, replanting trees as he cut. There were no laws forcing him to replant, but he did it anyway.

Shortly after they started harvesting trees on that parcel, people started talking about *indios bravos*—"wild Indians"—in a nearby national park. More than one timbering company had cut illegal roads into the area to extract peroba, openly defying the restrictions on cutting in parklands. Expedition teams from FUNAI were called in to investigate. The man who led those teams was named Antenor Vaz, and he quickly identified Altair's boss as a rarity—a logger with a firm respect for the law. Vaz and his team members would sometimes stop at his lumberyard before heading into the forest. If their trucks got stuck in mud on the way, they'd call his yard to ask for a tow.

Altair often cooked them lunch before the expeditions, and he was the one who'd tow them out of the mud when they got stuck. He did it gladly, because he couldn't get enough of the stories they'd tell about their jobs. Their work seemed to include all the benefits and none of the downsides of his job: it allowed them close contact with the jungle, without the obligation of destroying it. He had grown to loathe cutting trees.

Vaz rewarded Altair's curiosity by going out of his way to show him anything he'd find in the parklands during the expeditions: arrows, bows, pottery. After Vaz would leave the lumberyard, Altair would listen in disbelief as other loggers simply dismissed the evidence as a contrivance, something invented by Vaz to ruin their commercial prospects. Altair began to view their conspiracy theories as defense mechanisms, stories the loggers told themselves to protect their sense of purpose. After talking to the FUNAI guys, Altair didn't merely suspect there might be Indians living in the park; he *knew* they were there. Eventually he was proved right: the parkland, more than two thousand square miles in all, was officially designated the Massaco Indian Territory for an isolated tribe that had long made the area its home.

When Antenor Vaz heard that Altair's boss was thinking of getting out of the lumber business because of the Indian discoveries, the FUNAI chief pulled the young man aside to have a word. He told Altair that in Rondônia, FUNAI needed all the allies it could find.

Altair understood what Vaz was driving at, but he told him he didn't think it would work out. He didn't have a high school degree.

Vaz told him he didn't need one if he hired him on a contractual basis.

For the first twenty-three years of his life, Altair had rarely given a thought to indigenous cultures. It simply wasn't something that the people he knew cared about. Back in Santa Catarina, people talked about Indians in the same way cotton farmers talk about boll weevils. The settlers fought the native Xokleng tribe, whom they suspected of stealing their crops and cattle, and one provincial president in Santa Catarina had gone so far as to say of the Indians, "These barbarians, who think only of robbing us or attacking us in ambush, can never be treated with kindness or consideration. . . . I am increasingly convinced that it is practical, even necessary, to snatch these savages by force from the forests and place them somewhere whence they cannot escape." When Altair moved to Rondônia, he discovered that the same philosophy survived the westward migration intact.

He told his parents he was joining FUNAI to go on expeditions that might help protect the land of the region's Indians, and his father's reaction summed up the attitude of most of the people he'd grown up with on the rugged frontier.

"Why would you want to do that?" he asked.

More than five years later, in November 1996, Altair sat on a tree stump near the recently discovered clearing of the fourteen holes, and tried to soften the squelch on the radio.

"Marcelo? Do you read me?"

While Marcelo had returned to Vilhena and Vincent had checked into the tiny room in Chupinguaia to do his detective work, Altair had continued to explore the forest around the destroyed village with Purá and Owaimoro. Now he was calling Marcelo to offer a brief update on the additional Indian vestiges they'd found: an entire field of corn that had fallen into disuse, as well as several animal traps. Judging by the fill dirt accumulated at the bottom, the traps appeared to be a couple of years old.

While Altair was on the radio, Owaimoro ducked between two enormous roots that anchored the trunk of an enormous rubber tree to the ground. The roots completely hid her. From her crouch, she tried to demonstrate how an Indian would use this place as a hunting blind. Judging by the discarded animal bones found under that spot, it appeared that Owaimoro was right: someone probably had used it as a base from which to hunt and clean wild game.

Owaimoro and Purá felt comfortable around Altair, who had become their central connection to the new world that had opened up to them since first making contact a year earlier. Altair would spend weeks at a time in FUNAI's Rio Omerê camp, and the Indians often would hike a couple of miles to spend time with him. Members of the Akuntsu tribe did the same. Altair emitted an easygoing energy—always curious, never hurried, quick to smile—that put both tribes at ease. He loved gleaning tips from them, like new techniques for tracking animals or tapping resin from a tree, and they seemed eager to interact, eyeing his every move with an anthropological absorption that was at least as intense as his own. He might never have spent a day studying anthropology in his life, but all the idle hours passed in their company gave him more knowledge of these two isolated tribes than anyone else alive.

Altair was a newlywed. Fortunately, his wife, Jussara—a nurse specializing in indigenous health, introduced to him by Marcelo—shared his fascination with the Kanoe and the Akuntsu. Instead of pressuring him to spend more time at home, she stoked his curiosity, pressing him for details about the tribe members' lifestyles and personalities. She quickly became a regular visitor to the Rio Omerê camp. A couple of years later, when she was eight months pregnant with their first child, Jussara could be found sleeping next to Altair under the thatched roof of the FUNAI encampment. The sturdy comfort of their relationship impressed everyone in the camp.

Even Konibu, the old Akuntsu chief, once jokingly proposed a deal to Altair: he'd trade him *two* Akuntsu women for Jussara.

That November evening, before he drove Purá and Owaimoro back toward their village, they bivouacked near the cool mudbanks of a stream. Altair waded into the flow to wash off a day's worth of dust and sweat. The orange disk of a sun dipped below the tree line and bled into a violet sky. Shirtless, clean, and relaxed, Altair took his knife to a long piece of bamboo, jabbing it carefully with the point of the blade, while Owaimoro swung in a hammock. Her monkey, tied to the rope of her hammock, danced on her shoulders, kissed her ear, and searched the skin of her arms for nits. Wild turkeys roasted on a makeshift wood grill they had fashioned out of thin branches above glowing embers. When Altair tossed the bamboo aside, Owaimoro grabbed it and inspected the handiwork. She pressed her mouth to the end of the bamboo and blew: it was a deep-throated flute, a musical instrument that the Kanoe used to accompany the songs they sometimes sang in the evenings, after a meal. Purá walked over to give the flute a try.

To Altair, the simple melodies that Purá played floated upon the air with a beautiful precision, more melodic than any he himself might be able to coax from the instrument. But to the other members of the Kanoe tribe, Purá's musicianship sounded clumsy and raw, and it had nothing to do with the quality of Altair's craftsmanship.

To understand why Purá's playing sounded flat to the other Indians, a person needed to understand a little bit about the Kanoes' history in this forest, and it had taken a while for Altair to puzzle it out. Through translators he eventually learned how the Kanoe had gone from a strong tribe to a ragtag family of five survivors in a single generation. The story was at once tragic and triumphal. And it was the kind of story that was giving Altair and the rest of the Contact Front a clear window into what life was like for Indians on the run, including the one they were chasing from hut to hut.

The rain forest cradled in the vast lowlands between the Andes and the heart of Amazonia has always been a perfect place to get lost. Anthropologists believe that when Europe began to colonize the Americas, the area now called Rondônia was populated by perhaps dozens of different Indian nations, or tribes. Each consisted of several thousand members. The tribes spoke different languages and most lived independently of the others, but some formed shaky alliances. Nonallied groups, or clans, were generally hostile to one another. Cannibalism wasn't unheard of. Some of the groups might have been seminomadic, slashing and burning a small patch of forest to grow crops, then moving on when the soil lost fertility.

The density of the woodlands and a plentitude of rivers made isolation easy. The linguistic evidence indicates that many of the tribes stayed isolated for centuries. Rondônia remains a teeming petri dish of idiomatic trace material. More than thirty indigenous languages can be found in the state. Dutch linguist Hein Van der Voort, who has spent years working with the tribes of the Guaporé Valley, estimates that those include at least ten isolates—languages that have no relation to any other. That means the state of Rondônia alone has far greater linguistic diversity than the whole of Europe, where the Basque language remains the only isolate.

It's impossible to say how many tribes and languages disappeared over the years. Of the thirty languages in Rondônia, half of them now have fewer than fifty speakers.

After Europeans discovered the area, the Spanish ruled the lands that now belong to Bolivia, and the Portuguese claimed the lands in what is now Brazil. On the Spanish side of the Guaporé River, which forms the border at Rondônia between the two countries, Jesuits established what for a century was the largest missionary outpost in South America. The missions made deep inroads into the indigenous tribes, and many of those tribes dissolved. But on the Portuguese side, the dynamic was slightly different. Some Portuguese colonial leaders, wary of attempts by the Spanish Crown to claim their territory, encouraged the known tribes of the region to remain intact: they believed that if the Indians aggressively defended their native lands, Spanish trespassers might keep their distance. Essentially, they used the Indians as unpaid border guards.

When rubber tappers descended upon the area in the 1800s, many of the Indians on the Bolivian side who'd previously been contacted by the missionaries became slaves of the rubber trade. The rubber companies also made incursions on the Brazilian side, but more of the tribes there remained isolated, left to live alone in the forest, much as they had for centuries.

Candido Rondôn, perhaps the greatest Brazilian jungle explorer who ever lived, traveled throughout the Guaporé Valley in the early 1900s, traversing the forests of what decades later would become a state named in his honor. In 1909, he noted the presence of Kanoe Indians in the region—this tribe likely included the parents of the elderly Indian named Monunzinho, whom Marcelo had hired as a translator from a Kanoe clan in another part of Rondônia. According to Monunzinho, his branch of the Kanoe tribe was moved out of the region in 1940 and forced to work in rubber camps. But he said the elders of his tribe often talked of another group of related Kanoe who hadn't been enslaved. A 1943 Brazilian government report seemed to support that story when it mentioned that a group of Kanoe Indians were believed to live on the left bank of the Omerê River—the place where more than fifty years later the Contact Front had found Purá, Owaimoro, and the rest of the clan.

Brazilian linguist Laércio Nora Bacela traveled to Rondônia to carry out the first detailed study of the Kanoe language shortly after Marcelo and Altair established contact in 1995. He sat down with Purá's mother, Tatuá, and began to try to decipher their history.

Tatuá was about fifty years old, but she was an old fifty. Her face was scored with deep wrinkles, and her back was permanently bowed by a lifetime of burdens. As she began to talk, those burdens revealed themselves in the form of feverish memories of a tribe in decline.

Tatuá said that more than twenty years before, in the 1970s, the Kanoe tribe consisted of about fifty people, the majority of whom were females. The men of the tribe had been trying to reach out to other isolated tribes in the area to negotiate marriages, hoping to form a sort of partnership to keep their lineage alive for at least a few more generations. One day, all of the males—from old men to adolescent boys—went to look for other tribes, leaving the women and only the youngest children behind. Days passed, and the men didn't return. After days of uncertainty, two of the women decided to form a search party. A few days later, they returned with devastating news: the men had been killed. They had found their slaughtered bodies in the forest. The tribe's tasks had always been split distinctly between the males—who hunted, fished, made arrows, and built huts—and the women, who tended gardens, reared children, and handled many of the chores around the village. Now they felt lost, unsure that they could survive. They panicked. They collected a vine called *timbó,* which produces a poisonous sap that Amazonian Indians often pour into river inlets to stun fish, making them easy to catch. Convinced they and their children would suffer and die anyway without the men, the women brewed a timbó poison and agreed to commit collective suicide. The women gave the poison to their children before drinking it themselves. But Tatuá said that she was plagued by second thoughts. She didn't give the poison to Purá and his sister—she only pretended to do it. She drank very little of the poison herself, and forced herself to vomit. Struggling to summon her strength, she gathered her two children and ran to her sister and her niece. She helped them to vomit what they'd swallowed, and together they staggered away from the camp.

The two adult women and the three children were the only survivors, Tatuá said. But Tatuá's sister was never the same after the incident. She suffered from visions and refused to believe that the men of the tribe were really dead. A short while after the mass suicide, Tatuá's sister ran off into the forest to look for the men, convinced they were out there somewhere. The others never saw her again. That left Tatuá to raise her two children and her young niece, Owaimoro, by herself.

By the time the Contact Front encountered the group, nearly two decades had passed since the suicides. Tatuá had struggled to play the role of both mother and father to the children. She said she did her best to teach each of them how to handle not only the tasks traditionally managed by females, but also those that had been the purview of the tribe's men. She tried to preserve as much of the tribe's culture as she could, teaching the children the songs the tribe performed during frequent shamanistic ceremonies. Men traditionally played all the music at those events, which is why she tried to put young Purá in charge of that job.

"He isn't good with the flute," Tatuá said, "because I'm the one who had to teach him how to play."

* * *

Altair revisited the site of the destroyed village in the first week of December 1996 before heading out into the woods on another search for clues. The seeds that the ranch workers had been spreading on the day that Marcelo angrily confronted them had thrived, germinating into broad-bladed grasses that brushed the tops of Altair's knees as he walked.

Under all that grass, the holes could still be found. Based on the striations of dirt inside them, the team estimated they'd been dug many years before. Some of the tapping scars on the surrounding trees appeared to be more than a dozen years old. The size of the garden remnants suggested that the area had been a long-term dwelling site, perhaps for fifteen years or more. Most of the fourteen holes on the site were five and a half feet deep, just like those found in the individual huts near the lumberyard. The rectangular mouths of those holes at the village site were the same width—about thirty-five inches—as the holes found in the single-man huts, but they were approximately five times as long.

In each of the single-man huts, they had found the remnants of a stiff hammock draped over the width of the hole. For whatever reason, it seemed that whoever had lived there slept over the hole. If those holes had been big enough for one person, then the fourteen structures they believed once stood on the village site each might have accommodated five people. The structures might have been longhouses. Dozens of people might have lived there.

But Maria Elenice had told Vincent that only three Indians were believed to have lived on the site when it was destroyed the previous January. The Contact Front figured that might be true. Perhaps the decimation of the tribe hadn't occurred all at once. Maybe the destruction in January represented the final nail in the coffin of an already dying tribe. It didn't take a huge leap of imagination to think that one Indian might have been separated from the rest of the tribe during that destruction.

When Altair waded through that grassy clearing that morning, all of those inferences seemed reasonable, if uncertain. A few days later he undertook another expedition, and what he found convinced him that one of the inferences was unquestionably true: they now were tracking a single Indian through the forest, not a small group of them.

Marcelo returned to Vilhena to tend to administrative matters, while Vincent returned to the family he hadn't seen in weeks. Altair took charge of the expedition. He was accompanied by a FUNAI assistant named Adonias and a friend of Vincent's who carried a video camera, just in case they actually encountered the Indian. Monunzinho, the elderly Kanoe translator, also joined them. If the Indian who had built the huts didn't actually speak Kanoe, there was a chance he might speak a related tongue that Monunzinho might understand.

Monunzinho was a small man, no taller than 5 feet four, and he couldn't have weighed much more than 110 pounds. His cutoff shorts exposed a pair of spindly legs that appeared weak and unsteady, but they proved surprisingly resilient on long treks. His eyes narrowed to slits when he laughed. Those eyes were hard to see on hikes, though: he wore a dirty red baseball cap he'd gotten at a gas station, and he pulled the bill low, completely obscuring the top of his face. When he high-stepped over branches and puddles while crossing a muddy hillside ridge, it seemed a wonder he could see where he was going.

Monunzinho walked along the muddy edge of a steep ridge that was covered with thorny briar, descending to a ravine more than twenty feet below. Altair was right behind him. When they passed the ridge and descended a slope, Altair took the lead. He didn't walk far before he stopped, noticing a shallow bed of dark leaves.

Altair set his rifle aside and bent to clear the leaves, uncovering a hole. Insects darned the air within the perfectly smooth mud walls of the pit. At the bottom of the hole, razor-sharp stakes menaced. If anyone less observant had been leading the hike, the pit might have caused a crippling fall. Altair spread the leaves over the pitfall, leaving it as he found it.

As he set off on the trail again, Altair paid special attention to the leaves.

He slowly walked a few yards, then paused to listen, head angled slightly upward. The calls of unseen birds rained from high in the trees, sounding like spinning coins rattling to stillness on a tabletop.

At the base of a tree, Altair saw a patch of bare ground, the type of place his foot would naturally want to fall when hiking through brush. He stopped. Near the woody root, he saw a couple of smudges.

Only they weren't smudges. He bent to take a closer look, pointing them out to the men behind him. They were two footprints, human, and judging from the direction in which the toes were pointed, they led around the other side of the tree. Altair didn't say a word because the tracks were fresh.

Quietly, he slipped around to the other side of the tree and tried to soften the sound of his steps, slowly shifting his weight into the soles of his muddy brown leather boots. A few yards away, he confronted another pitfall. But unlike the one he had found just minutes earlier, this hole wasn't covered with leaves. A pile of loose red dirt spread from the lip of the hole. The dirt was moist. The excavation was shallow, fewer than two feet deep. Someone had dug the hole recently but hadn't yet finished the job.

It wasn't until Altair stood to ponder that work in progress that he saw a hut. It was only some twenty feet away. Barely visible among the trees, its architecture consisted of little more than an untidy heap of palm fronds atop a frame of slanting sticks.

"Come on," Altair said, whispering to the others as he approached with his rifle. Knowing someone had been in the area recently, his movements were slow and deliberate. He walked up to the hut and carefully spread apart the leaves covering the exterior to look inside: thin strands of golden light poured through the latticed thatch overhead, but other than a few flying insects, the hut was empty.

At the same time, Monunzinho spotted something near the fresh and unfinished pitfall, and he whispered just loud enough to get Altair's attention. "Look," he whispered. "More footprints."

They followed the tracks to a pile of cold ash, where someone had burned a few logs, probably the night before. When Altair joined him to look, he didn't have time to examine the tracks too closely. Beyond the nearest clutch of trees, Altair caught his first glimpse of the man they had been tracking for months.

The Indian didn't see them at first. He was kneeling outside another hut that appeared sturdier than the first, with walls of bundled palm boles and a peaked roof that jutted out in leafy eaves. Altair waved to Vincent's friend with the camera, signaling for him to come closer with his camera to get a better view of the Indian, who appeared oblivious to their presence.

They peered over the shrubs and ferns that separated them from him. The Indian sat on his haunches, with his elbow on his leg, and his chin resting on the bend of his wrist. His hair was long, though it appeared that he'd cut the sides close, probably using a bamboo blade or a scavenged machete, the same way the Akuntsu trimmed their hair. His face was neither young nor old: Altair guessed he was in his midthirties. He had a patchy assemblage of facial hair, including a thin mustache that framed his mouth. In those quiet moments before he noticed his visitors, he radiated a pensive attitude of untroubled relaxation. But he abruptly jumped up when he heard a twig snap under Altair's approaching boot heel.

The Indian wore nothing except a groin-covering breechcloth of dried grasses that hung from a fibrous rope tied around his waist. He appeared to wear neither body paint nor jewelry. He turned quickly, showing them his bare backside, then dashed behind the hut.

Altair whistled, trilling the note to make sure the Indian knew the whistle was meant to be heard. He hoped the whistle might convince the Indian that the group wasn't trying to sneak up on him, even though that is exactly what they'd done: Altair had wanted a closer look, and something had told him he should try to preserve the opportunity for stealth observation as long as possible. Now that his cover was blown, Altair said the only thing he could think to say was, "Whoa— *Ola!*"

Altair couldn't see the Indian, but he knew he was still back there, either inside the hut or around the other side.

"Hey, amigo!" Altair called, continuing to speak to him in Portuguese.

The only answer he heard was silence. But through the wall of the hut, he saw something protrude: the fluted tip of an arrow, the kind designed to pierce the thick hide of a peccary.

"Okay, Monunzinho," Altair said, turning to the elderly translator, "try to talk to him."

Monunzinho offered a greeting in Kanoe. There was no reaction, so he tried another greeting common to the Tupi family of languages, which included tribes such as the Akuntsu. Again, nothing. For the hell of it, they tried Spanish and got no reaction. Monunzinho launched into a little more Kanoe, hoping maybe he'd warm up to it. But the Indian didn't respond, and the arrow didn't move.

Altair wasn't sure what to do next. When he and Marcelo had found the Kanoe for the first time, the tribe had been friendly enough after that initial awkward exchange of hellos. Altair had no experience of anything but an amenable encounter. He pushed his baseball cap back on his head and drew a deep breath. If they left the Indian to try their luck on another day, there was no guarantee they'd easily find him again. The Indian might abandon the hut just as he had the others. It was impossible to guess how many expeditions might be required before they could get another opportunity like this one. So Altair stayed.

It was hot, at least ninety degrees, so he peeled off his sweat-soaked shirt and sat down for a second to think. A warbling of birdsong filled the silence of the forest. Near the hut, they'd seen a small collection of leaning sticks built over a fire. Next to the sticks sat a pot—blackened, misshapen, and dented, an artifact apparently manufactured from an anonymous hunk of scavenged metal, and it appeared to have survived many years of backwoods abuse.

"Maybe he was cooking," Altair said to Adonias, the FUNAI assistant.

Adonias looked at the pot. It looked as if there might be something in it—corn, maybe. They hadn't eaten all day.

"Hey there, friend," Altair called out, giving it another shot.

Adonias added, "Friend, you want to give us a little of that food?" he asked, smiling at Altair. "We're hungry, too!"

They stayed put for the next several minutes, reluctant to approach a man who clearly wasn't convinced they were friendly visitors. He'd withdrawn the arrow but hadn't revealed himself to them. They sat under a tree branch as the light of day grew slant, shining through the tiny holes that insects had bitten in the leaves that hung still above their heads. Every now and then, for lack of anything else to do, Altair would trill a melodic whistle, hoping it might be able to communicate benevolence on some unconscious, sublinguistic level. Adonias slapped away a cloud of gnats from his face and let out a deep, frustrated breath. It was dark inside the hut, and they couldn't tell if he was there. Monunzinho took off his shirt and again tried to address him in Kanoe, figuring the man might respond better to another Indian if he wasn't wearing white men's clothes.

"Do you have a machete with you?" Altair asked Adonias, who lifted his knife, still encased in a leather sheath. "Show it to him."

The idea was that if they showed him the machete in an entirely unthreatening way, maybe he'd recognize it as a peace offering. During FUNAI's first contacts, it was customary for sertanistas to offer gifts as a way of proving friendliness. Often they tried to leave tools, such as machetes and axes, on trails in the woods where Indians were believed to walk, as a way to attract them toward a nonviolent encounter. Adonias banged his machete—still encased—against a branch, hoping to attract the Indian's attention. Then he gave it to Altair, who stepped closer to the hut and unsheathed the machete, holding it by the blade and extending it toward the hut, handle first. He didn't hear a single rustle, but saw the tip of the arrow, and he dropped the machete on the ground and backed away.

The Indian had been inside the hut with his arrow drawn, but during the two-hour encounter he chose not to shoot. The team members eventually gave up, telling themselves they'd come back later with the others and be better prepared to encourage contact.

They set a pan next to his crudely battered one, then filled it with the manioc they carried as a gift. Altair then removed a leather necklace from the videographer's neck and draped it on a stick by the fire. Altair silently walked away, knowing he'd be back. No sound came from the hut as they retreated, only the hum of grasshoppers.

Altair told Marcelo everything they'd experienced, and two weeks later the Contact Front filed a report to FUNAI headquarters in Brasília that outlined their strategy: they would push for contact with the lone Indian, no matter how many expeditions it took. They feared that if they didn't encounter him first, land-grabbers would, and their version of contact might be swift and fatal. Now that the Indian's presence had been so thoroughly documented, Marcelo believed that the pressure to bring the situation to some sort of resolution would only intensify for all of them—the Indian, the Contact Front, and the ranchers.

"Information collected in our travels alerts us of the added responsibilities that we have to return again, with a certain frequency," Marcelo wrote to his bosses in Brasília. "After all, some of the ranchers are convinced that the use of violence against Indians is the only way to protect their 'rights' of ownership over the land. And the presence of the Guaporé Contact Front has always accelerated that process."

Purá Kanoe pictured in 2007 in his village.

Konibu, chief of the Akuntsu tribe, constructs an arrow while Pupak (background) watches.

CHAPTER SIX

Windows to His World

Purá sat on the wooden edge of a pavilion-style hut in the Kanoe village. The air was smoky, and his arms and shoulders ached. Both of these facts were related to the blackened carcass of a giant armadillo that was roasting over a smoldering fire a few yards away.

He had found the armadillo burrowing into the ground near a creek the day before. The animal was built like a mechanical excavator, weighing about a hundred pounds, armored with protective plates, and equipped with sickle-shaped claws. Purá watched it tunnel through the mud, and he resolved to catch and kill it: underneath the bony armor, the meat of an armadillo is tender and savory. He got down on his knees and began to dig. Nearly eight hours later, he captured the scaly beast in the pit of a deep hole, and he speared it in its soft belly.

A day later, sore all over, Purá needed a calm afternoon of restrained motion. With the armadillo, the Kanoe had enough meat for a couple more days. He didn't need to hunt or fish. He was free to concentrate on more sedentary labors.

At Purá's feet sat two sections of hollow cane tubing and one shank of palm wood. He'd already cut the three pieces into predetermined lengths. The palm piece was shorter than the others, and it wasn't tubular: it was a fluted, foot-long sliver that was sharpened to a point. The blunt end of the sliver was carved to fit snugly into the hollow of a piece of the cane tubing.

The three components united like the segments of a pool cue. Together they formed an arrow that measured about five feet, four inches—about the same height as Purá himself. This was the Kanoe way: an archer shoots an arrow that corresponds to his own height, ensuring maximum accuracy.

Purá rubbed some white string he had fashioned from tree fibers on a plug of brown resin. The cottony string turned brown and sticky. He wrapped the string tightly around the arrow's joints. Then he wrapped them with red string, which he had previously dyed using the pulp of *achiote* fruits he'd collected. This was decorative, as were the two thin strips of what looked like white plastic, but were actually the spines of tiny bird feathers, to create an ornamental border.

Near the notched end of the arrow, opposite its point, he sewed to the shaft a fletching of two feathers, which came from an eagle he'd found dead in the forest. He wound the feathers around the shaft in a subtle spiral. The flourish served an aerodynamic purpose: helical fletching causes the arrow to spin in flight and helps it fly true.

As a final touch, he pulled a small needle from another bag. It was the barb from a freshwater stingray's tail. He affixed it to the tip of the arrowhead to create an even sharper point than the one he'd carved.

Each tiny component of the arrow—the feathers, the tubing, the string, the tip—could in itself represent a full day's work. But because he had already stocked a complete inventory of materials, Purá was able to finish two arrows on this day.

He added them to his collection of several dozen. Many of the arrows were designed for large game, but others were lighter and featured multipronged tips for birds. A few of the arrows had several barbs curving from the arrowhead, which helped anchor it into the flesh of its target. Those barbed tips were designed for monkeys, the only prey in this forest that would try to yank an arrow out of itself after being hit.

Altair watched Purá work in humbled admiration. Humbled, because he'd tried to make arrows himself once and abandoned the project in frustration. After working on them for days, he walked into the bush to try them out. But with almost every step, he'd knock either his bow or his arrows into a branch or a bush or a tree trunk. He couldn't figure out how to walk without making an unholy racket. If there had been any animals within miles of him, he scared them away.

Purá never had that problem. And as he worked on his hunting tools, he was the picture of patience. He lost himself in the subtleties of the craft, deriving a slow-burning pleasure from the tiniest of details. The eagle feathers he had attached to the two arrows were beautiful, and he strummed a finger across them in admiration. Eagle plumes were harder to get than wild turkey feathers, and his pride in them suggested they were worth every bit of extra effort required.

Altair had learned how much the Kanoe prized such tiny details when Purá and his mother led him through the forest to point out an eagle's nest they'd spotted high in a tree. In addition to a full-grown bird, they believed the nest housed at least one eagle chick. If they could raise the chick to adulthood, they believed it could yield them a regular supply of arrow feathers.

Through sign language, they told him that the nest was too high to shoot down with their arrows. They wanted him to shoot it with his rifle. Altair refused—it was too high even for his gun. If he were able to knock it down with bullets, he told them, it would require several shots, and he'd probably kill the birds. If they wanted the nest to remain reasonably intact, he said, they'd have to chop the tree down. So Purá hacked away at the tree trunk for three full days. On the fourth day, the tree fell and the Kanoe captured a baby eagle.

The day after he chopped down the tree, Purá built a wooden cage for the eagle. Altair couldn't believe how large he'd made it.

"That's big enough for a lion!" Altair told him.

Purá reasoned that the bird needed room to grow into a healthy, feathery adult. But the bird never got the chance. Shortly after it was caged, a jaguar stole into the village at night, reached between the bars, and devoured the young eagle. The experiment failed, but it showed Altair just how much labor could be poured into a lifestyle that seemed so unadorned on its surface. The Kanoe could have made their arrows with less flair, but they believed lesser arrows would have been indicative of a lesser tribe. It was a quality-of-life issue. Details mattered greatly to them.

After the Kanoe began spending more time with the members of the Contact Front, Purá focused his acute attention to detail onto them. While Altair was observing the Kanoe way of life, Purá was studying him with even greater intensity.

Even before the Kanoe had made contact with Marcelo and Altair,

Purá had been fascinated with the modern world. Purá's mother told Altair that her son sometimes disappeared for weeks at a time when he was younger. It took her a while to figure it out, but she eventually learned exactly where he was hiding: he spent those days high in a tree on a hill that overlooked a camp full of workers from a neighboring ranch. He'd stay up in the tree until dark, scrutinizing the workers, studying the clothing they wore, the tools they used. But his obsession couldn't be slaked through mere observation; he had to get closer. When they washed their clothes in the stream and left them in the water to soak, Purá seized the opportunity to grab a few garments. Kanoe custom dictated that he leave something behind for them, so he laid a couple of arrows on the riverbank—a fair trade, he figured, considering all the work that went into making a single arrow. The unsolicited transaction alerted the workers to the presence of Indians on the land, of course, and they began placing guard dogs at the edge of their encampment. After that, the rumor of Indians in that area began to spread. Years later, Marcelo and the rest of the Contact Front followed those rumors to the forest trail where they found Purá and his sister.

It was Purá who'd made the salt-bag shorts the Kanoe had been wearing on the day of contact. He had replicated the design from the clothes he'd seen the ranch workers wear.

After contact, Purá's thirst for new clothing designs seemed unquenchable. He'd cut small sections of wire from the fencing that enclosed the nearest ranch, sharpening them into knitting needles. One day Purá showed Altair a new pair of shorts he'd made from some fabric he'd collected. He pointed to the needlework along the outseam: it was double-stitched. Altair was impressed; the tailoring looked surprisingly professional. Then Purá pointed to the outseam of Altair's Levi's. The double stitching was identical. Purá had silently noticed the design and had replicated it.

His mimicry wasn't limited to clothes. After he saw Altair and Marcelo build the Rio Omerê camp, Purá returned to the Kanoe village and constructed two new rectangular frame buildings in the same architectural style. Out were the conical, tepee-shaped thatched huts the Kanoe had traditionally constructed; in were the pavilion-style structures favored by the Contact Front.

The eagerness of Purá's absorption took Altair and Marcelo aback. Whenever he wore traditional adornments, such as feathered armbands, they'd shower him with compliments, hoping to instill a little native pride in him. It made no difference. He clearly preferred T-shirts and zippered pants, factory-made. Unnatural colors were his favorites. Hot pinks, neon oranges, psychedelic swirls—those were what caught Purá's eye. They tried to cure him of the impulse as if he'd come down with a touch of the flu, but they couldn't. He was a natural dandy. From the first time he spotted ranch workers in their colorful clothing, a genie had been let out of a bottle. There was no putting it back.

Every interaction raised questions of how much of their culture they should share with the recently contacted tribes, and how much they should shield from them. For most of the team members, the instinct was to shield. But where did they draw the line? If they were enjoying the benefits of a sharp steel machete, was it cruel to deny Purá use of a tool he clearly would like to use? If something as simple as a pair of scissors would cut several hours away from the time required to make a dozen arrows, was it fair to watch him toil unnecessarily just for tradition's sake?

The dicey interplay between technology and tradition was an ethical minefield. For centuries it had formed the unstable center in relations between the Amazon's tribes and newcomers. Since colonial times, whites had used gifts of tools and other energy-saving products to buy goodwill from Indians. Explorers developed a tried-and-true method: set a gift rack on a jungle trail and load it with machetes, axes, and bags of sugar. After receiving the gifts, the Indians might be more willing to meet peacefully. That practice was quickly hijacked by those with ignoble designs: whole tribes had been wiped out by people who laced sugar bags with poison and distributed them in the forest. That kind of thing happened with disturbing frequency. In 1957, rubber tappers loaded sugar bags with arsenic and later blamed the dead Tapayuna Indians found in the forest on "an epidemic." Six years later, a rubber company overseer in Rondônia dropped sugar packets from an airplane, and when Cinta Larga Indians gathered to collect the packets, he firebombed them.

Even so, the gift racks were still used regularly by FUNAI, and the Contact Front had initiated relations with the Kanoe using the method. They'd left machetes and axes in the forest even before the first encounter with Purá and Tiramantú on the trail, hoping to convince them they meant no harm. It was also how they hoped to initiate contact with the lone Indian they were now tracking. Maybe he would discover that the benefits of contact outweighed the dangers. Maybe he'd peacefully greet them. Maybe then they could protect him from what they believed was the *real* danger—men with guns who'd rather see the Indian dead.

In watching Purá and the rest of the Kanoe go about their daily lives, Altair and the others grew to believe that reasonable compromises were possible. If they showed prudence, they believed they could make peaceful contact with Indians—including the lone Indian—while preserving the basics of the culture.

One thing they knew for sure about the lone Indian's culture was that he was a honey gatherer. He probably diluted the honey in water and drank it as a sweet refreshment, like the Kanoe did. Marcelo and Altair had found numerous honey cuts crudely hacked out of tree trunks near the Indian's huts. An ax or a machete would make the process a lot easier. One of those tools might win his good graces. Such a gift might smooth the road to contact, and they knew from their experience with Purá that the custom would survive more or less intact.

When Purá went hunting for honey, he now always carried the ax they had given him shortly after they established contact. They followed him into the forest to learn his routine. It wasn't hard to imagine the lone Indian in Purá's place.

Purá scaled the forty-five-degree incline of a fallen tree as if walking up a ramp. About fifteen feet off the ground, he reached a small scaffold he had constructed earlier, using bamboo and natural twine. Stepping out onto the scaffold, he was able to reach the upright trunk of another tree, which was dead. A teeming beehive was affixed to that trunk. Ax in hand, Purá hacked at the trunk with a downward, slanting stroke, like a baseball coach hitting hard ground balls to his infielders. Just a few swings was enough to work up a lathery sweat, soaking his T-shirt.

After notching the trunk, he leveled his swing and bored straight in, cutting a wedge into the hollow core of the trunk. Thousands of stingless bees poured out, covering his hair, his shoulders, his face. He reached his arm into the trunk, and pulled out a clump of brown, honeycombed wax. He tried to throw it to the ground, but it stuck to his hand. He shook it furiously until it finally came free. Holding an empty bowl near the hole in the trunk, he reached in again. This time he pulled out handfuls of honey, letting the opaque golden liquid drip from his hand into the bowl. Squinting through a thick veil of swarming bees, he tried to shoo the teeming insects away. He ran his hand over his eyes to scoop up a handful of bees—a temporary solution, because the traces of honey he left on his face provoked them into an even more delirious frenzy.

After half filling the bowl by hand, he descended the slanted trunk and searched in the low foliage until he found two grassy stalks. Yanking them out of the ground, he shredded them to tassels in his palm, then wadded them into a pompon. He returned to the hole in the tree and used the wadded grass as a sponge to collect the honey. He wiped the pompon around the inside of the trunk, and when it was heavy with honey, he wrung it out into the bowl. After more than an hour, Purá returned to the village with one full bowl of honey.

If it took Purá an hour to collect honey with an ax, the team members suspected that the lone Indian toiled a lot longer for his taste of sweetness. Field experiments supported that suspicion. Researchers at the American Museum of Natural History found that while it took a person an average of 3 hours to cut down a tree with a modern steel ax, it took the same person about 115 hours when working with the stone axes traditionally used by Amazonian Indians. By giving Purá an ax, they had saved him hours, and he could spend those hours on other tasks—making arrows, hunting, fishing, whatever. The gift hadn't destroyed the Kanoe honey-gathering tradition itself, and they figured the spirit of the labor remained relatively unchanged: collecting honey was still no walk in the park for him. It was a compromise, they knew, but it was one their consciences could live with—if the Indians themselves were the ones determining the speed of the change. If an Indian wanted an ax, they couldn't blame him for muddying an unspoiled ideal that the Indian himself didn't believe in. Likewise, if the Indian didn't want those tools, they figured they had no right to force them on him. He, not they, should make the choice.

But those choices weren't always so clear-cut. Minor aspects of Indian culture could change without them even noticing it, as easily overlooked as the outseam on a pair of jeans. It was a messy business. But if contact might help save a culture from extinction, the cultural alterations caused by something like an ax or a T-shirt seemed minor in comparison.

Over the next several months, they continued to invite Purá and Owaimoro on expeditions into the Modelo Ranch to try to make contact with the lone Indian. They found more traps, honey cuts, and trails. On the trails that showed signs of his foot traffic, they left machetes, axes, and seeds for planting.

But when they would return to those spots weeks later, they'd find that the tools lay exactly where they had left them, untouched.

Marcelo and Vincent developed a theory to explain why the lone Indian, whom they had begun to casually refer to as "the Indian of the Hole," might be reluctant to accept gifts.

Marcelo remembered that years before, in 1984, a group of unidentified Indians living just miles from what later became the Rio Omerê Reserve had shot arrows at logging trucks. According to rumors at the time, some of the local ranch hands had maintained a glancing relationship with that tribe for several years. The ranch hands camped in the forest for extended periods, and sometimes they'd strike deals with the tribe, trading old machetes for corn, rope for fruits, sugar for manioc. Their relationship with the Indians never progressed beyond those simple transactions. But according to the stories, when logging trucks were hit by arrows in 1984, the owner of the nearest ranch feared that the known presence of Indians might threaten his ownership of the land. He supposedly ordered the ranch hands to distribute "gifts" to the Indians: bags of sugar laced with rat poison.

The story was apocryphal and was never proved. But it got Marcelo and Vincent thinking. That supposed poisoning allegedly occurred within a day's walk from the place where they had found the village with the fourteen holes. When they considered the proximity, obvious questions formed:

Could the lone Indian have been a member of the tribe who shot arrows at the logging trucks before being targeted with poisoned sugar?

After surviving the poisoning, was it possible that he and several other survivors from the tribe moved to the village of the fourteen holes?

Could the lone Indian be the only one to have survived the recent massacre that destroyed the village they had discovered?

The connections seemed plausible, and they might explain why the lone Indian would leave their gifts untouched on those jungle trails. But they couldn't be proven.

They tracked down an old logging driver who'd been part of the convoy of trucks attacked by the Indians in 1984. They hoped to collect a description of the Indians, but the driver wasn't much help. He explained to Marcelo that he'd seen the arrows bounce off of the windshield of another truck in his convoy, but he didn't get a good look at the Indians themselves before he sped away.

"When I saw it get hit with the arrows," he told Vincent and Marcelo, "no one could force me to stick around."

Without solid evidence, the theories about the massacres weren't worth a damn, true or not. The best way to get that evidence, of course, was to speak to the lone Indian himself.

Marcelo figured that if anyone could break through the lone Indian's resistance to contact, it was probably the members of either the Kanoe or the Akuntsu tribes. But if the introduction of a mere tool, such as an ax, created ethical traps, the introduction of another tribe could prove even more delicate.

After discovering the Kanoe and the Akuntsu and creating the Rio Omerê Reserve for them, the Contact Front had encouraged a bond between the two tribes. To outsiders, the two tribes might have seemed incredibly similar—both were victims of conflict, both had been reduced to a handful of survivors, both lived in the same general area, both had been discovered at roughly the same time by the Contact Front. But the two tribes had to overcome enormous differences to forge a bond. Even among Indian tribes isolated in the middle of the jungle, self-perception is a complex and highly relative matter. The Kanoe, for example, believed they had very little in common with the Akuntsu. They saw the Akuntsu as barbarously crude, a clan blighted by swinish habits, in need of a good scrubbing in the river.

The two tribes had been forced by circumstances to be friendly during the past couple of years, but trust remained shaky. Owaimoro, more than any of the other members of the Kanoe, found it difficult to hide her disgust with the Akuntsu way of life. With her pet capuchin monkey permanently ensconced on her shoulder, she'd watch how the Akuntsu treated their pets. The Akuntsu attached almost no sentimental value to their animals; if the tribe members were hungry, they had no qualms about slaughtering a pet for food. To Owaimoro, it smacked of savagery. She viewed the Akuntsu as members of a clearly inferior culture. The other members of the Kanoe were less open about showing their disdain, but they also seemed to harbor similar attitudes regarding their tribal neighbors.

But if the five members of the Kanoe hoped to have relations with any other Indians, the Akuntsu had become their only hope. That's why, despite the differences between the two tribes, the Kanoe in 1995 led Altair and Vincent through the woods to meet the Akuntsu for the first time.

The initial meeting with the Akuntsu occurred just weeks after the team had initially encountered Purá and his sister on the jungle trail. The Kanoe had spoken of the Akuntsu as savages, and they explained that they still didn't fully trust them. Nerves were tight as bowstrings when Owaimoro and Purá's sister, Tiramantú, prepared to lead Altair and Vincent across well-trod jungle trails toward the Akuntsu village. Just before they departed from the Kanoe village, Tiramantú paced nervously and confessed her anxiety to the elderly Kanoe translator whom the Contact Front had hired.

"I'm scared of them," Tiramantú said, touching her machete to her chin, measuring the words slowly. "They fight a lot. They're wild."

For the past two years, Tiramantú had served as something of a diplomatic envoy between the two tribes. She was the one who had initiated contact with the Akuntsu in the first place, believing it was the only way the Kanoe, who had dwindled to four people, could survive for another generation. She recognized that the Akuntsu were similarly threatened by the narrowing prospects for reproduction that didn't violate incest taboos: their tribe consisted of two males, an elderly female, two sisters aged about thirty-five and twenty-five, and a girl of about thirteen.

Tiramantú had arranged meetings with the eldest Akuntsu male, a chieftain named Konibu, who appeared to be in his sixties. The meetings had been tense, always, as they struggled to communicate without a common language. But Tiramantú successfully made her point to Konibu. Within a year, she became pregnant and had a boy—young Operá, who was now about two years old. Tiramantú never discussed the boy's lineage, but everyone knew that the father had to be one of the two Akuntsu males—Konibu or his nephew, Pupak, who was in his thirties. Despite the age difference, the members of the Contact Front assumed Konibu was the father. Konibu ruled over the Akuntsu with unquestioned authority, and if anyone was going to take charge of ensuring that his tribe live on in one form or another, it would be Konibu.

But even Tiramantú—who'd managed to be intimate with one of the Akuntsu—was nervous when the group approached the Akuntsu village. She explained that the reason Purá didn't come along was that Pupak viewed him as a rival and had threatened his life just the day before. The translator detected her unease, and grew a little edgy himself. When they emerged from the woods into a vegetable garden beside the Akuntsu village, the translator asked her, "If they are there, do you think they will attack us?"

Tiramantú held her arrows over her shoulder and scanned the huts. They appeared empty. "They're wild, yes, and yesterday they wanted to kill my brother," she said. "So you should also be careful. They could kill you."

She explained that the tensions between the two tribes had recently heated up when she approached Konibu about the possibility of Purá pairing up with one of the Akuntsu women. They were, after all, his only chance at finding a mate. But Konibu wouldn't allow it. Tiramantú got angry, and the animosity between the two tribes began to boil.

"I was so mad," Tiramantú explained, "I wanted to kill them all." She paused before turning to Altair and Vincent: "But after you have appeared here, I don't want to kill anyone anymore." Her face split into a smile, flashing an uneven row of discolored teeth, and she began to shake with laughter.

Her attempt at comic relief didn't go very far in comforting the others, who followed her and Owaimoro as they slowly approached the huts. Tiramantú listened carefully for any stirrings. Behind one of the huts they found Pupak, the Akuntsus' younger male. Pupak was with the elderly Akuntsu woman, who had adopted him as a son decades before.

The old Akuntsu woman wore no clothes aside from fibrous armbands that squeezed tight around her upper arms, and colorful necklace baubles and earrings made of shells. Pupak wore only a breechcloth of dried grasses. Their skin was painted with red urucum dye. To repel insects, they had rubbed the ashes from smudge fires onto their skin. The Kanoe considered the practice hopelessly squalid; Owaimoro was forever urging them to bathe.

Tiramantú grabbed the old woman by the hand and walked her to Altair, who smiled and nodded.

"These are the men who came to our village," Tiramantú said to the old woman. The elderly tribeswoman couldn't understand a single word Tiramantú said, of course. The Akuntsu spoke a dialect of the Tupari language, not Kanoe.

Tiramantú and Owaimoro used the translator and took charge of the encounter, trying to advise Altair and Vincent how they should treat the Akuntsu. Generally, their advice was that they shouldn't bother treating them well. It was futile to waste gifts on them, they said. The Akuntsu, according to the Kanoe, lacked the refinement to appreciate the white man's tools.

Altair and Vincent suspected jealousy.

"Go ahead and give her the pan," Vincent told Altair.

Altair grabbed a shiny new chrome pan he'd brought and held it out for the elderly Akuntsu woman. Owaimoro protested. She pointed to another black and dented pan, an old one Altair had used for himself, and suggested that it was a more appropriate welcoming gift for such a primitive tribe.

"Don't give that new pan to her," Owaimoro said, watching the old woman fondle the gleaming object. "She'll just break everything."

"And if you give them clothes," Tiramantú added, "they'll rip them all. Take that pan and hide it from her."

Owaimoro abruptly snatched the pan away from the old woman, then took off into the woods to hide it, leaving the Akuntsu woman speechless in wide-eyed confusion. A few minutes later, Owaimoro returned, grabbed the old woman's hand, and shoved a metal bowl into her palm. A consolation prize, Owaimoro seemed to say, and one she believed the Akuntsu should be happy to get.

But instead of the violent savages that the Kanoe had prepared them for, Altair and Vincent found the Akuntsu to be kind and welcoming, especially considering that they'd been surprised by strangers who couldn't have seemed more foreign had they arrived by spacecraft. Altair offered the Akuntsu crackers, and Pupak sat nibbling them contentedly while Altair unscrewed the cap on a jar of Nescafé and placed a pot of water over a fire. They sat in wordless communion, sharing food and drink. Pupak neither smiled nor frowned. He simply chewed his crackers and tried a sip of the coffee, staring at his visitors' faces. Tiramantú and Owaimoro sat in silence on the edge of the clearing.

Eventually Pupak led Altair and Vincent to the main Akuntsu clearing to meet the rest of the tribe. The elderly woman packed food and tools in twine bags she carried on her bent back, and picked through the forest with the aid of a long cane. After several minutes' hike, they reached the encampment, which consisted of four large conical huts.

Konibu sat cross-legged on one of the foot-long tree stumps that the tribe had arranged in the clearing as chairs. He and Pupak greedily puffed sweet tobacco that they'd rolled in brown leaves. Altair, wearing only shorts and his hiking boots, sat cross-legged near him, offering friendly smiles, hoping for acceptance from the chief. After a moment, Konibu reached over to Altair and began lightly grabbing at the skin of his forearm and legs.

"You're so hairy!" he said in the Akuntsu language.

The two men's broad smiles marked the beginning of what would become a long and often strange relationship between the Akuntsu and the Contact Front.

Over the following two years, Marcelo, Altair, and the rest of the team watched the Kanoe and the Akuntsu hold their sometimes strained relationship together. If those two tribes, with so many differences between them, could learn to live together, maybe there was hope for the single member of an unknown tribe living somewhere in the surrounding woods. Maybe one day, after being brought together in one protected area by the Contact Front, all of those tribes could live together peacefully.

As the three-way relationships among the Kanoe, the Akuntsu, and the Contact Front continued to evolve, the only one among them who seemed to regret FUNAI's efforts to encourage the new tribal bonds was Owaimoro's pet capuchin monkey.

He was a hyperactive little creature, a twitchy bundle of perpetual motion, eager to please from his perch on Owaimoro's shoulder. One day Owaimoro tagged along with Altair to hunt monkeys near the Kanoe village. The monkey, as usual, was on her shoulder. In retrospect, this was probably a mistake.

To attract monkeys, Altair imitated their whistled howls. He'd stand still in the forest and let loose with a call, then scan the treetops for any sign of a response. But on this day, his calls weren't working. Owaimoro's capuchin seemed amused by Altair's attempts at mimicry, and the monkey corrected him by offering a genuine whistle, as if he believed Altair needed to reference the genuine article. Altair encouraged the monkey to keep it up.

Before long, a small group of monkeys responded to the call by swinging through the treetops toward Altair, Owaimoro, and her pet. Altair waited until one got close enough, then aimed and pulled the trigger. A monkey fell dead from the tree. Owaimoro's pet watched everything unfold with an expression that Altair could only interpret as one of stunned horror.

From that moment on, Owaimoro's monkey couldn't stand being anywhere near a gun. If Altair or Marcelo approached with their rifles, he would hide behind Owaimoro and cover his eyes.

The members of the Kanoe and Akuntsu tribes themselves seemed to share none of the monkey's misgivings at having made contact with FUNAI. After Altair and Marcelo built the Rio Omerê encampment between the tribal villages, the Akuntsu and the Kanoe began to see much more of each other. The tribes often visited the team's camp at the same time to relax, socialize, and share meals. The tribes even began participating in joint shamanistic rituals together, once in the presence of Altair, Marcelo, and Vincent.

The ritual began when Konibu, the Akuntsus' chieftain, used a wooden pestle to mash *angico* seeds from the *paricá* trees in a small coconut bowl, creating an orange powder called *rapé*. He invited Tiramantú of the Kanoe to sit next to him. Konibu reached into the bowl and held a small mound of the powder on his index finger. He raised the finger to his nostril and snorted deeply, grimacing, coughing, and slapping his knee as the snuff burned through his rhinal cavities. The angico seeds are mildly hallucinogenic. Unlike the tobacco snuff that Konibu used habitually throughout the day, this rapé had a sacred purpose: it summoned spirits from the forest, they said.

Konibu continued to sniff and cough as Tiramantú, who'd stripped off her T-shirt for the ritual, reached into the bowl. They took turns sniffing the powder, letting the snuff penetrate their minds. Large black flies swarmed around their shoulders and bare backs, but they paid no attention to them. Tiramantú threw her head back and began whistling. She held both arms out to the side and began waving her hands and chanting: *babay-ah, babay-ah, babay-ah-ah-ah*.

As Konibu watched her in stoic silence, she took both hands to her mouth and inhaled large gulps of air: she was sucking the evil spirits out of the clearing. Then she puffed her cheeks and blew out, waving her arms in front of her: she was blowing those spirits away, far out into the forest. Konibu scanned the air around them, as if he could see them go.

Soon, Tiramantú rose from the wood stump she had been seated on and began running in circles with her arms flapping like the wings of a bird. Konibu mimicked the gesture from his seat on his own stump. They continued to blow away spirits. The two of them sat, they stood, they hopped up and down. Together they jumped in a circle, clapping their hands and slapping their thighs, until both collapsed on the ground. Konibu lay motionless, but Tiramantú chanted over him, stirring him back to life. After a few minutes, she leaped up and grabbed a bow and arrow. Her gaze suggested that she was staring at something hovering in the middle distance, by the tree line. But soon she collapsed on the dirt, moaning on her back. Flies descended on the sweat of her face. The ritual was over.

Altair and Vincent weren't sure what Tiramantú and Konibu had seen, but they themselves had just witnessed something historic: two enemy tribes coming together almost as one, sharing one of the most sacred spiritual rituals that each observed. What's more, the tribes had allowed the men to observe it all.

As they got to know the Akuntsu better and began communicating with them through translators, they grew to appreciate how lucky they were to have been accepted so quickly by the Akuntsu. If the Contact Front had approached the Akuntsu alone, without the Kanoe, the experience could have been disastrous. White men had approached them before but hadn't made a good impression.

The Akuntsu carried those impressions with them everywhere they went, literally. Konibu pointed to scar tissue that shone on the skin of his triceps like a glistening leech, and Pupak showed pockmarks on his back that Altair and Vincent recognized as the splatter pattern from shotgun pellets. Through a Tupari translator the team hired, Konibu told them how it happened.

"I'm alone now, with no brothers," Konibu said. "The white men killed all of my friends—*pow, pow, pow!*" He chopped a hand through the air, imitating a gun. "They killed them with guns, not bows and arrows. I am alone, which is why I have this fear of the people who live over there. That's why I ran away from them."

Konibu paused for a moment to clarify a point with the translator. "This guy here, and this one"—he gestured to Altair and Vincent—"I'm not scared of them. I'm afraid of the white men out there." He made a sweeping gesture, as if to indicate that "out there" meant beyond the forest, to the ranches that were cutting into the other side.

The translator pressed for more details, but Konibu said he needed to lie down. He withdrew into his hut and stretched out in his hammock. Altair and Vincent accompanied the translator into the hut and sat on the ground, which was soft and powdery from the ash of a dormant fire in the corner. Ururu, the elderly woman, entered and, placing both hands around her mouth, bent down to Konibu and inhaled deeply: she was sucking the poison of the bad memories out of his body, the translator explained, then blowing them to the winds. When she was finished, the translator asked if the white men had attacked the Akuntsus' former village during the day or at night.

"They attacked during the day," Konibu said, reclining in the hammock and pointing at the ceiling. "They attacked at midday—the sun was up there. They had come with their noisy machines. Later I only found dead bodies. But I never found the body of my brother. I don't know if maybe they had taken the body to eat it." The translator's face broke into a smile when Konibu offered the speculation, but the smile dissolved as the Akuntsu chief continued to speak. "The bodies of all the women were there, and the others. I looked and looked, but I didn't find it."

Altair sat at the foot of the hammock with his arms crossed over his knees, next to Vincent. Altair listened with an expression of blank horror, then asked where Konibu was when the white men attacked.

"I was away, over here," he said, drawing an imaginary circle in the air, indicating a location outside of the old village. "That's how I escaped. But their bullet caught me in the arm." He pointed again to the scar on the underside of his upper arm. "After that my arm was very hurt, very swollen."

Again Konibu assured Altair and Vincent that he bore the two of them no grudges—it was the ranchers who scared him. "When I see the white men, I am terrified. It feels like my heart is going to jump out of my chest. They had come with this machine that makes a lot of noise—*whee, whee, whee!* They came down very close to the people. We were left being very afraid."

From details they were able to pick up from Pupak and the rest of the tribe, Altair and Vincent determined that Konibu, Pupak, and the surviving females had been away from their village when ranch hands armed with chainsaws and guns began clearing the area. It occurred to them that perhaps the lone Indian they had been tracking had been another survivor of the same attack. Perhaps, they speculated for a moment, he even might have been the brother who Konibu presumed was dead but had never found.

But the Akuntsu never dug holes the way the lone Indian did, and they had never heard of any Akuntsu member doing such a thing. The attack on them had occurred at least a decade before, and from

Konibu's descriptions, the location of the former village was near the Yvipita Ranch, not the Modelo. Marcelo began to suspect that when he had his first arguments with the attorney Odair Flauzino in 1985, after he and his group of Nambiquara Indians found rifle and shotgun shells around the vestiges of a destroyed Indian village, it had been the Akuntsu who'd been attacked. The lone Indian, however, was almost certainly of a different tribe that had suffered a similar fate.

When the team members described to Konibu the general location of the destroyed village of fourteen holes they'd found, the chief said he didn't know a thing about it.

They told him they were trying to make contact with the lone Indian before he met a fate similar to that of Konibu's brother and fellow tribespeople. They asked him if—like Purá and Owaimoro—he and maybe a few of the Akuntsu women would be willing to join them on their mission. They explained to Konibu that if their group could get to the lone Indian before the ranchers did, the Indian might have a chance to survive in peace on a protected piece of land, just like the surviving members of his own tribe.

The idea made good sense for a couple of reasons. Even more than the Kanoe, the Akuntsu seemed to resemble the lone Indian, particularly the fact that he wore no clothes. Maybe the Indian would empathize with the Akuntsu. At the very least, the presence of more women on one of the team's expeditions might lend a more peaceful atmosphere to any encounter, to let him know they hadn't come to wage war.

Altair was tasked with convincing Konibu to join them, but first he had to convince him to ride in one of the Toyotas—a prerequisite for any expedition. None of the tribe members had ever set foot in a vehicle of any kind before.

When the Akuntsu first saw the truck, they refused to go near it. It was full of nasty spirits, they said—*listen to its roar, look at it shake!* But slowly, painstakingly, Altair worked to assure them it wasn't as bad as they believed. He opened the doors and walked them close to the truck, encouraging them to take a good look inside. After they gave it a once-over, Altair climbed into the seat and invited Konibu and three of the women to join him. It took almost a full afternoon of pleading—he tried everything short of falling to his knees and begging—

and they eventually relented. Altair gingerly shut the doors and took a seat behind the wheel. When he turned the ignition and the engine jumped to life, the Akuntsu lost their nerve. Konibu and the women began banging their fists against the windows. They said the noise was making them dizzy. They wanted out.

After that, Konibu categorically refused to allow any member of his tribe to accompany the Contact Front on an expedition. The Akuntsu and the Kanoe were able to live together only after years of diplomatic groundwork. Konibu believed that forcing a meeting with this Indian was only asking for trouble. He told the team members that if they wanted to find the Indian and establish a relationship like they had with the Kanoe and the Akuntsu, they'd have to do it without his help.

Maybe Owaimoro and Purá had already forgotten how dangerous a tribe could be when pushed to its limits, but Konibu hadn't.

Owaimoro Kanoe is shown with her ever-present pet monkey
during an expedition with the Contact Front in 1996.

CHAPTER SEVEN

Savages

In the first half of 1997, Brazil's environmental protection agency temporarily banned clear-cutting in the forest where Altair had encountered the lone Indian. The prohibition was a result of that encounter, but it was a hollow gesture: the government nailed a few signs to trees at the edge of the territory, and that was it. No one enforced the ban. The ranchers continued to cut down trees, and the Contact Front reported the violations, to no avail. The temporary restriction existed only on paper, not in the real world.

If Marcelo and his team really wanted to protect the land where they believed the Indian was living, they first needed the Justice Ministry to officially recognize his presence. To do that, FUNAI needed more than a mere physical description of the man. They needed a tribal name, a language, an overview of his customs—*anything* to prove that he represented a culture deserving of protection. There was one way to do that: the team members needed to establish contact with the Indian. Sydney Possuelo, the head of the Isolated Indians Division in Brasília, encouraged the Contact Front to launch more expeditions, gather more evidence, and—if possible—make contact with the Indian before pistoleros or ranch hands got the chance.

Throughout the second half of 1997, Marcelo and the rest of the team shouldered their packs over countless jungle trails, searching for signs of human life in places where no tribes had ever been officially recorded. Each month they launched an expedition, usually four or five days long, that took them through the forests claimed by the Dalafinis and their neighbors. From the start, those explorations conformed to a predictably monotonous template. They'd find a few traces of an individual Indian's presence in the woods around the Modelo Ranch—maybe a few bent twigs and a honey cut or two in a tree. But they never laid eyes on the Indian himself.

During a four-day trek in September, they came close. Marcelo, Altair, and Purá found ten different trees that had been tapped for honey near the banks of a narrow stream. The cuts were no more than two days old. In the same area, they spotted two spiny *jaracatiá* trees that had been felled no more than two weeks before. The trunks of those trees had been slotted and placed facedown in the soil—an Indian technique to attract edible insect larvae. Nearby they found a couple of *jiraus*—suspended platforms constructed of twigs, used to roast and dry meats over a fire. On the muddy slope of another stream they found day-old human footprints.

As they inspected the prints, Altair told Marcelo that he couldn't shake the feeling that they were being watched. He said he sensed that the forest had eyes—two of them—and they saw everything the team was doing. Before the explorers gave up and abandoned the banks of the stream for the day, they placed a machete and one of Purá's arrows on the ground as gifts. They returned a few days later; the machete and arrow lay untouched.

The hikes were becoming arduous exercises in frustration. Instead of solid evidence that could fill in the blanks of the Indian's backstory, they only uncovered more clear-cutting. In his expedition reports, Marcelo described new clearings that had bitten into the forest on the Dalafinis' property. He did everything typographically possible to draw attention to his indignation, punctuating his sentences with exclamation points, capitalizing words, underlining whole passages—and they were met with silence. No fines were levied, no charges filed. The Contact Front so far had failed to convince the country's regulators that any of it *mattered*. The Indian was an abstraction, not a real person who could inspire an emotional connection. It was a significant distinction; empathy doesn't stick to a shadow.

Marcelo couldn't conceal his resentment. During the evenings, after making camp for the night, he usually charted his team's course on maps and scribbled field notes. While the others collected firewood and roasted whatever meat they managed to scare up for dinner—usually wild pig, turtle, spider monkey, or fish—Marcelo poured his spleen out into his journal.

To Marcelo, the Indian had become a symbol, an embattled refugee on the run from a modern world rotten with depravity. In his journal one evening in September after he found more cutting in the forest, he wrote, "The situation of this Indian is a disgrace for Brazilian society. We could never pay the debt we owe them after decimating their entire population, and now at this moment we can't even guarantee the minimal conditions for survival. What greed it is that allows this barbarity and the impunity!!!"

Marcelo believed his cause was inviolate, that the cattle ranchers were law-breaking villains who needed to be brought to justice. That sort of righteousness can rub people the wrong way, especially if those people don't share your indignation. In Rondônia, Marcelo's harsh view of ranchers and loggers wasn't enthusiastically supported by the general population, because ranchers and loggers *were* the general population. The members of the Contact Front could cite the latest version of the constitution all they wanted, but it was just words on paper—like the temporary restrictions placed on logging in the Indian's forest. In his little corner of the world, it was still cowboys versus Indians, and the cowboys were the good guys.

Throughout its history, Brazil has struggled to decide what role Indians should play in its national story. Official policy and public sentiment have sometimes agreed on the matter, sometimes not.

In the last half of the nineteenth century and the first decades of the twentieth, a mode of thought called positivism spread from Europe and took a strong hold on Brazil's middle class. It quickly grew into something close to a theology. One of its high priests was Candido Rondôn, the legendary explorer of the country's backwoods who founded Brazil's first Indian Protection Service, and after whom Rondônia has been named.

According to the positivists, cultures evolved in specific stages, from primitive to mature societies. The native tribes of Amazonia represented the very first stage of cultural evolution, one marked by animism, or the belief that any natural object can have a spirit. The positivists believed that those tribes were incapable of rational thought. But from that stage of cultural primitivism, the positivists believed the tribes could evolve through more advanced stages of development: from animism to polytheism, then to monotheism, and finally to enlightened rationalism. Rondôn believed that with help, the Indians might be able to skip the middle stages of development and leap straight into the light of modernity. He instructed agents in the Indian Protection Service that pacifying Indians helped preserve the possibility of their successful transition to modernity. He came up with a motto intended to guide agents on their pacifying missions: "Die if you must, but never kill."

After he left the White House, U.S. president Theodore Roosevelt journeyed through the Amazon with Rondôn in 1914, and observed the effect of positivism among Brazil's tribes was often religious conversion—an outcome the positivists never sought, but one that seemed to please the former American president. "It may seem strange that among the first-fruits of the efforts of a Positivist should be the conversion of those he seeks to benefit to Christianity," Roosevelt wrote after his expedition with Rondôn. "But in South America Christianity is at least as much a status as a theology. It represents the indispensable first step upward from savagery. In the wilder and poorer districts men are divided into the two great classes of 'Christians' and 'Indians.' When an Indian becomes a Christian he is accepted into and becomes wholly absorbed or partly assimilated by the crude and simple neighboring civilization, and then he moves up or down like anyone else among his fellows."

Positivism's influence faded in the 1930s, at about the same time the idea of cultural relativism began gathering force in anthropological circles. Anthropologists began putting words such as "primitive" and "savage" inside quotation marks, arguing that they were loaded terms unfairly applied by Europeans to indigenous societies. The influence of the idea was transformative—but mostly academic. The intellectual theories that began to permeate popular thought *outside of* anthropological circles—theories including Freud's and Jung's—reinforced the idea that indigenous cultures represented a childlike stage of human development. Freud suggested that primitive Indians have a mentality roughly equal to that of a civilized child. Jean Piaget, a Swiss philosopher whose theories of cognitive development held wide sway over the fields of education and morality, wrote that members of many traditional indigenous cultures were, like very young children, incapable of distinguishing objective reality from their own subjectivity.

The notion of native as child thoroughly infiltrated Brazil and guided its policies. In the country's civil code of 1916, Indians were defined as "relatively capable persons," and granted the same legal status as minors and the mentally deficient. That status remained even after the country enacted the Indian Statute of 1973, which stipulated that Indians needed to live as wards of the state, in the form of FUNAI. In his 1988 book, *The Indians and Brazil,* Brazilian anthropologist Mércio Pereira Gomes summed up the result of the philosophies that over decades had combined to form the shifting backbone of the country's Indian policy:

> All things considered, the Indian has become a kind of bastard child of our civilization—furthermore, an ill bastard child, for he is seen as suffering from a terminal disease, inexorably condemned to death. The state's social and humanist, if not Christian duty, then, would be to ease the sufferings of these people and ensure that they meet death with dignity.

Marcelo hated the Indian-as-child concept. He subscribed to cultural relativism's notion that his own culture was simply different—not better or worse—than the Indians'. But as the local FUNAI representative, it was Marcelo's job to serve as their guardian. Because he was philosophically opposed to that notion, his job was riddled with paradoxes. He believed the Indians had a right to political autonomy. If some Indians wanted to cut themselves off from the rest of society and others wanted to fully integrate their tribes into the modern world, so be it—but Marcelo believed *they* should have the freedom to make the choice. Their cultures had the right to succeed—or fail—without interference from people like him. But unfortunately, the intrusion of modern society had already started, and Indian villages were literally being bulldozed in the process. Without people like him, the Indian cultures would never get the chance to exercise those rights. The job of the Contact Front, particularly as it related to the lone Indian, was itself a paradox: they needed to contact the isolated Indian so he'd have the right to be left alone.

By the time the Contact Front began searching for the Indian, Brazilian law had begun to dovetail with Marcelo's view that Indian cultures had an unalienable right to survive. Just months before Marcelo and Altair started on the lone Indian's trail, a jury in Rondônia found a man guilty of genocide against an Indian tribe—the first verdict of its kind in Brazil's history. The judgment was a long time coming: the guilty man, a rubber tapper accused of killing Orowin Indians and setting fire to their village, was handed his sentence more than thirty years after committing the crime. A few months later, another court brought genocide charges against men accused of attacking members of the Yanowami tribe.

Those verdicts illustrated how radically the legal views of Indians had changed in a single generation. In 1969, when Marcelo was in college, Brazil's permanent representative to the United Nations had argued that violence against Amazonian tribes didn't qualify as genocide if it was perpetrated for economic reasons, such as taking over their land. But after years of debate, now Brazil's courts and constitution had begun to place a higher value on indigenous cultures.

Unfortunately for Marcelo, the respect for individual cultures hadn't filtered down from high court rulings to much of the rest of the population. Even those who occupied positions of power seemed out of step with the courts. By the 1990s, it had become politically incorrect to publicly label Indians as hopelessly primitive savages who stood in the way of Brazil's manifest destiny. But every now and then a federal official indiscreetly mapped the distance between the country's constitution and his own views. Prominent sociologist Hélio Jaguaribe, upon being named a Brazilian cabinet minister in 1992, told reporters that Brazil needed to "get out of the swamp of underdevelopment and backwardness, or we will confront a social convulsion difficult to calculate."

Two years later, he took the idea further when he defined what role Brazil's Indians would play in the country's leap to a more advanced stage of development: no role whatsoever.

"There will be no more Indians in the twenty-first century," Jaguaribe said during a seminar. "The idea of congealing man in the primeval state of his evolution is, in fact, cruel and hypocritical."

* * *

Disentangling Amazonian Indian tribes from the stereotypical naked savages depicted in old dime-store novels is sometimes easier done from a distance than up close. Such clichés are often strongest in the areas where people live closest to the tribes, where some of the locals have seen for themselves that real tribes occasionally *do* partake in activities that seem brutal and fierce. The members of the Contact Front knew this better than most. They also knew that such examples didn't define tribal life any more, or any less, than a savage crime in a city such as São Paulo defined Brazil's nonindigenous culture. But occasional examples of indigenous violence remained a fact of life, and they helped explain why Rondônia's general population often found it difficult to view tribal cultures as anything other than primeval, anarchic, and menacing.

One afternoon in 1997, Altair was staying in the Rio Omerê camp when Purá's cousin, Owaimoro, passed through. She was walking from the Kanoe village toward the Akuntsu village to collect bananas from a cluster of trees that grew there.

The next morning at seven o'clock, when Altair radioed Marcelo to transmit his daily update, he mentioned that he'd seen Owaimoro depart for the Akuntsu village but never saw her return. The two tribes had been friendly, but a member of the Kanoe tribe would never spend the night in the Akuntsu village. It simply wasn't done.

Later that morning, Purá arrived at the FUNAI base, visibly upset. Owaimoro still hadn't returned. She had left her monkey at home, which suggested that she hadn't intended to be gone so long. Purá feared that something terrible had happened.

They all knew that Owaimoro had a knack for rubbing the Akuntsu the wrong way. She was strong-headed, and she was convinced that the Kanoe tribe was superior to the Akuntsu.

Altair, Purá, and a FUNAI assistant set off from camp in the morning along Owaimoro's likely route toward the banana grove. After about two miles of hiking they arrived in a cornfield near the Akuntsu village. There they spotted a basket lying on the ground, upturned. Bananas and papayas spilled out of it. Purá recognized the basket as Owaimoro's.

At the edge of the cornfield they saw tracks leading toward the

Akuntsu village. As they approached the village, they saw smoke rising from the general direction of the tribe's huts.

They reached the village and discovered that four of the tribe's five huts—all of them except Konibu's—had been set on fire. The fires had stopped burning, but plumes of smoke continued to rise weakly from each of them.

They scanned the village grounds for clues that might tell them what happened. It was a scattered mess. Trash was strewn across the ground. Some of the Akuntsus' things had been left in the huts, though most had been removed. In the middle of the clearing, they found that the dirt had been stained with what looked like gallons of dark paint. It was blood.

Purá froze. His eyes began to fill with tears.

Altair noticed a thin trail of blood leading to the periphery of the village clearing. It disappeared into a small patch of secondary forest that had grown over a garden plot that had been abandoned by the Akuntsu years before. He and the assistant followed the trail while Purá stayed behind in the village.

Several yards into the thick brush, they found Owaimoro's body. She had been hacked to death with a machete. Deep wounds slashed across her neck, her arms, her legs.

When Altair reemerged into the clearing, Purá searched his face.

"Owaimoro?" he asked.

Altair nodded yes, and Purá wept.

The Akuntsu had killed her. As tribal custom dictated, they had abandoned their own camp after taking another person's life and set fire to it—an attempt to cleanse the grounds of lingering evil spirits. They had collected most of their things and begun to build a new village a couple of miles away.

Altair could only guess at the Akuntsus' motives. Afterward, when he managed to speak with Konibu and the rest of the Akuntsu, the tribe acknowledged the act but refused to talk about it in detail. Eventually Konibu blamed Pupak, the tribe's only other male. Altair's best guess was that Owaimoro's bossy condescension toward the Akuntsu had finally pushed Pupak over the edge. But that would always remain a guess.

The day they discovered Owaimoro's body, Altair and Purá

returned to the FUNAI camp, and Altair radioed Marcelo to tell him what had happened. Altair then accompanied Purá to the Kanoe camp to break the news to the rest of his tribe.

The Kanoe were devastated. Purá and his mother gathered all of Owaimoro's belongings into baskets and began a funereal trek through the forest, back to the place where she had died.

They retrieved Owaimoro's body from where it lay and dragged it back to the only one of the Akuntsus' huts that hadn't been burned down. They placed her body inside the hut and all of her belongings alongside her. They planned to cremate her body.

Before setting the hut on fire, Purá led Owaimoro's monkey to the edge of the encampment. With a wooden club, he beat the animal to death. Then he carried its remains to the hut. He laid the monkey alongside Owaimoro and set fire to the hut.

Sacrificing the monkey was a final act of love toward his cousin. He wanted Owaimoro's most cherished companion to accompany her. In death, as in life, they would remain together.

CHAPTER EIGHT

Letting Go

Down to four survivors, the Kanoe village was enshrouded in quietude. Living under a legacy of both slaughter and suicide, the Kanoe always had been prone to long silences, but in the months following Owaimoro's killing, those silences seemed less reflective than lugubrious.

The Akuntsu had abandoned their charred village and built a new one a short trek away, but the fragile scaffold that had supported relations between the two tribes had collapsed. Just two years after the two tribes had begun to emerge from their extreme isolation by reaching out to the Contact Front, loneliness again began to constrict around them.

Without the social interaction between the tribes, the members of the Contact Front remained the only human links to the world outside each of the tribes' own thatch huts. Purá sometimes visited the Rio Omerê encampment, sat outside one of the FUNAI huts, and cried. The language barrier that separated him from the FUNAI workers left the finer points of his grief unexpressed.

The members of the Contact Front stayed out of the conflict between the Kanoe and the Akuntsu. But some of them couldn't help feeling a little guilty. There was no getting around the fact that the team's actions—the initial contact, the establishment of the Rio Omerê camp—had helped bring the two tribes together, maybe too fast. They had encouraged the alliance between the tribes and had compressed the rhythms of tribal interplay.

But even if FUNAI had unintentionally contributed to that conflict, its employees decided that taking an active role in the resolution of the killing might compound the problem. They believed that the tribes themselves should decide how to handle it. And each tribe independently decided that a cooling period was the wisest course of action. They indefinitely suspended relations.

The Akuntsu retreated from FUNAI, folding into themselves at their new village. But the Kanoe continued to look to the Contact Front for companionship. If anything, the personal connection between the team members and the Indians strengthened after Owaimoro's death.

Purá had seen the grisly consequences of reaching out to another tribe, but it didn't stop him from volunteering to accompany the team as they prepared for another expedition on the trail of the lone Indian on August 1, 1998.

It wasn't perfectly clear why Purá wanted to go. It never really had been. He had always been mildly curious about the Indian's way of life, but he didn't seem particularly interested in the possibility of getting to know the man. When Altair repeated the story of his single encounter with the lone Indian outside his thatch hut, Purá would smile and shrug, as if to say he thought Altair was a little crazy to approach an unknown Indian. So when Altair pondered what might lie behind Purá's enthusiasm to join the expedition, he thought it had something to do with camaraderie, or maybe the simple thrill of exploring new places. Often Purá would return from those trips with a basketful of supplies, such as pieces of *taquara* palm that could be used for arrow tips, or strange feathers, or rare fruits that weren't so easy to find near the Kanoe village. Whether they found the Indian seemed beside the point to Purá. It was the journey that seemed to interest him, not the intended destination.

By the beginning of 1998, the team had uncovered more evidence that the Indian was on the run. He seemed to be keeping one step ahead of the ranchers who continued to cut the forested sections of their properties. In the second half of 1997 and the early part of 1998, Marcelo and Altair found several additional huts that the Indian had abandoned as loggers cleared more of the forest around the Modelo Ranch. Some of his huts appeared to have been constructed in a day, then abandoned almost as quickly. During one expedition, in June 1998, they had found two huts. The location of those huts suggested he was moving over the property lines, reacting to the movement of the loggers. Sometimes he remained inside the Dalafinis' property, sometimes he crossed into forests claimed by other ranchers. In July 1998, workers on Jaime Bagattoli's property—which included the forest where they had found the first hut two years earlier—had told them they'd seen the Indian again, though he'd disappeared almost instantly.

The language in Marcelo's memos to FUNAI's headquarters throughout 1998 took on a new tenor of urgency, one that at times bordered on desperation. So far, the agency's official response had been one of wait and see. Marcelo tried to tell them that if they waited much longer, they'd see a tragedy unfold right before their eyes.

> The situation of the Indian is getting more complicated all the time in this atmosphere of permanent insecurity, with the frequent activity of non-Indians around his dwellings. Workers are encroaching on his huts and cutting down the wilderness where he hides, not even leaving him the minimum of tranquility to live or to hunt. . . . The people who are expelling him are illegally destroying hundreds of hectares of native forest, either unaware of the restrictions put upon the land by regulatory agencies, or else simply refusing to comply with those judicial decisions. FUNAI must officially recognize the Indian's existence and make policies that guarantee his right to survive where he is, at least until contact is made and other considerations can be made concerning his future. But at this moment in such a turbulent atmosphere, that possibility grows more remote and complex all the time.

FUNAI officials responded that their hands were tied: they couldn't officially recognize the Indian's presence until they knew more about him—a tribal name, a little backstory. They needed contact, in other words. In writing back to FUNAI, Marcelo made sure the bosses in Brasília recognized that they weren't the only ones toiling in less than ideal circumstances—tracking the Indian was like chasing a ghost. His tribal affiliation was still completely unknown. Marcelo had never heard of a more elusive Indian, and tracking him had become the most perplexing mystery he'd ever known.

FUNAI contracted anthropologists to try to piece together a speculative tribal description of the Indian based on the scraps of information the Contact Front had collected. For lack of a better name, they called him the "Indian of the Hole," latching on to the one characteristic of his dwellings that set him apart from the other local tribes.

The holes found in his huts led some anthropologists and indigenists within FUNAI to speculate that he might be a remnant of a band of Sirionó Indians, a seminomadic tribe from Bolivia whose only agricultural tool is a digging stick and whose only weapon is a bow and arrow. In the early 1900s, observers believed the Sirionós' culture was one of the world's most primitive. Early Jesuits in Bolivia brought some of them into their missions, but most were dismissed as hopelessly uncivilized. Years later, anthropologists developed a more charitable view of the Sirionó culture: it wasn't that the culture was barbarically crude, it was that it had been pushed to the brink of destruction by smallpox, influenza, and the destruction of their territory. Like the Akuntsu, the Sirionó spoke a language of the Tupi-Guarani root.

But the anthropologists and the members of the Contact Front eventually abandoned the idea that the lone Indian might have been the lone remnant of a band of Sirionó. No Sirionó Indians dug holes inside their huts as this Indian did. They also used much bigger longbows. And when Altair had confronted the lone Indian in 1996, he tried out a Tupi-Guarani greeting, to which the Indian didn't respond. The Sirionó theory was as shaky as any other. The team simply couldn't provide FUNAI with a tribal affiliation for the Indian without contact.

Marcelo urged his bosses to imagine for a moment what must be going through the Indian's mind as they tried to make contact with him. When he summarized the plight of Rondônia's isolated Indians in letters to his bosses, it was clear that Marcelo was referring to one Indian in particular:

> The first thing that's obvious is that the situation of these Indians is a calamity, a national embarrassment. They've been poisoned, shot at, been decimated, have had their houses and gardens destroyed,

and now they're prohibited from living anywhere in peace. Our work also has unquestionably been complicated by the innumerable expulsions from territory that they have been subjected to. We're stuck in an odd situation, on account of all this turbulence surrounding local agricultural development. It requires a lot of patience and determination to try to present ourselves as being different than all the other "civilized" people they've known. The Indians are obviously very distrustful and hide themselves very craftily, making our searches even more difficult.

Sydney Possuelo, the head of FUNAI's Isolated Indians Division in Brasília, sympathized with Marcelo. Possuelo believed that isolated Indians should remain isolated, and that contact almost always weakened the tribes. But given the speed and extent of the deforestation in Rondônia, Possuelo believed that in this case the lone Indian's death was inevitable; ranchers or loggers would kill him, sooner rather than later. In this case, contact was necessary, and Possuelo encouraged Marcelo and his team to get out into the jungle and keep trekking, which is exactly what they did.

FUNAI gives its sertanistas an *Operational Manual,* a seventy-one-page book of practical advice designed for contact teams preparing to enter the jungle and look for Indians who've never interacted with anyone outside of their tribe. Parts of it read like a locker-room pep talk, urging the teams to develop "a sense of companionship, solidarity, and esprit de corps." But most of it is flatly practical, full of packing checklists. It issues reminders to take nothing for granted, including the backwoods competence of the sertanistas themselves. On page fifty-four, would-be explorers learn, "To discover out in the middle of the jungle that one forgot to bring a sewing needle or a disposable hypodermic needle—where there is no longer the possibility of getting them—may produce a passing discomfort, or may cause a tragedy." A few pages later: "Watch out for brand-new jeans, they usually cause a rash on the inner part of the upper thigh."

Marcelo and his team relied more on their own judgment than the advice handed to them from headquarters in Brasília. They never wore the uniforms that FUNAI had dreamed up for its sertanistas—military-like fatigues, Bermudas, and long socks, which were supposed to be instantly recognizable to Indians, so the tribes could distinguish them from ranchers or anyone else. And instead of checking off the 230 items the manual suggested they pack for expeditions—a list that included everything from sunscreen to toothbrushes—they relied more on their own experience.

Their limits were defined by their individual backpacks: seventy-five-liter models made of a green canvas that was light enough to collapse well if empty, but sturdy enough to support a maximum of forty-five pounds of cargo. Altair and Vincent believed that a law of diminishing returns began to kick in at about thirty-five pounds—beyond that, the extra weight wasn't worth the luxury that any additional item might provide. Marcelo's target weight was a little lower—he liked to limit his pack to twenty-five pounds or less.

Hammocks were absolute must-haves for everyone. Theirs were lightweight nylon, weighing about twenty ounces, and they rolled up to about the size of a fat metropolitan Sunday newspaper. Hammocks are ideal for warm weather, but if the temperatures dipped below about sixty degrees at night, which was common, the cool air penetrated the thin fabric of the hammock's underside and seeped directly into the bones. If they wanted to sleep well on such nights, a thin six-by-ten blanket that could wrap completely around the body was key. If it was warmer, all they needed was an ultrathin cotton sheet.

Another necessity was a machete, the most useful tool an explorer could carry in the forest. Pocketknives occupied a slightly lower place in that hierarchy of necessity. Mosquito repellent was generally considered a waste of packing space, while a sheer square of mosquito netting was deemed judicious, because it was lighter than a can of repellent, less messy, and more effective. A plastic tarp that could be tied to trees and used as a rain shelter was a smart addition to any pack, but a full tent was excessive. Sewing kits, rope, first-aid supplies, and soap were essentials, but squandering space on drinking water was perhaps the worst affront against jungle-trek efficiency—creeks and rivers were easy to find, and the water was clean and cool. An extra pair of shoes or boots was considered an extravagance. But black electrical tape, used to repair shoes and boots, always had a spot in the corner of a pack. Fishing poles were superfluous because the forest provided an inexhaustible supply of cane rods, though fishing line and hooks were well worth their weight.

If the expedition was expected to last more than a couple of days, they hauled antiseptic powder and antibiotics, but usually left them behind on shorter journeys. Each of them packed a single change of clothes: an extra T-shirt, socks, and pair of pants. Towels were optional; Marcelo never packed one, figuring his extra T-shirt worked just as well.

A lot of the weight they carried was dry food such as rice, beans, pasta, sugar, and coffee—about fifteen to twenty pounds of it per person for a two-week hike. Sometimes they carried dried meat, but normally they relied on the forest for their protein. Wild pigs and spider monkeys were the preferred game, but sometimes hunting and slaughtering them didn't make sense. It took about three days for four people to eat an average-size spider monkey. That meant they'd be forced to carry the rest of the meat on their backs for at least two days. From a packing perspective, killing large animals usually wasn't worth the effort.

The *Operational Manual* makes it very clear that such matters are anything but trivial, and the obsessive emphasis it places on the finer points of expeditionary preparation seems to reach toward a mild paranoia: parts of the manual seem to suggest that the sertanistas not only should be prepared for disaster, but also expect it. When addressing the stress that accompanies first-time encounters between tribes and sertanistas, the sympathies of the manual's anonymous author at times seem to lie with the explorers, not the Indians.

> Nobody will ever imagine what moral strength a man needs to dominate the unbearable nervous irritation caused by his feeling himself incessantly besieged, watched and studied in his smallest acts by people he cannot see, of whom he doesn't even know the numbers, whom he doesn't want to harm or chase away, but rather please and attract, and yet who are just waiting for the right moment to assault and kill.

In her 1998 book *Indigenism,* Brazilian anthropologist Alcida Rita Ramos spotted what she considered a glaring omission in FUNAI's sertanista manual, one that she suggested betrayed the agency's fundamental flaw: "Symptomatically, the manual is almost silent about how these teams should or should not behave once they come face to face with the Indians."

Purá finished packing for the expedition on the morning of August 1, digging around inside his hut for a clutch of arrows to take with him. Marcelo, Vincent, and Altair waited with the rest of the Kanoe tribe in the clearing outside.

Tatuá had been nervous for days; she was worried about her son, Purá. She feared that the same bad spirits that had recently sickened her grandson, Operá, might hang over the expedition. Since Owaimoro's death, Purá was more important to the tribe than ever. If anything happened to the group's only adult male, the survival of the Kanoe would be thrown into peril.

Marcelo and Altair knelt down close to Tatuá and her grandson, whose stomach was aching. They tried to convince her that they'd take good care of Purá during the trip. Altair gently stroked the boy's hair, trying to deflect some of the tension in the air. He looked into the boy's eyes and smiled.

Purá emerged from the hut, ready to go. But before the group departed from the village, Tatuá motioned to Vincent, asking him to come to her. She wanted to tell him something, and Vincent concentrated on her body language to try to decode her message. She wore an expression of concern on her face as she motioned toward Vincent's midsection. She was clearly worried. But Vincent couldn't understand why.

At the same time, Purá grabbed a bite of turtle meat that had been smoking on the fire—a little snack for the road. Vincent, who had fought diarrhea from eating turtle the very first time he'd met the Kanoe almost three years earlier, assumed that Tatuá was trying to warn him to be careful of getting sick again. Vincent wasn't one to put much stock in tribal superstitions, and he didn't give Tatuá's concern much thought.

A few days later, he'd look back on that moment and consider the possibility that the woman might have been referring to something else, that her sixth sense had been picking up the signals of a more serious kind of danger. Then he'd laugh the thought out of his head. He was probably giving her too much credit. Her gesture could have meant anything.

Clutching his rifle in his left hand, Altair twisted through a tangle of ferns. It was August, the dry season. It hadn't so much as sprinkled in sixty days, leaving the air grainy with hints of smoke from the fires that charred the tree line miles away. Insects droned within the streaming bars of light that penetrated the forest's canopy. The papery rustle of leaves accompanied each footstep. Marcelo, Vincent, and Purá followed him deeper into the jungle, wiping the sweat out of their eyes as they walked.

They'd been hiking for three days when they found a lightly trodden path. After following it, Altair spotted a partially concealed pitfall. The loose dirt around it suggested it had been dug within the past twenty-four hours. While the others inspected the pit, Altair found ground markings indicating that someone had diverged from the path to follow a northeasterly course through the woods. In a patch of soft mud, he found a fresh print from a bare human foot.

Altair motioned to Purá to look at the print. Bending down to the ground, Altair placed both hands around the impression to measure it from toe to heel. When he held his hands out to show Purá how big it was, Altair held his hands about sixteen inches apart. *He's huge,* Altair was trying to tell him, *an absolute monster!*

Altair was joking. The footprint may have been wider than most, but it wasn't any longer than Purá's own. Purá returned Altair's smile.

When Altair joined the others around the pitfall, he found a piece of wood with a broad and sharp point. It was a digging stick, probably the same one the Indian had used to dig the pitfall. Altair held the stick and stabbed it into the dry soil, trying to imagine how the Indian might have created his spike-bottomed trap. Digging a hole like that would take a couple of hours of backwrenching labor at the very least.

They walked on, with Marcelo leading the way, until they spotted a small hut across a tiny clearing. The fronds on the roof weren't dried and browned like those that covered the other huts they'd found. These were green, as if they had been collected recently.

Purá stiffened and motioned to the others. He'd heard something.

"Quiet!" Marcelo whispered to the group.

They stood still and listened: a rustling. It was the Indian. He was near the pitfall they'd just abandoned, perhaps checking it for fallen game.

They ran toward him, but he vanished. It was as if he'd found a crack in the deep green curtain of foliage behind him and quietly slipped offstage.

Actually, he'd fled toward his hut. He was inside it.

They returned to the hut. Altair set his rifle down and approached the structure.

"Oi, amigo," Altair said. There was no response, but through a slight gap in the thatch Altair could see the man's eyes, peering at him.

Altair turned to the others. "He's there," he said, "standing inside the hut."

They couldn't see the Indian, but through the tiny cracks in the thatch they detected movement. Vincent aimed his video camera at Altair, who was inching closer to the hut. Through the small openings in the wall, he could discern that the Indian was standing up.

The men looked at one another for a moment, silently sizing up the situation, trying to figure out how to convince the man to come out of the hut and join them. Altair peeled his T-shirt off, thinking that maybe the Indian would relate to him more easily if he could see that underneath their clothes, these strange men were essentially the same as he. Altair took a few careful steps forward, until he was about ten feet from the hut. He noticed that something was protruding through the thatch, twisting in place.

"Look," Altair said. "An arrow inside." It was just like the one Altair had seen nearly two years earlier, during his previous encounter with the Indian. As Altair backpedaled a couple of steps, the tip of the arrow disappeared inside the hut.

"Easy," Altair said. "Easy, my friend."

Altair again stepped slowly toward the hut, and the arrow again emerged from the thatch. Squinting into the hut, Altair could barely make out the Indian's form: it appeared that he was standing with his bow drawn. Altair slowly backed up, showing the man his palms, meaning no harm. Once again, the arrow disappeared as Altair retreated. It seemed that the Indian was drawing an imaginary line in the dirt about ten feet around his hut. A line that said, *Keep your distance.*

"Come on out, amigo," Altair said, in Portuguese. "We're not here to hurt you."

Marcelo figured that it was time for Purá to try to speak with the Indian. He turned and called for Purá to step forward. Maybe the lone Indian would be calmed by the sight of another tribesman. "Speak to him," Marcelo told Purá.

Purá inched toward the hut as if approaching a tensely coiled snake. *"Mampi no,"* Purá said in the Kanoe tongue. *Don't shoot.* The Indian inside the hut didn't react.

Purá was scared, and took several steps backward. Marcelo tugged at the sleeve of Purá's T-shirt, signaling that he take his T-shirt off and try again; maybe the Indian would relate to Purá if he saw that he wasn't dressed in white men's clothes. Purá did so, approaching the hut for the second time, and the arrow popped out of the hut's wall again. This time the arrow emerged with a sudden thrust, as if to emphasize his warning to stay back.

"No, no, no," Marcelo said, pleading with the Indian and quickly jumping backward. Marcelo held an upraised palm toward the hut and offered a smile of reassurance. "Calm, calm."

The Indian showed no signs of wanting to interact, but Marcelo didn't want to let the opportunity slip out of his hands. After tracking him for two years, Marcelo finally had laid eyes on the Indian; he couldn't simply turn around and go home. If he could just break down the man's resistance, everything might fall into place. FUNAI could officially catalog his tribal affiliation, opening the possibility of permanently preserving his land and reducing the threats to his livelihood. If the man was the last member of a dying tribe, as Marcelo had begun to suspect, then anthropologists could study his culture and linguists could analyze his language before they sank into extinction. No one could guarantee that Marcelo and the rest of the team would ever get a chance for contact this good again. They needed to make the most of it.

If Marcelo was nervous, he didn't show it. He figured that if the Indian sensed that he was edgy, things might get dangerous. When Marcelo told the others, "He's still showing me the arrow," his voice had the lilting cadence of a kindergarten teacher who didn't want to excite the kids and who wants to seem as gentle as a lamb.

No one moved for a couple of minutes. No one spoke. Birdsong filled the silence.

Purá didn't appear nearly as calm as Marcelo. He began inhaling deeply, using his arms and hands to shovel the bad spirits toward his mouth from the air all around them. Then he turned and blew them away into the forest. He clapped his hands. He rubbed his palms together, and he shuffled his feet in a rhythmic dance.

If he had cleared the air of spirits, he hadn't erased the tension. The Indian's arrow was still sticking out of the thatch, its deadly point twisting in place.

The encounter had become a tense standoff. Morning turned into afternoon. The group built a small fire in the clearing and prepared lunch. Marcelo gingerly approached the hut and laid on the ground some taquara sticks that Purá had collected. He was offering them to the lone Indian as a gift. The thatch of the hut rustled violently, and Marcelo ducked behind a tree, fearing that the Indian might shoot: "No, no, no."

After a few more minutes, Marcelo offered him an ax. He approached the hut and held the ax out with one hand, handle-first. The sun was shining into Marcelo's eyes, washing out his vision. He shielded his eyes with his free hand and slapped at the insects that had begun to alight on his sweat-drenched face. Refocusing on the hut, he saw the arrow emerge once again.

After a while Altair decided to take a closer look. He got down on his hands and knees and began crawling toward the hut. He banged the ax that Marcelo had left for the Indian on the ground: a hollow thud. "Here, this ax is yours," Altair said. He tossed some food in front of the hut. "This water yam, too."

Again the group waited for a reaction from the Indian, but none came.

After another hour or so, Altair searched through the woods and found a fifteen-foot length of bamboo. It looked like something a pole-vaulter might use. Altair hung a pot of food on the end of the pole, and—standing behind the imaginary line the Indian had drawn around his hut—dangled the food toward the hut's opening. The Indian didn't budge.

Frustration was turning into desperation. They believed that the Indian's safety depended on making contact, but he wouldn't open up. All they needed was a little crack in his defensive shield, something that would prove to him that he wouldn't be harmed by reaching out to them. But he continued to stand on guard, poised to strike.

Vincent, meanwhile, walked around to the side of the hut. Peering through the lens of his digital video camera, he aimed its focus through one of the cracks in the thatch. The thin, lucid thread of a spider's web ran across the crack, catching the sunlight. Vincent zoomed in on the Indian's face. The man was staring intently at Marcelo and Altair, who were now inspecting the side of the clearing, noticing that the Indian had planted some manioc there.

Zooming in closer through the hole in the thatch, Vincent got a clear shot of the man: it was undoubtably the same Indian his assistant had filmed during Altair's encounter two years earlier.

He wore his dark hair long. Sparse wisps of facial hair bordered his mouth. A small scar jagged across the high ridge of his right cheekbone.

Altair again tried to approach close to the entrance of the hut on his hands and knees. Vincent could see the Indian release his right hand from the bow. He raised that hand slightly, and Vincent saw that he was holding an old, broken-handled machete that he had probably scavenged from one of the camps of ranch workers. It appeared that he was raising the machete up to bring it down on Altair if he tried to enter. When Altair got close to the entrance he saw the upraised blade and backed away.

The team regrouped, unsure what to do next. The Indian seemed to be paralyzed by uncertainty. Even though he was armed, the man didn't seem eager to fight. He was defensive, not offensive. This allowed them to continue pressing for contact, hoping to help him reclaim a little bit of stability in what must have been a terrifying existence.

They began to consider possibilities that might explain his indecision. Maybe, they thought, it wasn't that he was *choosing* not to speak to them; maybe he was physically unable to speak. Maybe he was part of the tribe who had been targeted with poisoned sugar, and maybe it had left him deaf and mute. They knew those hypotheses were long shots, but *what if?* They felt as if they couldn't just give up now.

As the standoff stretched toward its fifth hour, desperation began to eat away at Altair's inhibitions. Caution disappeared, and he dropped to his hands and knees again, getting within a couple of feet from the hut. The arrow was pointed right at him.

"No, you don't need that arrow there," Altair said, pleading. "Come on. We're not going to do anything to you."

Altair began probing the hut's opening with the bamboo pole, trying to get a look inside. The man hacked at the pole, probably with his machete. Altair dropped the pole on the ground and grabbed a banana. "Mmmm, a banana," he said. "Mmmmm, *good*. Banana."

The banana didn't interest the Indian, so Altair tried some corn. He walked back to the rear of the clearing, bundled several ears of corn together, and draped them over the end of the pole. As if he were fishing, he dangled the corn toward the hut, managing to maneuver it *inside* the opening.

Altair pulled the pole out, and the corn was no longer on the end. The Indian, it seemed, had accepted an offering at long last.

But a few seconds later, the corn flew out of the hut, uneaten. The Indian had ripped the ears to shreds. The act seemed colored with anger. Maybe they had pushed him too far.

The arrow reappeared out of the hole in the thatch, and Marcelo and Altair tried to calm the Indian down by speaking in Kanoe, repeating, *"Mampi no."* Vincent moved a little closer with his camera to try to get a clearer view. The arrow moved, then whizzed out from the hut.

"Watch out, Vincent!"

The arrow flew past Marcelo and hissed toward Vincent, narrowly missing the cameraman's torso.

Purá had seen enough.

He turned and ran as fast as he could through the forest, terrified.

After six hours and one near-death experience outside of the Indian's hut, the group gave up. But before they left, Vincent wedged his camera into the crotch of a palm tree and pointed it at the hut. He left the camera running, and told the others he'd come back a little later to retrieve it. Maybe it would capture more images of the Indian after they had left, when he was calm and alone.

"He probably thought the camera was a weapon of some kind," Vincent guessed.

They carried the arrow he had shot at Vincent on the long trek back to their camp, where Purá was waiting for them. He was quiet but unrepentant. He'd been frightened, and he wasn't ashamed to admit it.

It was, as Marcelo described it in his expedition report, "a long, sad night."

After a full six hours spent trying to convince the Indian that they meant no harm, that they were nothing like the other white men he'd met, all efforts had ended in failure. There was no other word for it. *Failure.* They'd given him every opportunity to approach them. They'd offered smiles, food, tools. And the only message he sent them in return was an arrow.

Marcelo tried to put himself in the Indian's place, looking out from that hut at the gallery of strange faces. What sort of fevered notions must have been flashing through his mind when he drew the bowstring? When the Indian let the arrow go, what did he believe the consequences of that act might be? The arrow had missed Vincent, but only by a couple of inches at most. Had he intentionally missed? Was he simply trying to scare the team away? Or, when he released that arrow, was he declaring war? Had he been pushed so far that he was willing to risk all in a lopsided four-against-one battle?

Only one certainty could be drawn from the expeditions: the Indian might have temporarily escaped the encroachments of loggers and ranchers, but the persistence of the seasoned jungle trackers in the Contact Front was keeping him on the run. Every time they found one of his huts, he would abandon it for good, never risking a return. Their continual search for clues meant he was never able to settle in one place. The desire for contact was more of a hindrance than a help.

Later, they recovered Vincent's video camera from the palm tree where he had left it. The image on the tape showed the hut, and the large frond serving as a front door was centered in the frame. The sound of the team's footsteps faded as they left the Indian alone. Insects darted between the camera and the hut. On a single limb visible in the foreground, beetles crawled up and out of the frame. The hut was completely still.

After about six minutes, some of the fronds of the hut rustled. At the 6:12 mark of the tape, a dark figure crawled out of the back of the hut, bows and arrows in hand, and disappeared into the forest.

The rest of the tape revealed nothing more than a static image of the thatch hut. The Indian had abandoned it forever.

A patient drizzle fell on their camp through the night, and the team members reached a painful conclusion: their good intentions had no value. Everyone who wanted the team to establish contact—the anthropologists and linguists who wanted to study his culture, the FUNAI officials who needed more information before they could reserve his land—none of their wishes mattered as much as the Indian's. It was clear to the members of the Contact Front that their work was only making things worse for him, and that no matter what they tried, he was unlikely to cross the boundary he'd established. If put in his position, each of them guessed that they might have resisted contact, too.

Marcelo had to tell his bosses that he knew no more about the Indian than he had before the expedition. But he questioned why FUNAI needed to know any more about the Indian to offer him protection. It was obvious that he was an isolated Indian, and according to the constitution that alone gave him the right to his land and the right to live according to his customs. Contact, Marcelo believed, was no longer the best strategy.

"He's alone," Marcelo wrote that night in camp, "and it seems that he wants to die that way. It's his right."

Marcelo had given up one tactic, but he was determined to find another. He resolved to try to save the Indian's land *and* his right to be left alone.

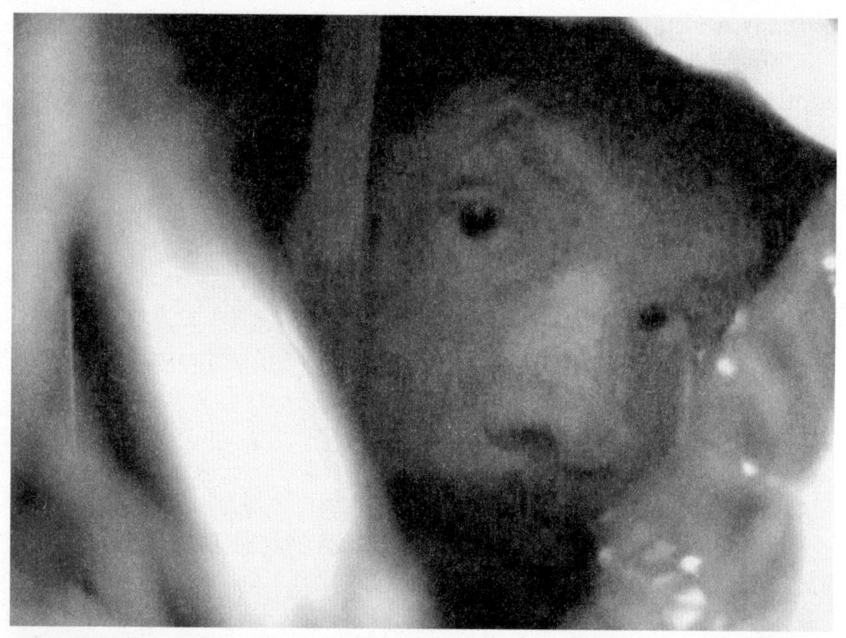

The lone Indian is shown peering out of one of his huts in November 1998.

CHAPTER NINE

Battle Lines

Throughout the 1990s, business boomed in Vilhena. Its grid of dirt roads was paved over with asphalt. The general stores scattered next to the BR-364 were crowded out by clothing emporiums, jewelry boutiques, sporting goods stores, and ice cream shops. Hotels with names such as the Mirage and the Colorado upgraded their rooms for visiting buyers making deals with local ranchers, farmers, and logging companies. Postmodern office towers bracketed the streets downtown. New residential neighborhoods sprang up all over the city, and though their architectural styles were dizzyingly diverse, almost all the houses shared one thing: the same rosy hardwood that helped make this city the mercantile capital of southern Rondônia by the mid-1990s.

In one of the oldest neighborhoods in the city lived a doctor named Newton Pandolpho. He'd lived there for years, and he'd watched the city double in size in less than a decade. Pandolpho was a little bit hard of hearing, but his ears had become attuned to a peculiar pitch: the electronic squawk of his next-door neighbor's two-way radio. Every time he'd hear it, he'd drift over toward the property line separating the two houses.

The radio belonged to Marcelo dos Santos. Up until the frustrating expedition in August 1998, he often used it to receive updates from Altair and the other members of the team on the situation with the lone Indian. Pandolpho couldn't get enough of the story. If the radio blared to life, Pandolpho tried to eavesdrop. Pandolpho would pepper Marcelo with questions, schooling himself on the Indian's backstory and the team's latest adventures.

To Pandolpho, who often volunteered his medical services for the area's acculturated Indian tribes, the story perfectly encapsulated the conflicts that were changing Vilhena: the battles of the new versus the old, the modern versus the traditional, development versus the natural environment, frontiersmen versus Indians.

Marcelo and Pandolpho had become close friends, and when Marcelo returned from his latest expedition he showed the doctor the video footage of the team's encounter with the lone Indian. Marcelo also explained his new plan: he was preparing a formal document that he would present to the Justice Ministry to try to temporarily preserve about twenty-three square miles of the forest for a single man. Although deforestation was already prohibited thanks to a temporary injunction, that ban needed to be renewed every couple of months and was ignored by most of the ranchers anyway. Marcelo hoped for something with more teeth: a lasting prohibition that the landowners would be forced to abide by. In a letter he drafted to the federal prosecuting attorney's office, Marcelo reviewed the team's expeditions, its investigations into the alleged massacres, and its decision to suspend efforts to force contact with the Indian.

> We feel embarrassed by our insistence in trying to contact him. The face of the Indian—always sullen, anxious, worried and permanently silent—had made it clear to us that he wants to be left alone. Despite clearly demonstrating our conciliatory intentions, we continued to challenge his obvious decision. . . . We finally concluded that we were assailing his rights. We resolved to suspend the attempts to contact him and shift our work in another direction—guaranteeing his right to be alone and to survive in a patch of forest free from the threat of systematic expulsion. We won't abandon all attempts to get close to him, but it's obvious that we'll have to act with more caution. We won't get so close to his hut and we'll leave the decision of whether or not to make contact up to him. But to do that, we need—or, rather, he needs—a minimum of tranquility, free of the presence of loggers, ranchers and hunters.

"They're going to fight it hard," Pandolpho told Marcelo when he heard what his neighbor was proposing. "They'll say you planted that Indian there. That's what they always do."

That wasn't news to Marcelo. He was well aware that by formally asking for an indigenous reserve for the lone Indian, he was inviting the wrath of an entire political class. He did it anyway.

At first, things went Marcelo's way. FUNAI supported his efforts to declare a temporary ban on development of twenty-three square miles where the Indian roamed. In early 1999, the agency asked federal judge José Henrique Guaracy for the prohibition of any physical alteration of the land, including deforestation, the creation of new pastures, or any construction projects. The land included parts of two ranches—the Modelo, owned by the Dalafini brothers, and the Socel, owned by a man named Celso de Sordi. The judge ruled in FUNAI's favor. The Contact Front considered it a temporary solution, but the ranchers took a harsher view: they considered it a travesty of justice.

"It's incredible."

Denes Dalafini was outraged. A reporter from the biggest newspaper in Brazil, *Folha de S. Paulo,* asked him about FUNAI's attempt to declare his property off-limits to development, and the rancher didn't hide his contempt of the legal maneuver.

"I don't know why, with so many more serious problems facing this country, that the justice system would buy the crazy thesis presented by the Guaporé Contact Front," Dalafini said.

The other rancher whose land was affected, Celso de Sordi, tried to distance himself from the story, telling the newspaper that he'd let the legal process take its course. But the Dalafinis indicated that they weren't going to give up rights to their land without a fight.

Denes Dalafini labeled the case "a farce" and said that the story was pulled out of thin air, that it was a complete fabrication. If there was an Indian on his property, he said, then the Contact Front must have put him there.

"There never existed a village on our property, not even a hut," Dalafini said. "The Guaporé Front is creating scenarios and forging evidence. I don't know how this farce has been constructed, but it is a farce. Who can guarantee me that they didn't place Indians there themselves?"

The ranchers pulled out all the stops. They argued to Judge Guaracy that the Brazilian government itself had sold the plots of land to them after issuing "negative certifications" verifying that no Indian tribes were known to live in the area.

"If they didn't find savages at that time, how are they finding them now?" Dalafini said.

As they had done before, the landowners and local business organizations in Vilhena called attention to the fact that the Contact Front had received funding from a World Bank project locally known as Planaforo. The project had been authorized by the international lending institution to assist the Brazilian government in providing "a coherent incentive framework for sustainable development in Rondônia." Dalafini suggested the Contact Front's link to the Washington-based World Bank was damning evidence that proved Marcelo's team was part of an international conspiracy to take the Amazon out of the hands of Brazilians.

"Everyone comments about how this group depends on foreign resources," Dalafini said. "That money is being put to good use."

But of all the arguments the ranchers aired against the Contact Front, they seized one with particular vigor. The video images that Vincent had captured of the Indian during the team's latest encounter with him showed that he had facial hair, including a mustache. *An Indian with a mustache?* The ranchers had never heard of such a thing. Of all the pictures they had seen of Amazonian Indians, they couldn't remember ever seeing one with facial hair. Amazonian Indians can't grow mustaches, the ranchers argued; therefore the "Indian" couldn't be an Indian at all. It was proof, they said, of an elaborate hoax. The Contact Front was trying to pass off an imposter as an isolated Indian.

When Marcelo, Vincent, and Altair first heard the mustache argument, their instinct was to laugh. It seemed so flimsy. They knew that some Amazonian Indians can grow facial hair, even though most choose to appear beardless. Purá, for example, looked clean-shaven, but that was because he plucked any whiskers before they grew too long. It was a matter of aesthetics: he thought he looked better without facial hair, and that belief had been reinforced by the collective opinion of his tribe. Many tribes throughout the Western Hemisphere felt the same way. Plucking was common, and long had been chronicled in publications ranging from anthropological journals to James Fenimore Cooper's *The Last of the Mohicans*. But to the surprise of the members of the Contact Front, the mustache argument was taken seriously. People all over Rondônia—public officials among them—were citing the existence of the Indian's patchy mustache as evidence of inauthenticity.

Marcelo's boss, Sydney Possuelo, had been lauded by the ranchers as the most trustworthy sertanista in Brazil—only because he'd been the one who reported in the 1980s that he'd found no evidence of Indian tribes in a patch of forest that later became part of the Rio Omerê Reserve created for the Kanoe and Akuntsu tribes. When reporters brought up the ranchers' mustache argument to Possuelo, the well-traveled sertanista dismissed the ranchers' argument outright. "There are tribes that do have beards," Possuelo told *Folha de S. Paulo*. "That's the case with the Araras, in the state of Pará."

The press also consulted eighty-one-year-old Orlando Villas Boas, a living legend in the history of Amazon exploration and the sertanista who had established the first Indian reserve in Brazil's history. Like Possuelo, Villas Boas advised reporters that the mustache argument wasn't the damning piece of evidence that the ranchers were saying it was. "He's certainly an Indian," Villas Boas told a reporter after being shown the images that Vincent had shot. "I saw many people similar to that during expeditions through the Amazon region." He listed a couple of tribes off the top of his head that he'd seen with similar amounts of facial hair. "There always were native communities there in the south of Rondônia, even though the State's process of occupation there ignored their needs. It's not impossible that, now, there would appear a man like this one who has been separated from his relatives."

When the reporter from *Folha de S. Paulo* talked to Marcelo, he asked him how he felt about being accused of fabricating the whole story.

"I do not invent facts," Marcelo told him. "I just dig around where nobody else is interested in going. And I end up finding things there."

On the morning of March 7, 1999, a series of stories regarding the lone Indian were published in *Folha de S. Paulo*. The lead story among them was titled, "Court Interdicts 60 km2 for an Indian."

> One man—naked and withdrawn, about thirty-some years old, with straight hair, dark skin, with small and slightly slanted eyes, with black sideburns and mustache—prompted the Federal Court to interdict about 60 km2 of land in southern Rondônia. The area is about the same size of the municipality of Osasco in the state of São Paulo, which has 65 km2 and 623,000 inhabitants.

The Contact Front had won one battle but not the war. The court's ruling wasn't the permanent victory that Marcelo had hoped for—the judge simply extended the existing prohibitions against development. The ban would still expire within a year. The interdiction, as the article explained, was intended to allow the Contact Front to continue to carry out their expeditions on the property until they figured out a long-term solution. The article reported:

> The court understands that, as a result, the Indian will be protected and FUNAI will have time to approach him, identify his language and tribe, learn the whereabouts of his relatives and then evaluate whether it is suitable to convert the area (totally or partially) into an indigenous reserve.

With enough time, Marcelo hoped that the Indian might eventually grow comfortable with the Contact Front's periodic presence in the forest and that *he* might reach out to them. The judge's ruling bought the team members more time to cultivate a peaceful atmosphere, but they hadn't reached Marcelo's goal of creating an Indian reserve yet. The only real step toward that goal had been a bureaucratic one, but that alone had sparked a firestorm of questions among Brazilian officials tasked with regulating the country's land and indigenous policies.

Protecting a tribe by protecting land was common, but what if the tribe had only one member? Was it still a tribe? Could there really be such a thing as a one-man Indian nation? The lone Indian's culture, or what was left of it, had no hope of survival beyond his own life. So wasn't that culture already dead?

Even within FUNAI, people were asking such questions, and few were sold on the idea that the land might eventually become a one-man reserve. "It isn't possible to save his society anymore," said Roque Laraia, the director of agricultural issues for the agency. Keeping the Indian isolated and "protected" from contact with outsiders was, in Laraia's view, a form of "cruelty."

Within the pages of *Folha de S. Paulo* and other newspapers, the case became a matter of debate because it cut straight to the heart of a basic moral dilemma that has confounded societies for centuries: are the rights of a small group worth protecting if more people might benefit from the elimination of those rights or protections?

Moral psychologists call it the Trolley Problem, a name that's based on an imagined scenario that they created to illustrate the dilemma:

Imagine that a runaway trolley is rolling down a track, and ahead of it you see five workmen who don't notice they're in its path. You are standing at a fork in the track, and you can pull a lever to save the five workers and divert the trolley onto a second track, where only one man is standing. Do you pull the lever?

Now imagine that you are standing on a bridge, looking down on those tracks. You spot the runaway trolley hurtling toward the five workmen. Without access to the switch, the only way you can stop the trolley is to throw a heavy object in its path. The only object heavy enough to stop the trolley is a fat man standing next to you on the bridge. Do you push the man off the bridge and onto the track, killing him to save the five workers?

The answers respondents give to the Trolley Problem have proved immensely interesting to researchers. Biologist Marc Hauser and psychologists Fiery Cushman and Liane Young published an Internet-based survey in 2006 among more than two hundred thousand people from more than a hundred different countries, and the responses were consistent with numerous other studies that posed the same questions. In the first scenario, almost everyone answers "yes," they'd flip the switch. But in the second, the majority of respondents in survey after survey answer "no," they wouldn't push the man onto the tracks. The respondents had various religious backgrounds, ethnicities, and educational levels, and the results were unequivocal: 90 percent of people judged that pulling the switch was morally permissible, while only 10 percent of people said that pushing the man off the bridge was acceptable.

In real life, moral dilemmas are almost never so cut-and-dried. But in Rondônia the case of the lone Indian became a Trolley Problem. A thorny and twisted ethical issue concerning indigenous preservation was reduced to an essential question that Brazilians could wrap their heads around: do you preserve a piece of forest, even though it might provide sustenance for dozens of farmers and their families, to protect the life of one man?

In Brazil, the indigenous population makes up about 2 percent of the total population, but they inhabit more than 12 percent of the country's land area. Those who believed that the tribes had too much land had become a vocal lobbying bloc within the country's political arena, and the case of the lone Indian seemed a distilled example of an injustice carried out in the name of fairness. Opponents of the reserve, which included ranchers and conservative members of Congress, began arguing that by choosing to "save" the lone Indian, Brazil was sacrificing a greater number of people who'd benefit from economically productive land. In framing their arguments, the opponents of the reserve tried to take the human element out of the equation as much as possible and present it abstractly: in their view, opening the land to development wasn't like pushing a man off the bridge to stop the trolley; it was like flipping the switch. Reserving land for Indians might seem politically correct, they suggested, but was it really serving the greater good of the population at large?

It wasn't so simple, of course. The case of the lone Indian couldn't be abstracted to a problem on paper. The benefits of developing the land couldn't be predicted. No one could guarantee that development would "save" anyone through economic opportunity, just as no one could say that it would spell certain death for the Indian. It was possible that the Indian, if removed from the land and placed on a faraway reserve, might discover a happier life among other tribes. Or he might not. The only reasonable certainty at this point was that the Indian himself wasn't interested in leaving the area.

Ambiguities aside, the argument that reserving land for Indians was undermining the common good of the larger population gained traction throughout Brazil. As landowners in Rondônia attacked the idea of reserving land for the lone Indian, similar arguments were applied to other reserves all over the country by Congress members linked to ranching and mining interests. Eventually the Supreme Court would be saddled with more than a hundred pending cases challenging the legality of Brazil's scattered indigenous territories.

Among the most powerful politicians in the state of Rondônia in the 1990s was a man named Amir Lando. Between 1972 and 1974 he'd been the head of INCRA, the agency that later would dole out the property titles in Rondônia. But by 1998 he had become a senator representing the state in Brasília.

Because he had been involved in the distribution of property titles, the law prohibited Lando from owning ranch land. But every time Marcelo or Altair asked local workers for the name of the man who owned the Convento Ranch—part of which had been incorporated into the Rio Omerê Reserve for the Kanoe and the Akuntsu—the workers would say the senator's name. Lando himself didn't do much to hide his connection to the property. A sign had been hung over the gate leading onto the property, and it read PROP. AMIR F. LANDO.

One day in 1999, Altair noticed that someone had been cutting trees in the section of forest that fell within the Convento Ranch's property lines, even though the courts had prohibited logging there. He estimated that at least two hundred cabriúva trees had been felled. He and Marcelo filed a complaint to the courts in Porto Velho. But Lando denied owning the ranch. And when they checked the property records, they saw that the owner was listed as someone named Leandro Lopes.

The local newspapers caught wind of the criminal complaint, and Lando denied involvement. He didn't own the property and therefore couldn't be punished. But when newspaper reporters questioned the people who lived near the property, they were told the same thing as Marcelo and Altair: Amir Lando was the owner.

Eventually the identity of Leandro Lopes was revealed: he was the nephew of Lando's ex-wife. Marcelo suspected that Lopes was a *laranja*; this Portuguese word for "orange" is a slang term describing someone, usually a distant relative, a politician uses as a legal surrogate to circumvent conflict-of-interest laws.

Lando's denials of wrongdoing infuriated Marcelo and Altair, and in a jointly signed report to FUNAI, they tore into him. After explaining that the Indian had chosen to avoid contact with their team, they told their bosses that they believed the local politicians were trying to exert pressure within the government to remove the Indian from the land. They believed that Lando, who previously had not been publicly involved in the court battles over Indian land, was working against them behind the scenes. They suspected that the senator was taking interest in the case of the lone Indian as a form of retribution against the Contact Front.

> A senator of the Republic, who has personal interests in this case, insistently issues requests that FUNAI speed up contact with this Indian, with the clear intention that he is removed, thus freeing the land for the ranch managers. Responsibility has been turned upside down—it seems that the blame rests with him, the Indian, just for having survived the innumerable instances of violence that have decimated his people.

Right around that time, in 2000, a lot of politicians began complaining about the work of the Contact Front. In governmental offices in Brasília and Porto Velho, a group of pro-ranching lawmakers decided it was time to delve much more deeply into the matter.

CHAPTER TEN

The Corridors of Power

The headline beside Marcelo's picture in Rondônia's *Expressão* newspaper on April 29, 2000, read, "The War of the Pale Faces."

> In addition to the many indigenous nations that have been decimated by the furious greed of invading ranchers, those who protect the Indians have also become threatened. Such is the case of Vilhena resident Marcelo dos Santos. Last year he received the "Knight of the Rio Branco" commendation from the hands of President Fernando Henrique Cardoso. A recognition of his 24 years of work in studying and preserving the customs of indigenous tribes. But in Rondônia, it's a different story. Marcelo revealed to *Fantastico* that he is being threatened with death.

Fantastico is a nationally broadcast newsmagazine program that, like *60 Minutes* in the United States, attracts millions of viewers each Sunday. A journalist with the program spoke to Marcelo early in 2000 as part of a general feature about isolated tribes throughout Brazil. During the interview, Marcelo mentioned that he recently had received threatening telephone calls as a result of his work on behalf of indigenous tribes, and he suspected that ranching interests were behind the threats. After the broadcast, the local press in Vilhena followed up on the story.

> Among the many ranchers "damaged" by Marcelo, one is very powerful. Aside from being an experienced lawyer, the rancher is a national senator. Amir Lando is said to own 4,000 hectares of land in Corumbiara where ten Indians live.

A sign outside the Convento Ranch in Rondônia alerts visitors that the land is owned by Senator Amir Lando.

The article went on to say that Lando apparently had used his ex-wife's nephew as a laranja to circumvent conflict-of-interest regulations and that Lando didn't deny his involvement in the ranch completely. He admitted he knew that two hundred cabriúva trees had been felled at the ranch, which is what attracted the attention of the Contact Front in the first place. Lando explained that he had donated the wood to charity.

The article also mentioned that Marcelo's disputes with Lando and other landowners had prompted talk of a possible transfer out of Rondônia. Marcelo told the newspaper that he didn't want to leave, because he equated it with surrender. "I'd rather resign," he said.

On the morning of October 10, 2000, Congressman Antonio Feijão walked into Rondônia's Legislative Assembly building, which dominates a city block in Porto Velho. Feijão wasn't familiar with the building—he normally worked in Brasília, representing another state in the national Congress. But as the head of a national congressional investigation into FUNAI's activities, he took a seat at the front of the cavernous hearing room.

He and several fellow legislators, many of whom shared his view that the country's Indian reserves were too large, had come to Rondônia to probe Marcelo dos Santos's role in demarcating Indian territories. The hearings were scheduled for two days, and several local ranchers had been summoned to testify.

Searching for hints of misconduct by Marcelo, the congressmen focused primarily on his work in demarcating the Rio Omerê Reserve, where Lando—or his family, at least—owned land. The stakes of the inquiry were clear to the members of the Contact Front: if the protected status of the Rio Omerê Reserve could be reversed by challenging Marcelo's credibility, then a temporary interdiction for the lone Indian wouldn't stand a chance of being renewed.

To the ranchers who assembled in the hearing room, Feijão represented a friendly face. The congressman had become one of Brazil's most vocal critics of Indian reserves, arguing that the natural resources found in some of them should be exploited for the good of the country's economic development. His résumé was music to the ears of any rancher eager to develop land. He had denounced several international nonprofit groups that supported broadened indigenous rights and Catholic missionary organizations, saying their advocacy was just a cover that hid their true goal: to undermine Brazil's sovereignty. He had personally filed lawsuits against anthropologists, accusing them of manipulating Indian leaders to stir conflicts with the rest of Brazilian society. Feijão also had proposed a law in Congress that would evaluate the "degree of acculturation" among the Indian tribes who had already been granted reserves; if it was determined that their tribal cultures had already incorporated much of the lifestyle present in the larger society around them, they could lose their claim to the land. A year earlier, in 1999, Feijão also had sponsored a bill that would punish any Indian tribes who harmed the environment, arguing that the country's environmental laws were unfairly one-directional and solely targeted non-Indians.

For years, Feijão had been an energetic opponent of a large reserve in the state of Roraima, near the Venezuelan border. Gold miners wanted access to the land, which was occupied by the Macuxi and Wapixana Indian tribes. The tensions between the tribes and the miners had exploded in the early 1990s. After a group of Indians kidnapped two miners in 1993 and demanded that their land be declared off-limits to development, the miners responded by kidnapping five Indians and threatening to lynch them. After Roraima's Roman Catholic bishop spoke in support of the Indians, angry protesters set his lawn on fire. A man went on a local radio program and offered to kill the bishop "for the right price." A *New York Times* correspondent traveled to the region to report on the conflict, and an adviser for a group of ranchers and miners explained to him, "The Bishop is still alive—that shows how tolerant we are, right? Of course, we pray every night that he will die in his sleep."

Feijão wasn't from Roraima, but he jumped to the miners' defense in their battle against the Macuxi and the Wapixana. Before entering politics, Feijão had been an official in the union that represented the wildcat miners who traversed the Amazon in search of gold. He had come of age fighting environmentalists and the international backlash against his profession. In trying to put the miners' culture into context within the rest of the country's social fabric, the *Christian Science Monitor* used the following shorthand description:

> Many people say that the miners, known as garimpeiros, are heroes because they create jobs for the poor and have made Brazil one of the world's biggest gold producers. But anthropologists say the garimpeiros, who have overrun Indian land throughout the Amazon, are decimating entire tribes, mostly with disease, but also with guns. Environmentalists worry that the garimpeiros' use of mercury to separate gold from gravel is polluting the Amazon's rivers for years to come and contaminating wildlife. The miners dismiss this. A hard-drinking, free-spending lot, they are gripped by visions of what gold can buy.

The mining camp that the reporter visited for that article was run by none other than Antonio Feijão.

Now a dozen years later, in 2000, he was helping to spearhead the congressional inquiry in Porto Velho. The investigation seemed to be his way of keeping a promise he'd made the year before: in 1999 Feijão had told reporters that he would not launch a congressional inquiry into the Indian affairs agency if the demarcation of the Roraima Reserve was legally revoked. And here he was in Rondônia on the morning of October 10, calling ranchers to the stand as part of a search for misconduct on the part of FUNAI.

For an introduction to Marcelo's activities in Rondônia, the panel called on Antonio Duarte to testify. He was a rancher who owned part of the land that had been interdicted to form the Rio Omerê Reserve for the Kanoe and the Akuntsu. He and several other ranchers in the area had hired Vilhena lawyer Odair Flauzino to wage a legal battle against the reserve a couple years earlier, but the appeal was unsuccessful. Now he was being given a second chance to air his complaint, and he didn't hold back.

Before he launched into a prepared statement that targeted Marcelo's character, he explained to the panel that his voice was just one of many among the local ranching community, which included Senator Amir Lando and other ranch owners. Duarte wasted little time in levying their central complaint: he suggested that Marcelo had planted the Kanoe and Akuntsu Indians on the land. Armed with a cache of official documents, he said that his suspicions were inflamed when he looked into Marcelo's background.

"Indian trafficking is not something new in Marcelo's history," Duarte told the panel. He said that in 1981 FUNAI had interdicted a large parcel of land in the state of Mato Grosso as an Indian reserve. But, Duarte said, no Indians lived on that land at the time of the interdiction, so Marcelo loaded a group of Indians in his truck and moved them onto the territory himself. Duarte told the panel that Marcelo's actions provoked a federal police investigation that confirmed those facts. What's more, the owner of the land, Luis Morimoto, sued FUNAI in 1983 and explained to the court that his land had been free of Indians until Marcelo had trucked them onto his property.

Technically speaking, Duarte was telling the panel the truth. Some important context, however, was lacking.

Marcelo *had,* in fact, transported the Indians to Morimoto's land. It also was true that the area had been completely free of Indians prior to that relocation. But before any of that happened, the Indians had begun lobbying for the interdiction of Morimoto's land. They said they had occupied the territory years before Morimoto arrived, and then were chased away. After hearing the Indians' case, FUNAI legally interdicted the ranch and declared it Indian territory. *After* that interdiction, Marcelo drove the Indians to the area, where they reestablished their dwellings. The officer who evaluated a preliminary police investigation concluded that Marcelo hadn't committed a crime. He dismissed Morimoto's criminal charges.

But when Duarte submitted that evidence to the panel, the story was presented as an implication, one that was designed to tie Marcelo's credibility in knots. The portrait of Marcelo that began to emerge inside the hearing room suggested that he was a longtime fabulist, conjuring Indians out of thin air to attract funding from international agencies and derail decades of progress and development.

The ranchers who testified repeatedly referenced the 1986 "negative certification" report by Sydney Possuelo—invariably prefixing his name with the identifying phrase "the illustrious sertanista." Possuelo's original report, which stated that he found no evidence of Indian presence in the area at the time of his visit, was cited as gospel. Possuelo's subsequent remarks explaining that the report didn't discount the possibility that Indians might have been in the area before or after his expedition weren't mentioned.

Not surprisingly, the fact that the Contact Front had received funding from the World Bank's Planaforo Project also was presented as a condemnation. They suggested that by inventing stories of persecuted Indians on the run, Marcelo was exploiting the international community's soft spot for Indians to get cash for his Contact Front. They implied that by doing so, Marcelo was toying with matters of national security. Because his Indian reserves sat near the national border, they could create a military weak spot for Brazil's territorial defense.

The congressional probe into Marcelo's activities didn't end with the inquiry in Porto Velho. Legislators championing development had found a whipping boy, seeing in Marcelo someone deserving of public dishonor on a national stage. Afterward, a separate Senate panel in Brasília also delved into his work, and legislators called three witnesses to testify about him: the head of Vilhena's soy producers' alliance, an anthropologist named Carlos Antonio Siqueira, and an ex-FUNAI employee named Osny Ferreira.

Ferreira was the first to testify. When contact with the Kanoe was made in 1996, Ferreira—an ex-FUNAI employee—had argued that Marcelo had uprooted Purá and the rest of the Kanoe from the Cinta Larga tribe and replanted them in the Rio Omerê territory. His accusations, though thoroughly dismissed by FUNAI's leadership in Brasília, had provided the basis for lawyer Odair Flauzino's public campaign questioning the identities of the tribes.

Ferreira told the senators that the morning after Vincent's footage of the Contact Front's initial meeting with the Kanoe aired on television in 1996, a group of Cinta Larga Indians showed up at his house. The Indians, he said, suggested that the newly discovered Indians might be relatives who'd gone missing from their tribe years before. Though Ferreira had been fired from FUNAI for stealing property—charges he later described as politically motivated—he drove the Cinta Larga Indians to southern Rondônia and hiked with them to the site of the newly discovered Kanoe village. There, they encountered two members of the Kanoe tribe—Purá's mother and his sister.

Ferreira said the Kanoe seemed hungry. He theorized that they had recently been planted on the land by Marcelo and Altair, and were therefore unaccustomed to the region, unable to gather or grow adequate food. Ferreira said that after meeting with the Kanoe, he walked about eight kilometers and discovered the FUNAI camp. There he found Marcelo and Ines Hargreaves, a nurse who worked for FUNASA, Brazil's National Health Foundation. They were surprised to see him, he said.

"As a member of the Christian Congregation of Brazil, I'm accustomed to giving testimony in front of the Lord," Ferreira told the panel, prefacing what he was about to say. "Marcelo put his hands over his head and said to me, 'Osny, you ruined everything. I have been working on this for so much time, and you have come here to ruin it all.' Ines Hargreaves did the same thing, and treated me very badly. . . . After a few months, Marcelo issued a complaint against me in the Public Ministry, saying I had exposed the Indians to the flu. And I spent, with very little resources, seven months trying to defend myself without a lawyer against [federal prosecutors] who accused me of taking flu to those Indians."

Ferreira told the senators that he would provide them with videotaped testimony of the Cinta Larga Indians who accompanied him on the trip, which he said would back up his statements. That testimony, however, had already been viewed years before by the late Orlando Villas Boas, perhaps the most well-known sertanista in Brazil's history, and dismissed as bogus. According to Villas Boas, Ferreira had manipulated the Indians' statements, essentially putting the words into their mouths.

But the members of the panel treated Ferreira as a reliable source. Senator Valdir Raupp, who himself had worked as a rancher in Rondônia between terms as governor and senator, responded to Ferreira's testimony with some opinions of his own. Raupp said that he believed that FUNAI agents had been forging evidence of Indian presence to expel ranchers from their land. "It seems like FUNAI is hunting for problems, stirring confusion there to create conflicts."

Next up was Carlos Antonio Siqueira, who identified himself as a retired anthropologist from FUNAI who now worked as a consultant for nongovernmental organizations. He told the panel that like Ferreira, he had visited the Rio Omerê Reserve to investigate the veracity of the Indian tribes. Siqueira said he had pored over Marcelo's early expedition reports, and he told the panel that they contained several "procedural imperfections." The first expeditions on the trail of the Kanoe, he told the panel, were "extra-official," and some included more members of NGOs than government employees. Additionally, one of the expedition reports had been typed on "Ministry of Justice" letterhead, not official FUNAI stationery.

Siqueira said he believed the Kanoe village had been constructed by Marcelo and Altair. The video evidence that Vincent had captured of the initial meeting with Purá and Tiramantú struck him as contrived, he said.

"This sort of thing just doesn't happen," Siqueira said. "It's ridiculous! It's theater!"

Finally, Nadir Razini, a rancher and the head of a local soybean farmers' business alliance, testified. He said he first met Marcelo in 1995. Marcelo had wanted to enter his property, which also was near what eventually became the Rio Omerê Reserve, to hunt for evidence of Indians. Razini, referencing Sydney Possuelo's report, didn't allow him onto the property without a warrant. About fifteen days after Marcelo returned with a warrant, a mysterious group of four foreigners showed up at Razini's gate, wanting access to the property. Although Marcelo wasn't with them, Razini told the panel he suspected they had some connection to the sertanista because of the timing of their visit. He told the senators that the foreigners were interested in conducting a mineral analysis of the soil there.

"None of them spoke Portuguese. One was Dutch, another Belgian, all young people who wore earrings, had long hair and looked like hippies," Razini told the panel.

Senator Augusto Botelho asked Razini if he believed the Contact Front members had planted the Indians on the land. When Razini said he suspected that they had but couldn't be certain, Botelho told him that he shouldn't harbor any doubts.

"These are tactics used by the NGOs to destabilize production, because they don't want the Amazon to develop," said Botelho, who later would introduce legislation attempting to open Indian land in Roraima to development. "And Rondônia is at the forefront of all the states in terms of development. So therefore more of this activity is pursued there."

* * *

Marcelo wasn't called to testify during the Senate hearing. When he testified during the investigation in Porto Velho, he told the panel that his investigations weren't meant to stir problems for ranchers but to protect Indians, which was his job. He explained that after the negative certification was issued in 1986 based on Sydney Possuelo's report, a farm employee had told him that Indians were living on property next to the inspected area and had been violently expelled. That's what sparked his initial interest. He tried to explain that because of all the logging throughout the 1980s and 1990s, it was natural that any Indian groups there would be forced to regularly migrate. But, he believed, they had lived on that land.

"In the beginning of 1986, the farmers had made one clearing of ten thousand hectares exactly in the place the Indians used to live, and all of their grounds were destroyed," Marcelo said. "Considering that four hundred chainsaws were operating there, and facing all the activity around them, the Indians had migrated."

If someone who knew nothing about the battle between development and preservation of the Amazon had sat in on that hearing, the observer might have left with the impression that the tension was solely a result of Marcelo's work. The ranchers had presented a convincing, if one-sided, case that he had single-handedly ripped the land titles out of the ranchers' hands, consulting no one.

Of more than twenty legislators participating in the hearing, only one asked Marcelo questions in his defense.

"Marcelo, do you have the power to interdict these areas yourself?"

"No, I don't have that power," Marcelo replied.

"So what do you do?"

"I can only pass the information I collect up the hierarchy of FUNAI, through the bureaucracy that regulates these matters according to law."

"And this area was interdicted for what reason?"

"It was interdicted because the presence of Indians was proven," Marcelo said. "The anthropologists that visited there proved this. The federal prosecutor that visited also participated in the process. Other people also went there to study the situation—other indigenists. All of them confirmed this. But technically, it was the anthropologists who went there who filed an anthropological report. Using that report, the president of FUNAI interdicted the area. Not me."

After the investigation in Porto Velho, FUNAI's leaders concluded that Marcelo had become a lightning rod of controversy, and his opponents had made it impossible for him to work effectively in the region. Marcelo, reluctantly, had to concede that they were right.

He remained unapologetic until the end, convinced he'd been slandered and railroaded. Years before he might have staked everything he had on clearing his name, there and then, despite long odds of success against some of the most powerful men of the region. But he didn't this time. He decided that Altair might be in a better position to finish what he'd started. Marcelo adopted a pragmatic outlook. Perhaps it was because he had fallen in love.

Just before the ranchers began to try to run him out of the state, he had met a woman named Divina, the sister of a nurse he'd worked with twenty years before among the Nambiquara tribe. As Marcelo endured the government inquiries and accusations, he found refuge in her.

Divina had family in Goiás, almost fifteen hundred miles away from the Indians of Rondônia. Goiás offered him a chance to start anew after an experience that felt like a bitter end in Rondônia. They bought a quiet little house and a piece of land.

To the ranchers, it was a victory.

Shown are several of the palm wood spikes that the lone Indian places at the bottom of his pitfalls. These spikes were discovered near one of his huts before they were implanted in a pit.

CHAPTER ELEVEN

Neither Beast nor God

While Marcelo was being run out of Rondônia, the lone Indian was being run out of the section of forest owned by the Dalafini brothers. Despite the temporary ban on deforestation, logging had continued at a devastating rate. By the end of 2000, approximately 80 percent of the "protected" land on the Dalafinis' property had been cleared. Most of the woods where the Indian had been living were reduced to pastureland.

Altair and Vincent believed that the team's work shouldn't be upended by Marcelo's disputes with the politicians. They continued to launch expeditions to monitor the Indian's survival, fearing that the steady reduction of his habitat exposed him to more danger than ever. Noncontact had become such an important part of their approach that the group had changed its name. No longer was it the Guaporé Contact Front; it was now the Guaporé Ethno-Environmental Protection Front.

They found more of his huts and discovered that the Indian had moved to a section of forest owned by Celso de Sordi, whose Socel Ranch bordered the Dalafinis' property. But Altair and Vincent soon realized that his forced migration was a wholly unexpected blessing, thanks to a surprising arrival on the scene: a group of landless squatters, who wanted to claim part of the Socel Ranch as their own.

The peasants were part of the Movimento dos Trabalhadores Rurais sem Terra (Landless Workers' Movement). The MST was made up of groups of poor, landless farmers who would move into unauthorized encampments on what they considered unproductive territory. After setting up their camps, the groups would try to legally expropriate the land, arguing that it was socially unjust to keep the title in the hands of someone who wasn't maximizing its potential. In a country where about 3 percent of the population owned about two thirds of the potential farmland, the group quickly became a political institution. By 2000 more than a million MST members were living in thousands of encampments throughout the country. Their colorful clusters of roadside tents polka-dotted the national landscape. It spread to other countries and eventually grew into Latin America's largest and most powerful social movement. For landowning ranchers, it was a nightmare.

Before the MST showed an interest in pitching their tents on the Socel property, the members of the Protection Front thought of Celso de Sordi as just another problematic rancher. But when the MST entered the picture, Sordi realized that the temporary interdiction of

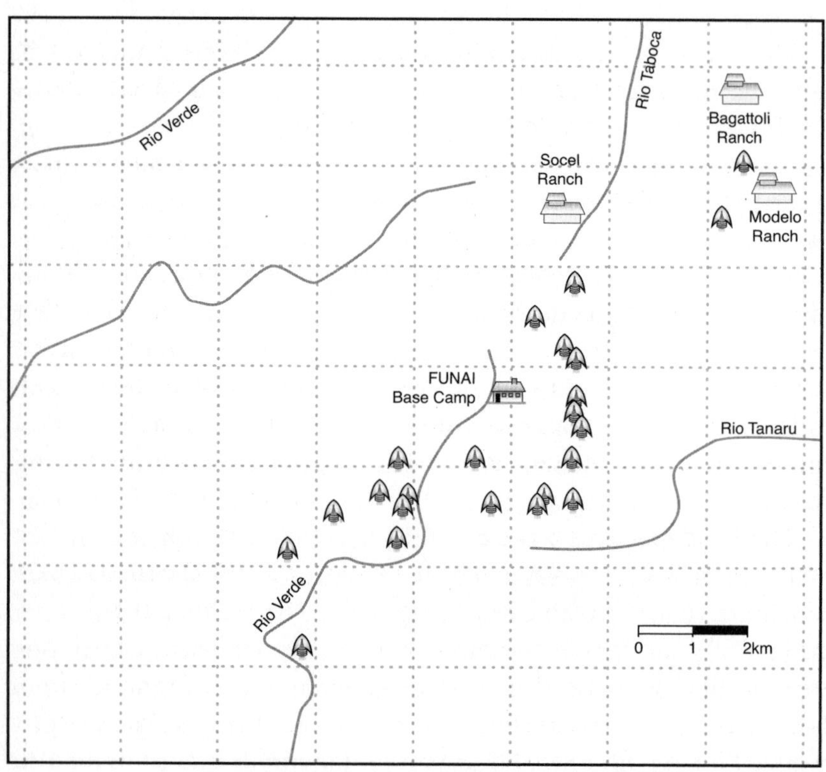

the forested area of his property might work to his advantage. Before the landless farmers could establish their makeshift village, Sordi called on the police to expel them. He argued that land they were trying to occupy wasn't simply another unproductive property—it was Indian territory, specially protected by Brazilian law. If the MST was looking for a place to set up a new squatters' village, there were plenty of other properties they could pick. But this one, Sordi argued, had already been claimed by an Indian. In stark contrast to the Dalafinis, Sordi began respecting the ban on all physical alterations of the forest.

Ever since the incident with the arrow, the Protection Front had continued to leave gifts for the Indian, in the hope that he would one day realize they were a friendly presence and that he could, if necessary, call on them. In 2000, for the first time, the Indian began accepting those gifts. He gathered up seeds, machetes, and fruits. During one expedition, Altair noticed that he had planted some of the seeds they had left for him and created a thriving garden.

The Indian's acceptance of their presents felt like a tiny victory after a long losing streak. It seemed that he had finally concluded that the Protection Front didn't want to harm him.

Altair believed the Indian might choose to initiate contact soon. If the Indian believed they were harmless, he might decide that forging a relationship would be in his best interests. Marcelo's conflict with the politicians couldn't have come at a worse time, but he made sure Altair and Vincent carried out the necessary fieldwork that he couldn't oversee. Three weeks after Marcelo testified in Porto Velho, Altair and Vincent visited Sordi's ranch. They wanted to see if the rancher's apparent change of heart concerning the Indian's presence on his land was genuine and what new opportunities it might open for them.

The headquarters of the Socel Ranch was a humble grouping of stables and shacks in the center of a soggy pasture. The rusting husk of a small propeller airplane, barely visible above the tall grass, had been left to rot beside the main stable. Ranch hands, mounted on sweaty horses, rounded up cattle. When Altair and Vincent found Sordi inside one of the shacks, he invited them to sit at a scarred wooden table, and poured them each a glass of coffee.

Altair and Vincent could hardly believe it. No rancher had ever welcomed them so warmly. Then again, Sordi was the first rancher who actually wanted his land to be interdicted for the benefit of Indians.

Sordi sat on a bench and listened intently, taking deep drags on a cigarette, as Altair explained that the Indian—from what they could determine—seemed to be living a more stable, fixed existence since he wandered onto Sordi's property. Instead of ignoring the team's presents, the Indian was now accepting the corn and manioc they'd left for him, and he had actually planted some of it. But Altair explained that FUNAI's temporary interdiction of the land would expire again in a few months. If the Indian still hadn't made contact with the Protection Front by that time, Altair wanted Sordi's word that he wouldn't come to harm.

Sordi had no complaints. The team had his permission to fully explore his land whenever they wanted and do whatever they needed to do to protect the Indian. He grabbed his box of cigarettes and tapped it on the table.

"The thing is, this Indian is a human being just like we are, right?" Sordi said. "I guess we have to have patience with him."

Altair picked up a deck of playing cards that had been sitting on the table and riffled them, nodding his head in agreement. Then he began to chuckle. "Well, it's good that you think like that," Altair said, "because your neighbors around here don't think that way."

Their meeting had been short and simple, but it was the sort of interaction that kept Altair's spirits up when it seemed like the case of the lone Indian was a lost cause. Because after all they'd been through, if a rancher could genuinely be sympathetic to their cause, then anything might be possible.

At six o'clock on a wet November morning in 2000, Altair and Vincent set out from Sordi's ranch and hiked into the forest to verify that the lone Indian was still living there. Paulo Pereira, the contract worker who regularly joined them on expeditions, also accompanied them, as did three members of the Sakirabia tribe of Indians. The Indians lived on the Mequéns Indigenous Territory, several hours' drive west of the Rio Omerê Reserve.

The Sakirabia, a group that numbered about eighty people in all, spoke a language that belonged to the same Tupari linguistic family as the Akuntsu. After years of living in the Mequéns Reserve, many of the Sakirabia also spoke fluent Portuguese. Altair optimistically figured that if they encountered the Indian and he wanted to talk, it couldn't hurt to have the Indians along. Perhaps he'd find a connection in them that he hadn't found in Purá.

They slogged through the jungle, their boots heavy with mud, their jeans soaked all the way to the knees. Mosquitoes flitted around their faces. Altair led the way, marching with his backpack and rifle, his bare back pocked with puffy red bites. Paulo followed him, carrying a bundle of palmwood they intended to leave as a gift for the Indian. The Sakirabia Indians carried baskets piled high with vegetables.

Altair tracked their progress on his handheld GPS, double-checking their route by flipping open an old brass compass. After a few hours, Altair found the spot where he had left tools and seeds twenty days before. The gifts were gone.

They scouted the area, following some of the natural trails that spoked through the forest until they passed a *jatobá* tree that caught Altair's eye. A ring had been cut around its trunk—the marking that often signaled that one of the Indian's huts could be found nearby. A few yards away, they found a spike-filled pitfall. A couple of minutes later, they found a hut.

It had been abandoned already. Altair ducked inside and saw the familiar hole in the center of the hut. The cold, scattered ashes of a fire littered a corner. An old bowl fashioned from dried and hardened banana leaves sat on the ground.

"What do you think we should do?" Paulo asked.

Altair looked at the hut and noticed that it was a lot like the others he'd found on the Modelo property: small, hastily constructed, covered with a slipshod overlay of sparse thatch. It wasn't nearly as sturdy as the wood-sided hut the Indian had lived in when Altair first laid eyes on him back in December 1996. He and Vincent assumed that the Indian built the smaller huts when he felt threatened, and only made the stronger huts when he felt more confident that he wouldn't need to quickly abandon them. The fact that the Indian had been accepting gifts and living in a section of forest that wasn't being cut suggested to them that he might now be living in a more permanent shelter.

"Let's walk on," Altair said.

They proceeded single file through the forest. After finding two hunting blinds, Paulo held a finger to his lips.

"Shhh."

He'd heard something, and he followed the sound. After walking several yards in the direction of the noise, they entered a small clearing that had been planted with corn, manioc, and papaya.

At the edge of the clearing, Altair placed a hand on the trunk of a paxiuba tree for balance as he leaned forward to peer across the garden. On the other side he spotted another hut. Because the Indian had been accepting their gifts, Altair decided it was appropriate to move in a little closer, in case the Indian was ready to reach out for contact. But Altair didn't want to startle him, so he turned to the others and held out his palm, signaling for them to stay quiet. Following Altair's lead, the group slowly and silently moved forward. The mud of the clearing was stamped with fresh footprints. A thin curl of smoke was spiraling from the top of the hut, as if someone might be cooking something inside.

"I think he just left the hut," Altair whispered to the others. "He heard us coming."

The others stared wide-eyed over Altair's shoulders, vigilant for any signs of movement.

"Let's go over there to hide and wait for him," Altair said, pointing to a vantage point hidden by trees. "Maybe he'll come back."

They disappeared into the cover of trees and gathered around the base of another paxiuba, taking care not to make slapping sounds as they swatted mosquitoes away from their faces. After several minutes of watching the hut, Altair suggested that they leave gifts for him at his door, including new cutting tools they knew he would find useful.

"We'll leave the axes and machetes for him," he said.

Altair and Paulo approached first, making sure the hut was empty before giving the others the all-clear sign. Altair took a closer look inside the hut as the others joined him. The smoke was rising from a wooden grill, where the ribs of a wild boar and the carcass of an armadillo smoldered. The pork had been roasted to a golden brown. It appeared as if they'd interrupted the Indian just as he was ready to eat.

Another banana-leaf bowl sat on the ground, this one full of the yellow pulp of *pupunha* fruit, sometimes called "peach palm" in English. Wild turkey feathers sat on the ground—they had already been separated, presumably to be used as fletching for arrows. An ample stack of completed arrows sat in a corner, near some latex that had been collected from caucho trees for illumination torches.

In the center of the floor lurked the hole. Two long planks ran along two of its sides, framing the fibrous strands of rope that hung over the mouth of the hole. It looked as if the Indian had draped a slack stretcher over the hole. It had to be where he slept.

Altair snapped some pictures, and placed the tools near the hut's entrance. Then they returned to the edge of the clearing to wait. As they walked past the corn and the manioc, Vincent noticed that the plants appeared as if they'd been maturing for some time.

"I'd say he's been here for at least three months," he guessed, sizing up the stalks.

They waited for an hour, watching the hut, then gave up. If the Indian had wanted to initiate contact, he would have approached them.

The entire time they waited, and even as they trudged away to make a camp for the night closer to Sordi's ranch, Altair couldn't shake the familiar feeling that they were being watched.

Over the four years that they had tracked the Indian, the bits and pieces they'd collected of his everyday life, the clues observed in his surroundings, had come together like the fragments in a kaleidoscope. They recombined in new ways with each discovery. They had learned what he ate, where he slept, how often he hunted, how far he roamed, the crops he valued and those he overlooked—nearly every element of his lifestyle. Each of the sertanistas had spent enough time in the jungle to be able to imagine that ruggedly independent way of life vividly: they knew what smoked armadillo tasted like, they had drunk from the forest's glassy streams, they had spent quiet nights huddled around the golden glow of a caucho torch in the middle of a vast jungle, knowing that no one else would hear their cries for help if something went wrong. But what they hadn't been able to comprehend was the fathomless extent of the Indian's emotional solitude.

Whereas they could at any time fall back on the support of a vast network of colleagues, friends, and family who were never farther than a radio call away, the Indian had no one. The thought of him existing within a vacuum of complete solitude, day after day, week after week, *year after year,* without the companionship of another soul, without any communication whatsoever, boggled the mind.

Humans are social animals. We are hardwired for company. When we are separated from others against our will, we undergo a biochemical transformation. Even moderate isolation, such as being separated from a group for a short time, generally kick-starts the production of more stress hormones. Blood pressure levels often elevate. Clinical depression and suicidal tendencies can become pronounced. Thinking can become clouded. Cognitive specialists have discovered that dendrites, conduits through which information flows to brain cells, can shrink or disappear completely when interactions with other people are cut off. If left alone long enough, a person's mind literally changes.

Yet as everyone who's ever sought privacy to collect their thoughts knows, a little bit of solitude can do wonders for a person's sense of clarity. Mystics, hermits, and philosophers—from the desert seekers of early Christianity to Henry David Thoreau—have forever extolled the benefits of voluntary solitude. Rousseau claimed that only when alone did he feel he became fully "what nature willed." More recently, influential American Catholic author Thomas Merton praised solitude as a noble aim in itself. Solitaries "withdraw into the healing silence of the wilderness, or of poverty, or of obscurity," Merton wrote, "not in order to preach to others but to heal in themselves the wounds of the entire world."

Yet there's a big difference between a contemplative walk in the woods, or a short camping trip, and hacking out an existence completely alone in those woods, forgoing human contact—either by necessity or choice—for years. The mere idea of that kind of solitude—of being *completely* alone—has beguiled and bedeviled thinkers for centuries. When faced with the concept, some of them have rejected it outright; to exist in such a state is so contrary to human nature that anyone subjected to it would, in a sense, cease to be human. Aristotle explained, "But he who is unable to live in society, or who has no need because he is sufficient for himself, must either be a beast or a god." In other words, every man is incomplete and needs others to make him whole—"the other half," as Plato termed it in the *Symposium*. The contemporary European philosopher Tzvetan Todorov, like Schopenhauer before him, draws a line between the concepts of life and existence: a person can live alone, but he only *exists* with the help of others. "Man *lives* perhaps first of all in his skin, but he does not begin to *exist* except through the gaze of others, and without existence life itself dies out. Each of us is born twice, in nature and in society, to life and to existence. Both life and existence are fragile, but the dangers threatening them are not the same. Certainly man is an animal, but that is not all he is."

Such philosophical musings can seem abstract and ethereal because history has provided very few real-life examples of truly isolated individuals; the hypotheses remain as good as untested. The Indian of the Hole's solitude was so extreme as to be practically unprecedented. Contemplating exactly how a human would respond to such a circumstance is, for the most part, virgin territory for the sciences, partly because a truly isolated individual would—by definition—be extraordinarily difficult to observe in a scientifically useful way.

There have been scattered attempts, however, to study the behavior of people who've survived extended periods of isolation, though the subjects—castaways, prisoners, astronauts—never experienced isolation as prolonged or as extreme as the lone Indian had. Some of those studies, limited as they might have been, shattered some widely held assumptions. In 1932, a girl dubbed "Isabelle" by University of California researchers was rescued after spending her first six years accompanied only by her mother, who was deaf and mute. The child, born illegitimately, had been kept in a dark attic every day of her life with the mother, who had been shunned by the rest of the family. Researchers assumed that the absence of communication with anyone surely must have harmed the child's brain—an assumption that seemed reasonable given the fact that the girl, at age six and a half, seemed unable to speak, only grunt. At first, specialists guessed she might be deaf, like her mother—in much the same way that Marcelo and Altair had suspected the Indian might have been deaf, because he seemed so unresponsive to their entreaties. When the Berkeley researchers initially tested Isabelle's verbal ability, the results were the lowest possible. But then a curious thing happened that caused the researchers to reconsider their assumptions that she was feebleminded: she began to learn, with astonishing speed. Two months after she managed to vocalize her first word, she began stringing sentences together. After nine months she could read, write, and retell a story after hearing it. Seven months later she had a vocabulary of fifteen hundred to two thousand words. Within two years, she had reached the educational level of a normal eight-year-old. Her IQ had trebled in a year and a half.

But projecting Isabelle's example onto another survivor of extreme isolation is tricky because the reactions of solitaries vary widely, according to the limited research. In the 1950s, the U.S. government's intelligence agencies, worried about the effects that forced isolation might have on Americans subjected to Communist brainwashing, concluded that the effect of being thrust into such a situation was almost impossible to predict; it would depend on the individual. "Individual differences in reaction to isolation are probably greater than to any other method," stated a Central Intelligence Agency memorandum addressing forced isolation. "Some individuals appear to be able to withstand prolonged periods of isolation without deleterious effects, while a relatively short period of isolation reduces others to the verge of psychosis."

Of those who emerge from the experience relatively unscathed, most had grown to accept their circumstance from the outset, instead of fighting it. A 1963 clinical study that examined survivors of prolonged forced isolation found that "the isolate, if he is to survive, typically adopts an introspective or internal resilience in order to cope with the terms of aloneness. . . . Typically these persons acquire a deep-set conviction that they will master the experience; they become highly motivated and devote most of their working hours to acquiring new scientific or technical skills."

A key to retaining sanity in such a situation seems to rest in how a person reacts to a prospect that some people find horrifying: a future full of vast stretches of unstructured time. If a person isn't immediately shattered by that daunting prospect, some studies suggest that their continued experience with isolation can help toughen their mental resolve, allowing them to better deal with challenges that might send others into depression. Researchers in Norway found that people who spent their lives on extraordinarily geographically remote farms, separated from everyone but members of their own family, responded much better to some forms of stress than did more socialized subjects. After being subjected to five hours of sensory deprivation, for example, those accustomed to long periods of isolation suffered significantly less from the experience than did others who grew up in an urban setting.

If there's one generalization that can be drawn from the various studies to help predict responses to extreme isolation, it's this: what matters most isn't how isolated a person actually *is*, but rather how isolated that person *feels*. Those who have been isolated for long periods often come up with imaginative replacements for human connections to protect themselves from psychological trauma. "Case studies of people undergoing extreme isolation suggest that they fairly quickly begin holding conversations with imagined people, religious deities, or animals," according to a study published in the *Journal of the Association for Psychological Science*. Imaginary or not, those connections help.

"The mind is a terrific device and it can generate other people in our environment, even if other people don't actually exist there," said Nicholas Epley, a social psychologist from the University of Chicago and one of the authors of that study. "The only thing that matters for physical health is perceived loneliness, not actual loneliness. You can be alone in the woods, all by yourself, but still feel very connected if you are deeply religious, for example. You feel like there's another agent there with you. In the same way, you can be married for forty years and feel totally alone."

From all the evidence the members of the Protection Front had found, they had no doubt that the Indian spent much of his day occupied with the hard business of basic survival. But it didn't consume twenty-four hours of his day. He had to have idle moments, times when he wasn't dedicating himself fully to practical labor. Each time they found one of his huts, they were sure to find a tree nearby with a ring cut around the trunk, about head-high from the ground. The cuts weren't made to gather honey or latex, and they weren't deep enough to cause the tree to eventually fall. They asked Indians from other tribes what purpose the rings could possibly serve, but no one had an answer. They seemed to have no practical purpose whatsoever. And that didn't seem such a bothersome answer to the other Indians. The rings, they suggested, were probably spiritual markings, the outward signs of whatever belief system ruled his inner world.

Maybe that belief system helped sustain him. The other Indians, including the Kanoe and the Akuntsu, automatically assumed that the lone Indian followed a spiritual code passed down to him from his elders. Every tribe known in the region told stories that helped explain their place in the world. They had origin stories, their own Adams and Eves. They peopled the forest and rivers with spirits. A single tree might assume an almost holy significance among the jungle's flora, might be rich with backstory, might drip with myth and meaning.

Some of the region's tribes say that two brothers were the creators of the world. Others say the sun and the moon were the first humans, before they were dispatched to the sky. More than one tribe tells the story of a great flood that wiped out most of humanity; some speak of one couple who lived through the rising of the waters, ensuring the human race's survival. The Nambiquara said that agriculture sprang from a boy who unsuccessfully tried explaining to his father the concept of manioc. When the boy died, his body was transformed into all of the crops the tribe would eventually cultivate: his leg bones became manioc stems, his ribs became black beans, his eyes became squash, his teeth became corn kernels, and so on.

Back in the first half of the twentieth century, French anthropologist Claude Lévi-Strauss traveled among the known tribes of this region, and he studied their mythologies. He discovered that many of them believed in the existence of a strange and invisible spirit fluid, something that pervades the forest and that may be either good or evil. The Indians often "captured" these spirits by gesticulating with their arms. After grabbing hold of the spirits, tribal shamans often attempted to cure illnesses by sucking and blowing such spirits into the bodies of their patients. Decades later, the tribes were still doing the same thing. Every member of the Protection Front had seen these rituals in action. The Kanoe and the Akuntsu performed them all the time. Purá had tried to summon those spirits when he had stood outside the lone Indian's hut, waving his arms with a mounting urgency as he watched the Indian's arrow protrude from the hut.

"Ghosts play a considerable role in the beliefs of the Guaporé River Indians," Lévi-Strauss wrote in *Handbook of South American Indians*. "According to the Aruá, ghosts are the souls of the dead returning from the Kingdom of Minoiri to harm their enemies and to protect their friends, chiefly shamans."

The tribal myths passed on moral codes from one generation to another, detailing the hideous punishments—being devoured by worms, swallowed by snakes, raped by tapirs—that befell those who'd been guilty of adultery, incest, gluttony, or cannibalism. The Aruá tribe of Rondônia told the story "The Man Who Ate His Wives," of a legendary figure who ultimately cannibalized himself after discovering the tastiness of his own flesh. His ghost transformed himself into a jatobá tree when he died, and from that time forward, arrowheads of a stunningly high grade grew from the tree. The Indians could pick the arrowheads from the tree as if they were low-hanging fruit. The tribe enjoyed those arrowheads until one Indian—known to history as "the Stubborn One"—refused to accept the tree's bounty. According to the myth, the jatobá tree never again produced good arrowheads—only ugly ones, of a useless quality. Brazilian anthropologist Betty Mindlin in 2002 recorded that story as told by Awünaru Odete Aruá, a member of the Aruá tribe in Rondônia:

> The master said:
>
> "My son-in-law and I, the man who ate his wives, had already taught the people who will be born in the future—they wouldn't have had to work to make arrowheads. All they had to do was come and get them. But because the Stubborn One didn't listen to me, these will be the arrowheads of those who have yet to be born."
>
> He took one of the ugly arrowheads and threw it on the ground. A taquara (bamboo) grew and that is how the arrowheads we use came into being.
>
> "The children of the ones who have not yet been born will have to work hard to make arrows!"
>
> And that's how it is today: it is a lot of work for us to make arrows.

The lines between the mundane and the magical were blurred by such stories, and they were so common that the lone Indian almost certainly at some point had been schooled in a similar mythology.

Those shared myths, which he now shared with no one, would have been coupled with a personal store of memories. Altair, Marcelo, and Vincent imagined scenes of carnage and horror. Seeing the rest of his tribe die would have stained his every memory, they believed, tainting the past with anger and sorrow.

Then, during an expedition in late 2000, Altair found a tiny bow in one of the Indian's abandoned huts. It was unlike the ones he used for hunting. It was too small to serve a practical purpose. It looked like a toy, similar to the one Purá had once made for Operá, his young nephew.

What was it? Why would a man living on the bare edge of survival go to the trouble of carrying around something so impractical? What meaning could he possibly find in a child's plaything, when no children existed in his universe?

A couple of possibilities arose. It might have been a memento that the Indian had taken from his tribe's destroyed village, a keepsake to remind him of a boy he'd once known. Or he might have made the bow himself, perhaps for the same reason: to allow him to touch a distant memory.

Altair couldn't be sure. Most tribes buried or burned a person's belongings alongside his corpse, but would the same rules apply to the last survivor of a tribe?

The possibility that the Indian might be longing for the company of relatives he had lost seemed devastatingly sad, and it could stop the team members' conversations cold. Sitting out in the middle of the jungle at night, eating armadillo, and trying to imagine what it must be like to be in his position—these were the kinds of thoughts that could make even the most hardened backwoods explorer lapse into a glum, prolonged silence.

Shortly after Altair found the child-sized bow, Paulo Pereira—the Protection Front's regular assistant—traipsed through the woods near the Socel Ranch with another batch of gifts for the Indian. He approached the same hut that the team had discovered during the previous visit, when they found the armadillo and the ribs of the wild boar roasting inside. Again, the Indian wasn't at home, but his arrows and bowls were there. All of the signs suggested that he was still living there. For the first time, he hadn't fled after the team discovered one of his huts.

It marked another milestone. Paulo guessed that it meant the Indian was growing more comfortable with them, that his fear was subsiding, little by little. The thriving corn and manioc, presumably planted from the seeds they'd given him, reinforced the sense that they were beginning to forge a relationship with him, one that finally had started to show the faintest signs of mutual trust and respect.

Paulo walked away from the hut feeling buoyant, excited. Several yards into the woods, he heard a voice.

"Ho!"

Paulo froze. He turned and saw the Indian, standing among the trees about fifteen yards away. Just as suddenly as the Indian's shout had rung out, he disappeared. He didn't run, but calmly walked around a tree and vanished into the forest.

Paulo, stunned, collected his scattered wits. Then he noticed that he was standing near the lip of one of the Indian's spike-bottomed pitfalls. Standing frozen in place, he realized that the Indian had yelled to warn him of the dangerous trap, to save him from falling into it. Altair had stepped into one of those pitfalls during a trek in 1997—only to be saved by his bulky canvas backpack, which stopped his fall and saved him from certain impalement. Paulo wasn't wearing a pack; he would have fallen onto the sharp spikes with his full weight if not for the warning.

The Indian was transforming from an abstraction in to a personality, from a complete stranger into someone they began to think of as a friend. Yet he was still nameless. They still referenced him through generalities: he was either "the Indian of the Hole" or "the lone Indian" or simply "the Indian."

Did he really need another name? If he maintained relations with no man, what was the point? In his world of one, where no name was necessary to establish him as an individual person, did he think of himself as *the* man?

For the Indians of the region, names were slippery things. For example, the Nambiquara Indians didn't have a name for their tribe before Candido Rondôn "discovered" them in 1907. They didn't even think of themselves as a tribe at all. The Brazilians gave them their name. Among themselves, they were simply "people."

That same ambiguity was evident on the individual level within the tribes of this region, including the Kanoe. Purá hadn't always been called Purá—he'd been named Operá until he loaned that name to his sister's newborn son. Similarly, Konibu of the Akuntsu tribe had been called Baba before he was bitten by a poisonous snake that the tribe called a *konibu*. Names weren't considered permanent, and they weren't invested with much significance. A person's individuality wasn't tied to his name; not knowing someone's name didn't mean his identity or existence was any less defined.

It was similar to the Aristotelian concept that existence or identity depends on other people, or the metaphysical concept of subjective idealism that is often summed up with a philosophical riddle: if a tree falls in a forest and no one is around to hear it, does it make a sound?

The Indians didn't believe that existence or identity depended on another person's perception. The tree that falls in the forest *always* makes a sound.

The Protection Front never gave the lone Indian a name because he didn't need one. They didn't invent him. He existed, even if no one knew his name.

It had been two years since Owaimoro's murder. After a period of cloistered retreat, the Akuntsu had reestablished contact with the Protection Front. Once again, they were regular visitors to the FUNAI encampment. They had even reinstated relations with the Kanoe, a thaw that had more to do with necessity than anything else.

One evening in early 2000, a storm had ripped through the jungle, a powerful display of sound and fury that dumped heavy rains atop the huts and severed the trunks of trees to their bone-white cores. The forest was alive with the howl of the wind and the tortured cracks of splintering trees. The seven members of the Akuntsu tribe huddled through the night in their three huts until a large tree at the edge of their clearing tilted and snapped. It fell directly on top of two of the huts. The youngest member of the group—a girl of about fourteen years old, a niece of Konibu's whom he'd adopted as a daughter—was killed instantly.

Konibu also had been hurt, and the rest of the tribe pulled him from under the downed tree. His body was scratched and bruised, and his right leg was crushed. The femur had shattered under the weight of the trunk. Two days later, after attempting to treat him with herbal medicines and compresses, Pupak walked to the FUNAI camp for help. Adonias and a nurse from Brazil's health service hiked the six miles back to the Akuntsu camp with him; then Adonias trekked back to radio Marcelo and Altair, who were in Vilhena.

At four o'clock in the morning, Altair left Vilhena with another nurse and a group of three Nambiquara Indians whom he brought along to help in case they needed to carry Konibu out of his village. They arrived at the FUNAI camp at eight o'clock, and it took them another three and a half hours to hike through the muddy forest to the Akuntsus' huts. Konibu was delirious with pain. For the next five hours, Altair, Adonias, and the Indians took turns carrying him through the forest in a hammock. When they reached the FUNAI camp, the other members of the Akuntsu tribe begged Altair not to take their leader away from them, but through improvised sign language, he assured them that Konibu would be back soon, and he finally convinced them to let him drive Konibu to the regional hospital in Vilhena.

After dropping Konibu and the nurses at the hospital, Altair drove three hundred miles across muddy roads to another Indian reserve to find a Tupi-speaking Indian the group had previously used as a translator with the Akuntsu, and he rushed him back to the hospital in Vilhena by the next afternoon. The doctors had recommended emergency surgery, and said they would need to transfer Konibu to a larger hospital nearly five hundred miles east, in the neighboring state of Mato Grosso. That afternoon, Konibu—a man who'd refused to ride in a vehicle of any kind until the day before—was put on an airplane and flown to Cuiabá, a city with a population of more than half a million.

Twelve metal pins were set in his leg. After about a month of therapy at an Indian center, Konibu finally returned to his tribe. The others had been devastated by his absence. Pupak had come down with pneumonia and the women were having trouble keeping any food down.

For Konibu the experience in the city had been overwhelming. Through a translator, he told Altair that the modern life he'd been exposed to didn't interest him. He wanted more than ever to return to the comfort of the forest. But after the experience, he arrived at a difficult conclusion: if he and the rest of the tribe were to survive in their isolated setting, they desperately needed the help of a shaman who could help them overcome any medical threats. Because he was the only member of his tribe trained in the spiritual arts—and because he needed assistance as much as anyone—Konibu was forced to call on the only person he knew of who fit the bill: Tiramantú, Purá's sister in the Kanoe tribe.

In the two years since Owaimoro's murder, relations between the two tribes had completely frozen. But coincidentally, at the same time that Konibu was recuperating, the members of the Kanoe were stricken with a serious bout of stomach illness. Tiramantú and her son had suffered so much that the Protection Front ferried them to Vilhena for medical treatment. Purá and Tatuá had feared that they might die.

The health threats had forced both tribes to confront the fragility of their existence. In February, the Kanoe and the Akuntsu gathered at the FUNAI encampment. Tiramantú and Konibu broke the ice with a rapé ritual. They cleansed the air of whatever bad spirits might be floating between them.

Over the following months, the two tribes began seeing more of each other. By the end of the year, they were as friendly as they'd ever been.

The Kanoe believed that every other tragedy paled in comparison to the escalating threat of tribal extinction, and they were willing to forgive anything, even a murder.

The Spix's macaw is a long-tailed blue parrot that depends on the rare *caraibeira* tree, native only to a small sliver of Brazil's Northeast, for nesting. By the 1980s, after the bird became a prize for collectors and much of its habitat fell to development, the Spix's macaw was considered practically extinct. The few known survivors of the species lived in captivity, in the hands of collectors. Then, in the early 1990s, residents near the town of Curaçá started reporting sightings of a bird in the forest that looked remarkably like a Spix's, spurring ornithologists and activists to undertake a massive search in the forests of northeastern Brazil. With the help of video footage shot during an expedition by field researchers, experts determined that the bird that had been spotted was the last known survivor of the species in the wild. After collecting molted feathers, an Oxford University professor eventually performed DNA tests to determine that the bird was a male.

The news of the lone macaw's existence stirred people into action all over the world. Brazil's federal environmental agency formed a group they named the Permanent Committee for the Recovery of the Spix's Macaw. Fund-raising drives held in Britain and the United States raised money for its protection. International symposia debated strategies to save the bird. Newspapers nicknamed him "Mr. Lonely."

The bird had tried to mate with a parrot of a different species, but its reproductive efforts were doomed to failure. After debating whether to capture the bird to try to breed it in captivity, the committee determined that it should remain in the wild, in its natural habitat: if the species had any chance of natural survival, the subsequent generations of birds would need a "teacher" to serve as an example of how to survive on their own. They decided to try to introduce the lone survivor to a female that had been bred in captivity. Ornithologists worked with the female for months to prepare it for release into the wild, and she was eventually set free in 1995. Initial reports of the two birds' compatibility stoked optimism, but they didn't successfully mate. After seven weeks, the female died, apparently the victim of a collision with a power line.

Five days before Marcelo was grilled by the congressional panel in Porto Velho, scientists spotted the only wild Spix's macaw for the last time. By the end of November, newspapers and television stations around the world were reporting that the bird was believed dead, probably killed by a predator.

"The bird had clung on grimly despite all odds for a whole decade, and its death is an absolute tragedy," said Tony Jupiter, a British environmentalist who helped lead the conservation efforts. "The conservationists had ten years to try to secure this species in the wild, and it certainly raises the question of whether or not more could have been done."

As the international media lamented the bird's demise, Purá, the last male of his tribe, continued his own campaign to save his bloodline. If he was ever going to have a child, his options for a mate pretty much began and ended with Inoté, an Akuntsu girl who was about seventeen years old. Shortly after the two tribes reunited, Purá began to broadcast his interest loud and clear. He'd slyly smile at her, then stroke her hair. They would sit and talk, neither really understanding what the other was saying, and he'd massage her palm as he stared intently into her eyes. She seemed flattered by the attention and did nothing to stop his advances. But Purá was nothing if not gentlemanly: he never touched her unless Konibu was present to supervise their courting. According to custom, if the two were to mate, their union needed Konibu's blessing. As Purá petted her forearm, the elderly chief sat just a few feet from them, keeping an eye on every move. So far Konibu had decreed that any coupling between the two tribes would have to wait.

The lone Indian, too, was the last of his tribe, and when he died, his bloodline and the unique attributes of his culture would die with him. The Protection Front had united the Kanoe and the Akuntsu, and that alliance was allowing both tribes to survive, and possibly even grow. But the members of the Protection Front couldn't help but wonder if they'd given the lone Indian every opportunity to avoid the outright extinction of his tribe, his language, his traditions.

When a new interpreter able to speak with the Akuntsu visited the Rio Omerê camp in November 2000, Altair recalled the failed attempt to try to convince Konibu and the Akuntsu women to accompany them on an expedition to try to find the lone Indian. They'd balked in fear of the Toyota, but now that Konibu had traveled in a truck and even on a plane, Altair thought it might be worth another shot. What if the so-called Indian of the Hole laid eyes on the Akuntsu women and got the same romantic ideas Purá had?

When the translator broached the subject with Konibu, the chief responded that he couldn't approach the lone Indian without being invited by him. Altair let the subject drop, and moved on to other topics. He didn't get a chance to pick it back up, because within weeks the president of FUNAI—the same man who had appointed him to replace Marcelo just weeks earlier—informed him that he was fired.

As soon as news of Altair's dismissal hit the press, FUNAI agents throughout Brazil cried foul. When Marcelo had been driven out of Rondônia, many of them had privately voiced suspicions that Amir Lando was the driving force behind it. Now that Altair had been fired, without explanation, they took their suspicions public. Leading the charge was Sydney Possuelo, the head of the agency's Isolated Indians Division and the man who'd been Marcelo and Altair's direct supervisor. The dismissals, Possuelo said, were done without his consultation. *Folha de S. Paulo*'s wire service on December 18 disseminated Possuelo's assertions across the country.

Possuelo charged that Altair's dismissal resulted from an under-the-table deal between Lando, who was the chair of the Budget Committee in Brazil's Congress, and the president of FUNAI, Glenio da Costa Alvarez. Possuelo told the news service that Alvarez had told him he'd received political pressure to get rid of Altair. "Senator Lando, who owns land in the area, is behind it," Possuelo said.

Both Lando and Alvarez denied Possuelo's allegations, but their denials were met with skepticism in some parts of Rondônia. In early 2001, the editorial page of Vilhena's *Folha do Sul* drew a bold line between Lando and the dismissal:

> After making life hell for Marcelo dos Santos, forcing the indigenist to move out of the state, Lando got the dismissal of his substitute, Altair, "The German." Coincidentally, the federal budget allocation for FUNAI doubled after "The German" was stripped of his position.

Losing Altair was a more devastating setback than Marcelo's move to Goiás. Everyone with the Contact Front had hated to see Marcelo go, but Altair and Vincent still had every intention of bringing Marcelo's work to fruition. Their mission seemed straightforward, and it felt noble. With a little optimism, they could almost rationalize Marcelo's move as a blessing in disguise: Marcelo seemed happy with Divina, and it might do him good to put some distance between himself and the ranchers of Rondônia for a while. But when Altair's job was pulled out from under him, a lot of hopes were shattered. With Altair gone, Vincent had lost his only remaining connection to FUNAI. All three of the men who'd opened the case of the lone Indian years before suddenly found themselves powerless in Rondônia.

Unlike Marcelo, Altair had never been viewed as a polarizing figure among the locals. He had earned a reputation as a patient and good-humored agent, and his actions had never been the subject of the kind of scrutiny that Marcelo had endured. He'd done nothing that might be construed as a firing offense—other than being a close confidant of Marcelo's. Altair's dismissal seemed wholly arbitrary, and it galvanized NGOs and indigenous advocates, who protested the decision as patently unfair. But they couldn't overturn it. Altair was allowed to keep a job with FUNAI, as long as he stayed outside Rondônia—an absurd stipulation with which he was in no position to argue. He moved first to Mato Grosso and then to the state of Minas Gerais, where his wife had family and where he joined a new FUNAI regional team.

Altair searched for a bright side. Brazil was an enormous country, with a lot of areas to explore, and there was always a chance he might be able to establish close ties with other indigenous tribes in his new territory, just as he had with the Kanoe and the Akuntsu. He could bemoan the fact that FUNAI had betrayed him as long as he wanted, but that same agency had provided him with a respectable livelihood and a position of relative authority, even though he lacked any sort of educational degree.

Vincent wasn't so charitable. He was disgusted with FUNAI, believing it had effectively sentenced the lone Indian to death by dismissing his most passionate protectors. His visits to Rondônia ceased. In his mind, the story of the lone Indian had effectively ended. And it was an unqualified tragedy.

But at FUNAI's headquarters in Brasília, at least one employee hadn't given up. Sydney Possuelo—the man whom Rondônia's ranchers couldn't praise enough after his 1986 visit to the region—was determined to try to finish the work he'd been monitoring from afar for years.

The sixty-year-old Possuelo had explored more of the Amazon's interior than anyone alive. As he pondered how to move forward now that his top agents in Rondônia had been removed, he decided to take a more active role. The more he studied the case of the lone Indian, the more he believed he had found a conflict that perfectly encapsulated the tensions he had seen coming to a head throughout the Amazon for decades.

A young Sydney Possuelo

CHAPTER TWELVE

Larger Than Life

In 1959, Sydney Possuelo was eighteen years old and itching for adventure. Up to that point, he'd lived in the suburbs of São Paulo, wishing he were somewhere else. When his friends wanted to play soccer, he wanted to run around with his slingshot through a little tract of woods. He would spend hours reading about Brazil's wild open spaces in *O Cruzeiro* magazine, and then dream of slashing his way through ropy jungles, mapping uncharted territory, discovering new lands. The city where he lived was enormous, but life there seemed small. Even as a kid, Sydney had a taste for the epic.

To put those dreams to the test, the teenager boarded a small military plane that delivered mail to Brazil's backcountry, and he strapped into the rear along with the boxes and envelopes. He was headed for the new Xingu National Park, which was little more than a big blotch on the map, a clumsy spill of green ink. The only people who lived there were Indians, and it was about to be explored by the most famous adventurers of the day: the Villas Boas brothers. The four siblings were ethnologists who had been traversing the wildest landscapes of South America. For months, Sydney had been writing them, begging to join their team. He had discovered where their sister lived in São Paulo and staked out the house. He became a hovering gadfly, offering to help her out in whatever way an anxious teenager with unlimited energy could, just for a chance to meet the men he already had grown to consider heroes. When the brothers visited her, he'd run to the store to buy them cigarettes. He was desperate for adventure, and they finally surrendered.

When the plane landed, it skidded toward the edge of the landing strip, burrowing nose-first through the mud. A storm of envelopes settled around Sydney as it shuddered to a halt. He and the plane's other passenger, a sergeant in Brazil's army, jumped out of the hatch and were greeted by a man who quickly fetched a tractor to help haul the plane out of the mud and onto more solid ground. The man hooked one end of a steel cable to the tractor, and the army sergeant hooked the other end to the plane's tiny rear wheel. But before the army sergeant had securely fixed the cable to the plane, the man with the tractor started to pull away. Sydney, standing next to the sergeant, watched the cable pull taut. The sergeant's finger got caught between the wheel and the cable, and it popped off into the mud at Sydney's feet, completely severed.

Sydney ran for help, straight to an outpost near the landing strip. There he experienced his first of countless encounters with Amazonian Indians.

He slipped in the mud just as he reached the outpost and commenced a long and comically dramatic fall—feet scissoring in search of something solid, arms pinwheeling for balance, mouth agape. He landed with a splat. Pulling himself up, he saw a hundred Kayapo tribesman laughing at him.

His first impression of Amazonian Indians was precise and unequivocal:

Sons of bitches.

One of the most celebrated careers in the history of Brazilian adventure began embarrassingly, with mumbled curses. Sydney had entered his line of work for adventure, plain and simple. Indians were an afterthought. It was his relationship with his mentor, Orlando Villas Boas, that began to change all that.

The Villas Boas brothers are believed to be the first nonmissionaries to live permanently with Amazonian Indians. Starting in the 1950s, Orlando, particularly, was cast by Brazil's media as a latter-day incarnation of the revered explorer and national hero Candido Rondôn. In fact, near the end of his life Rondôn had tapped the Villas Boas brothers as his protégés.

When Sydney landed in the jungle, the brothers were laying the groundwork to create South America's first-ever Indian reserve, the twelve-hundred-square-mile Xingu Territory. It is about the size of New Jersey and Connecticut combined.

For years the brothers had been pushing the idea of reserves, telling authorities that the Indians deserved a land buffer to protect them from modern society. Like most of the indigenists who came of age in their wake, Sydney adopted the Villas Boas philosophy: the Indians might have to adapt to the modern world, but they should be the ones to set the pace of that change.

Before Orlando Villas Boas died at age eighty-eight in 2002, he'd been awarded highest honors for humanitarian work given by a wide-ranging cast of international entities, from the Royal Geographic Society in London to the government of Germany. But Orlando also had collected more dangerous laurels, and those were the ones that had seized Sydney's imagination and led him to follow the same path.

Some of Orlando's most obvious battle scars came from his bouts with malaria, and he wasn't shy about letting people know about them. He claimed that he'd battled the disease more than 250 times during his career as an explorer and Indian advocate.

During his own career of more than forty years as an explorer, Sydney, who called himself "the tick on Orlando's neck," never let a bout of malarial shivers pass him by without adding it to his own personal tally. The malarial count became a sort of measuring stick for his adventuring. Sydney could easily awe new acquaintances with stories about one of his encounters with isolated tribes in the middle of the jungle, but he'd abruptly stop himself if his listeners appeared too wonderstruck. "You know, Orlando had malaria more than 200 times," Sydney would say, trying to inject some sobering context to the conversation. "I've only had it 39 times, so far." He'd appear coy and diffident, but he clearly viewed bouts with tropical disease as badges of honor, and he wore them as proudly as the cylindrical vial of antimalarial medicine that dangled from the chain encircling his neck.

By 2000, Sydney's thinning curly hair and wildly unkempt beard were flecked with gray and his face displayed the seams of a hard-lived life. Back in the 1970s, during a run-in with a colonist, five of his teeth had been knocked out by the butt of the man's revolver. In the 1980s he'd been kidnapped by Mentuktire tribesmen who were angry at FUNAI's plan to reduce the size of their portion of the Xingu Reserve. He'd broken ribs during crash airplane landings, and during his expeditions over the years he'd seen eight of his men die. His left eyeball had literally popped out during a motorcycle crash in 1998, but it had nothing to do with jungle exploration: he'd been visiting the Taureg, a nomadic tribe in the Sahara, after traveling to the region to receive a humanitarian medal from the king of Morocco.

In the early 1990s Sydney had served briefly as FUNAI's president, but gave up the post to return to his true passion: leading FUNAI's Isolated Indians Division, which he'd founded in 1987. He still traveled regularly, but his home base was in Brasília, in one of the city's boxy high-rise apartment buildings. Pictures from his expeditions hung on the walls, but they weren't the defining features of the decor.

Don Quixote statues sat on tabletops. Don Quixote paintings hung on the walls. Various editions of Cervantes's seventeenth-century epic sat on shelves.

Sydney had a soft spot for epic quests, and no story had resonated with him like the one about the idealistic man from La Mancha. He'd first read it when he was eight or nine years old, in a Portuguese edition that had been abridged for children. When he reread it as a teenager, the image of Don Quixote had been fixed in his head as a model of virtue: a man who always fought for what he believed was right, even if the whole world thought he was insane. Don Quixote believed he could change the world, and Sydney couldn't imagine anything more heroic. There was a simple elegance to the knight's code, fighting for justice, defending the weak, tipping the hat to the ladies. Even if the rest of the world considered such things to be the oxidized remnants of a bygone era, Sydney believed those were the terms on which life should be led. Fighting for the good of the country's tribes became his noble quest, and he plunged himself into the role with complete dedication.

Some of his colleagues in FUNAI rolled their eyes at his theatrical romanticism, but he didn't care. Each of his three ex-wives came to realize in their own time that he'd found his true love early in life; despite his charm and chivalry, his heart had already been claimed by Indians and his quest to help them. He cut himself free of his marriages as if he were clearing a jungle trail with a slash of his machete. If someone asked him about his three ex-wives, he responded, "They don't make Penelopes anymore."

Marcelo, Altair, and some of their peers had looked up to Sydney as a sertanista, but they didn't always agree with his take-no-prisoners style. For years they'd send him expedition reports and update him on the latest twist in the trail of the lone Indian, and Sydney's reaction was usually the same: push it; make contact before the loggers do.

Sydney had become famous for advocating an official policy of protecting Indians by leaving them alone, a philosophy that more than one writer had labeled "quixotic." But he believed the lone Indian faced an imminent threat to his life, and it was only a matter of time before he succumbed.

Sometimes there were exceptions to the rules, Sydney believed. The lone Indian needed to be saved. As the last of his tribe, he was an extreme case, practically unique in the world's history.

In the early 1800s, the Indians of the Island of San Nicolas, about seventy miles off the coast of California, were reduced from about three hundred members to just seven. Alaskan fur traders had decimated the tribe when the waters surrounding the island proved rich with otters and seals. In 1835, a group of padres from a Catholic mission in Santa Barbara, California, commissioned a schooner to fetch the survivors and ferry them back to the mission. According to some nineteenth-century accounts of the rescue, just minutes after departing from the rocky coast of the island with the Indians on board, they realized that one baby had been left behind. The captain of the boat decided that turning around in the stormy surf wasn't worth the risk. Desperate, the baby's mother jumped overboard and swam toward the island's windswept coast. The men aboard the boat quickly lost sight of her. She was believed dead, drowned in a roiling sea. Other accounts, less dramatic but perhaps more likely, suggested that the schooner's crew simply left one Indian behind; they hurriedly departed from the island in the face of a mounting storm without doing a careful head count of the Indians.

Either way, eighteen years later, an otter hunter reported seeing human footprints on the otherwise uninhabited island. Whether she had swum to shore from the boat or simply was left behind by the crew, one woman was living alone there. She had outlived everyone from her tribe—all those who had been successfully transported to the mission had died by the time the otter hunter found her footprints.

A search party arrived on the island in the summer of 1853 and found her, dressed in cormorant feathers, skinning a seal. She appeared to be about fifty years old, and she spoke a dialect that was all her own. If a baby had ever been with her, that baby was now dead. With only a sparse selection of foliage, mostly roots and tubers to eat, the woman had survived by hunting and foraging in the island's tidal pools, eating shellfish and seals. She had weathered nearly two decades of violent storms and isolation.

She was transported to the mission. A priest baptized her and gave her the name Juana Maria. She quickly became a local curiosity, and wowed visiting audiences with her singing and dancing. But just weeks after arriving at the mission, she developed dysentery and died, before the details of her survival could be pieced together.

Fifty-eight years later, the last "wild" Indian in America was discovered near Oroville, California. He was from the Yahi tribe, a group whose population dropped sharply during the Gold Rush. A massacre at the hands of cattlemen in 1865 left only thirty survivors. Over the next forty years, the Yahi dwindled in number until, in November 1908, a single Indian stood alone. He appeared to be about fifty years old. He remained without human companionship until the morning of August 29, 1911, when barking dogs outside of a slaughterhouse awoke a group of butchers and alerted them to an emaciated man crouching against the corral fence, wearing nothing but a scrap of covered-wagon canvas.

The local sheriff locked him in the Oroville jail. "The Wild Man of Deer Creek" was an instant sensation. Newspapers detailed how he'd been plucked straight from the Stone Age and deposited into the modern world. An anthropologist from the University of California at Berkeley named Alfred Kroeber read the articles and was reminded of the stories he'd heard about the "Lone Woman of San Nicolas." Kroeber sent a telegram to the sheriff requesting that the university take custody of the Indian. Kroeber's colleague anthropology professor Thomas Waterman traveled to the jail and discovered that the Indian spoke a dialect of Yana, a language that Waterman had studied.

The anthropologists transferred the Indian to San Francisco, where they began to decipher his history. Three years earlier, surveyors had found a village inhabited by four Yahi Indians—the man, his mother, his sister, and an elderly male. The Indian and his mother hid undetected by the surveyors, while his sister and the old man fled, never to be seen again. The surviving Indian later told the anthropologists that he believed his sister and the old man died soon after; either they had drowned while trying to cross a creek or had been eaten by mountain lions or another predator. His mother died almost immediately after they were forced to abandon their village, he said.

On the university's campus, the anthropologists outfitted the Indian in modern clothes, dressing him in pants, a button-down shirt, a coat, and a tie. He lived in the new anthropology museum, alongside the mummified remains of Egyptians and the skulls and bones of other Native Americans.

The fact that the Indian didn't have a name quickly posed problems. Kroeber, knowing that California Indians almost never spoke their own name, told reporters that assigning the man a name was inappropriate and futile. But that explanation didn't satisfy public demand that the Indian be named, so Kroeber reluctantly called him "Ishi," the Yana word for "man."

Ishi privately plucked his facial hairs with tweezers he made of split wood, refusing to imitate the white man's preference for beards. In his first days at the museum, he explained that he felt himself an outsider in his new world. "I am one; you are others; this is in the inevitable nature of things," was how Kroeber translated his view of life with his newfound acquaintances.

Soon vaudeville impresarios and carnival companies flooded Kroeber with offers to take Ishi on the road. Motion picture companies clamored for a chance to film him. The museum was swamped with visitors wanting to take pictures and shake the hand of a living, breathing Stone Age relic. The man who had spent almost three years with no human contact was suddenly surrounded by clamoring crowds. He had literally become a museum exhibit.

His public appearances at the museum were limited to two and a half hours on Sunday afternoons. Sometimes he would demonstrate how to string a bow, or chip arrowheads. He constructed wooden drill rods he had used to make fire. Kroeber took him for car rides to the ocean, and he practiced archery in Golden Gate Park. A newspaper invited him to attend a vaudeville show at the Orpheum Theater; Ishi accepted and sat in the front row of the balcony box seats, and he laughed along with the crowd when a rhyming performer onstage declared, "And sitting in the box you see/The Indian from the universitee." He learned to tie a four-in-hand cravat after a single demonstration. He refused to be photographed naked. He was fascinated by penny whistles, kaleidoscopes, and matches. He learned a little English, which he used with an unpredictable sort of flair. When a lady asked him if he believed in God, he said, "Sure, Mike!"

For the next five years, scientists studied almost everything about him. They marveled at the way he walked barefoot in the woods without snapping twigs underfoot. "He springs from the great toe which is wonderfully strong in its plantar flexion and abduction," wrote Dr. Saxton Pope. "His method of locomotion is that of rather short steps, each foot sliding along the ground as it touches. Neither the heel nor the ball of the foot seems to receive the jar of the step. The foot is placed in position cautiously, not slammed or jammed down. He progresses rather pigeon-toed."

Four and a half years after he was discovered, Ishi died in the museum, of tuberculosis.

Kroeber believed that Ishi wouldn't have wanted his body dissected in an autopsy, and he requested that his remains be cremated. He feared that Ishi might become even more of a curiosity piece after death than he'd been in life. "We have hundreds of Indian skeletons that nobody ever comes near to study," Kroeber explained upon Ishi's death. "The prime interest in this case would be of a morbid romantic interest." He had good reason to be concerned, because history was full of stories of native survivors who had been sentenced to macabre afterlives on Earth. The last surviving native Tasmanian man, for example, was alternately dug up and reburied after his death in 1869 by physicians who believed he was a missing link between humans and apes. One doctor cut the head off the Tasmanian's corpse, another the hands and feet, another the ears and nose. They kept the body parts as souvenirs. One of the doctors used the tribesman's skin to make a tobacco pouch.

Kroeber's request went unheeded, and doctors performed the autopsy. A San Francisco newspaper published a poem "To the Late Mr. Ishi" a week after his death.

You did not fit. Your ways were other.
This madhouse life was all too strange.
It was a shame they found you, brother.

For years, rumors circulated that Ishi's brain had been acquired by the Smithsonian Institution. The rumors were true. In 1999, the brain was discovered, pickled in ethyl alcohol, in a Maryland storage facility for the National Museum of Natural History. Responding to public outcry, the Smithsonian shipped the brain to members of the Redding Rancheria and Pit River tribe, deemed to be descendant relatives of the Yahi. Ishi's brain was buried in a private ceremony in Deer Creek Canyon in August 2000.

Sydney Possuelo knew that when it came to gracefully shepherding "last tribesmen" out of the wilderness and into modern life, those in charge almost always screwed it up. History's list of people who have endured the kind of isolation in which the lone Indian had been living was extremely short, but there was one man still alive who came close to experiencing a similar depth of solitude. Sydney happened to know him well.

His name was Carapiru, an Indian who was separated from the rest of his tribe in northeastern Brazil after settlers opened fire on his village and then burned it in 1978. As far as Sydney was concerned, what happened to Carapiru after that separation provided rare proof that the modern world had the capacity to get things right every now and then. If fate cooperated, the clash of civilizations didn't always have to end in tragedy.

Carapiru's tribal village was near a coffee-colored stream in the northern state of Maranhão, and its destruction was swift. A group of settlers attacked and shot several tribe members and sent the few survivors scattering in different directions through the woods. Only one survivor was found: a boy of about eight years old who had gotten entangled in a barbed-wire fence after fleeing the village. A local

FUNAI post took custody of him, placing him with other Indians on a nearby reservation.

Carapiru had been alone in the forest at the time of the attack. After he saw that his village had been ransacked and destroyed, he began walking through the woods with no plan other than to survive. For ten years he walked, south through the wooded hills of northern Brazil, all the way to a town called Angical, in the state of Bahia. He walked more than nine hundred miles in all.

During those years he avoided civilization as much as he could, though often he found himself skirting towns and settlements, walking along railroad tracks, crossing roads. He carried his bows and arrows, and a straw pack that held two cooking pots, a rubbing stick to make fire, and an alternating collection of other necessities.

In October 1988, the residents of Angical, a modest town of simple brick houses, heard a squealing pig dashing madly through the town. A long wooden arrow was sticking out of its side.

The people in town knew the arrow was a sign that there was an Indian nearby. It made sense: for weeks, the townspeople had noticed that some of their animals—pigs and chickens, mostly—had gone missing. If an Indian was lurking outside of the village, preying on their animals, they wanted to find him.

They organized a search party and fanned out across the countryside. They found Carapiru in the bush. Instead of resisting their advance—he easily could have fled—he actually seemed happy to see them. He smiled as they approached. He surrendered his bow and arrows without complaint.

They walked him into their neighborhood of houses, and clothed his naked body in a pair of shorts. He accepted their food, and smiled as the men, women, and children crowded around to get a good glimpse of a real, wild Indian.

It wasn't long before FUNAI got word of the story. Agency officials weren't sure what to do other than call Sydney, who had founded the Isolated Indians Division a year earlier, in 1987. Sydney wasn't sure what to do either, but he was more than game to meet the Indian.

With another sertanista, Wellington Gomes Figueiredo, Sydney drove to Angical and found Carapiru living among the residents.

At first, the Indian's tribal identity was a mystery. Years eariler,

Sydney had endured a grueling thirty-seven-day expedition through the virgin rain forest of the state of Maranhão to find members of the remote Awá-Guaja tribe. When he saw Carapiru he suspected the Indian might be Awá-Guaja. Carapiru's language sounded similar, and his hair had a slight curl to it—an uncommon feature among most Brazilian Indians, but not unheard of among the Awá-Guaja. They couldn't leave Carapiru in the village, and with nowhere else to take him, the two sertanistas loaded Carapiru in Sydney's car and drove him back to Brasília, about 220 miles away.

As they drove past fields and farms and eventually made their way into a city of 2.5 million people, both Wellington and Sydney wondered what Carapiru might have been thinking. Without the ability to understand his language, they could only guess. But Sydney was pretty sure Carapiru had to feel overwhelmed by the urban landscape unfolding before his eyes. Of all the cities in the world, none could have seemed more otherworldly to someone unaccustomed to the modern world than Brasília. The capital had been created from scratch in the early 1960s, between Sputnik and *The Jetsons,* to be "the City of the Future," and its uncompromisingly modernist architecture prompted Australian art critic Robert Hughes to label it a "utopian horror." But Sydney believed that because the country's foremost ethnological experts and indigenous services were based in Brasília, it was the best place to bring him, at least for a couple of weeks, until FUNAI officials could determine exactly where the Indian belonged.

Carapiru absorbed it all in silent wonder, staring wordlessly out the window as they approached the boxy high-rise apartment building where Sydney lived with his wife, daughter, and youngest son. For the next couple of weeks, the sixth-floor unit would be Carapiru's home, too.

Inside the apartment, Sydney rifled through his closet and dressed Carapiru in a blue button-down shirt. Carapiru stood in front of one of the windows and spit at the glass, amazed at its transparency. Tap water was a miracle. The television seemed to be almost too much to handle: he didn't pay much attention to it, watching the family's reactions to the screen more than the screen itself.

Sydney's wife and their housekeeper helped Carapiru into the shower, slowly rubbing him with soap. Sydney used the toilet to show Carapiru what the porcelain bowl was for and how it spirited away the dirty water with a flush. At dinner, they introduced him to cups, spoons, and forks, helping him cut his meat.

Sydney's three-year-old son, Orlando, made fast friends with Carapiru. Orlando was accustomed to being around Indians. It wasn't unusual for a houseguest at the Possuelo apartment to wear a feathered headdress or a wooden plate that stretched the lower lips into the shape of a tea saucer. But Orlando had never had a housemate like Carapiru: a constant companion who never seemed to tire of play. When Sydney went to the FUNAI office during the day, Carapiru would play with Orlando in the living room, watching *Tom and Jerry* cartoons. Orlando would burst into a children's song, and Carapiru would accompany him on percussion, banging a spoon on the table. Sydney's wife would watch them play together and imagine what the life Carapiru had left behind must have been like. The way he behaved with Orlando and her daughter, Fernanda, she figured that Carapiru must have had a family of his own once upon a time.

Carapiru couldn't sleep in a bed, so Sydney strung a hammock for him in the spare bedroom. About two weeks after Carapiru moved in with them, Sydney noticed a foul smell coming from the room. Sydney guessed it might have been old food. During the first meals they had served him he observed Carapiru hoarding meat, wrapping it in his shirttail to carry back to his room. He stopped doing that after they explained that he could simply go to the kitchen for food anytime he was hungry. Sydney searched the room for a stash of rotting food, looking in closets, under piles of clothes, in the corners—and found nothing. Yet the smell persisted. Finally, Sydney looked out the window. Several feet below the window a concrete ledge protruded from the building. A large pile of human excrement—about two weeks' worth, as it happened—sat moldering on the ledge in the sun. Carapiru had been dropping it out the window. Sydney couldn't reach the ledge to clean it, so he ran a hose from the bathroom to wash it away, creating a literal shitstorm as the muddied water ran down the side of the high-rise. The neighbors below them were not pleased.

As soon as Carapiru had arrived in Brasília, FUNAI began trying to determine what tribe he might have come from and called in specialists to listen to his speech patterns. Specialists with the Summer Institute of Linguistics, a United States–based nonprofit that documents languages around the world, said he was probably from the Awá-Canoeiro tribe from central Brazil, though Sydney maintained he was probably Awá-Guaja.

Sydney had tried to contact an Awá-Guaja tribe member named Gei to ask him to come to Brasília, but he couldn't find him. The only Awá-Guaja–speaker FUNAI could find was a boy about eighteen years old. He also spoke Portuguese, having spent most of his life on a reserve in Maranhão. The people there called the boy Benvindo, the Portuguese word for "welcome."

"*Benvindo* is his name?" Sydney said over the phone to a FUNAI agent in Maranhão. "Benvindo. Okay then, listen—get on the first bus that leaves São Luis and come here. I'll pick you both up at the bus station."

When Benvindo was introduced to Carapiru, they understood each other well. They seemed to share a deeper bond than a simple language. Benvindo locked eyes with Carapiru and stared at him silently for a full thirty seconds before turning to Sydney. "I recognize this man's face," Benvindo said.

Sydney was surprised, but he figured the story wasn't so outlandish—if Carapiru was Awá-Guaja, then it wasn't out of the question that Benvindo might have come from the same village and recognized Carapiru from his youth. But the boy continued, and the story got stranger: "I think he's my father."

They bore a striking physical resemblance, but Sydney didn't believe it. The coincidence was too wild. Sydney asked him if there was any way to prove it, if he remembered anything distinctive about his father. Benvindo said his father had a scar on his back, just below the halfway point on the spine. The two of them lifted Carapiru's T-shirt. Sydney saw a scar, exactly where Benvindo had described it.

The linguists from the Summer Institute were skeptical when they were told the story. They believed that Benvindo's story must have been a case of wishful thinking. The specialists stuck to their theory that Carapiru came from the Awá-Canoeiro. To solve the matter, FUNAI found Portuguese-speakers from that tribe and brought them to Brasília to try to talk with Carapiru. Benvindo also attended the meeting. Television stations covered the meeting as if it were a sports event.

"I couldn't understand anything," Butikal, one of the Awá-Canoeiro Indians, told a television reporter after listening to Carapiru speak. "I just heard gibberish."

But Benvindo understood everything. Anthropologists agreed that Carapiru was, in fact, an Awá-Guaja Indian. He was from the same destroyed village that Benvindo had fled as an eight-year-old, when he was discovered in a nearby field, impaled in barbed-wire fencing. Carapiru accepted the son that he thought he had lost forever.

A few days later, Sydney accompanied Carapiru on a journey to the Carú Indian Reserve, where Benvindo had been relocated shortly after he'd been found. They flew to Maranhão, then paddled in a canoe down the Pindaré River toward the reserve. At noon, the couple dozen Indians who lived there gathered around Carapiru, who smiled in wonder as they sang welcoming songs.

A decade after he set out on his own, Carapiru was back among Indians, though only one was from his own tribe. The transition to his new life wasn't easy. Shortly after moving into the reserve, he built his own hut in the forest, slightly removed from the village where the others lived.

In his fifties now, Carapiru is considered a living example of how an isolated Indian can emerge from solitude and readapt to community, if handled properly. He still lives on the grounds of the reserve, maintains a close relationship with Benvindo, and is friendly with the Indians from the other tribes. But sometimes he'll disappear into the forest for up to a week at a time.

The FUNAI officials in charge of the reserve say they think he sometimes hungers for the solitude he had learned to live with for so long.

After Sydney founded FUNAI's Isolated Indians Division, he earned an international reputation as the face of Brazil's policy of noncontact. The movie *Amazon,* shown worldwide in IMAX theaters, featured Sydney as an iconic protector of isolated cultures. *National Geographic* had run a cover story about one of his expeditions and quoted him as saying, "Once you make contact, you begin the process of destroying their universe." In 1998 *Time* magazine named him a "Hero for the Planet." The *New York Times Magazine* described him as a lone voice in the wilderness, waging an almost single-handed war against opponents who believed isolated Indians should be incorporated into society at large. The article continued:

> But for all his savvy, Possuelo stands practically alone, in his own way isolated as much as the Indians he tracks. He, too, belongs to a vanishing breed. There are fewer than a dozen sertanistas in all of Brazil worthy of the name, he said, who did not get their titles as political rewards. And many of them would just as soon see his project disappear.
>
> Indeed, it is impossible to imagine Possuelo's vision without Possuelo. . . . Possuelo knows that his critics include not only industrialists, politicians, generals and academics but also fellow sertanistas. Like that of the anthropologists, their glory has always grown from presenting new cultures to the rest of the world, as if they had given birth to them. Yet as impossible as his quest may seem, Possuelo is determined to change peoples' minds. "I'm proposing the exact opposite," Possuelo said. "I say your glory is in not discovering them."

But in the case of the lone Indian in Rondônia, Marcelo and Altair had been fiercer advocates for noncontact than Sydney. He believed that the threat to the Indian's environment was so severe that risking contact had become an unfortunate necessity. Relocation to another reserve had worked for Carapiru, and Sydney thought it might work in this case.

Sydney was in charge of finding a replacement for Altair to lead the efforts to resolve the lone Indian's dilemma. The sensitivity of the Indian's situation demanded that someone dedicate himself fully to the task. But Sydney didn't trust many of the agency's sertanistas to do the job right. He needed someone to uphold the "Possuelo Vision." Eventually he decided that to find that person, he needed only look a few doors down the hallway in his own home.

Orlando Possuelo, the son whom Sydney had named in honor of the greatest sertanista he'd ever known, was only a teenager. But

Sydney had been a teenager when he'd boarded that mail plane and headed to Mato Grosso. In his son, Sydney spotted the same itchy, adventurous spirit that had guided his life, as if it had been passed on in the blood. The kid knew the outdoors: he'd spent more time in the jungle before he hit puberty than a lot of explorers do in a lifetime, and his experience with Indians had been, to say the least, one of a kind.

Sydney knew that if the lone Indian could hang on for just a year or so for Orlando to finish high school, then Sydney would be able to appoint the perfect person to head a newly energized Ethno-Environmental Protection Front in Rondônia.

In the months after Altair was dismissed, Sydney kept an eye on the situation in Rondônia, overseeing a team that made sure the Indian's land wasn't destroyed. A little more than a year later, Sydney began taking Orlando with him on FUNAI expeditions, grooming him for a leadership position in the Isolated Indians Division.

By the time he was twenty years old, in late 2004, Orlando Possuelo became the team leader in charge of the expeditions to contact the lone Indian. Orlando boarded a plane for Rondônia. It landed safely, without the drama that his father had experienced when he'd embarked on his first journey as a sertanista-in-training.

Still, Orlando's flight also was the beginning of a great adventure.

Sydney Possuelo and his son, Orlando, are pictured in Sydney's home in Brasília in 2007.

Orlando Possuelo (center, front row) leads a 2005 expedition in search of the lone Indian accompanied by a group of Indians from the Massaco Indigenous Territory in Rondônia. The group is pictured in front of one of the characteristic holes dug by the lone Indian.

CHAPTER THIRTEEN

One More Shot

Orlando Possuelo was just getting settled in Rondônia, and already he was flat on his back in a hospital bed.

His temperature had started the climb the morning he rented a house to serve as the Guaporé Ethno-Environmental Protection Front's new headquarters. While he was driving across the muddy roads and back to the Rio Omerê camp for the night, he broke out in a drenching sweat. After trudging across a sloppy trail to the main hut, he filled a bath bucket with cold water and sat down in it. It didn't help. He skipped dinner and tried to sleep. His whole body clenched with pain. Throughout the night, he hauled himself to the bathroom, again and again. The romance of a jungle adventure. This wasn't it.

Orlando was worried that he might have dengue fever—a potentially fatal mosquitoborne disease that had been tearing through Brazil with unusual ferocity in 2004 and early 2005, sickening people from Rio to Rondônia. He suffered through another day and sleepless night in the camp, then climbed in the truck to drive to a small hospital in the town of Jiparaná. His neck was so sore he could barely turn his head.

At the hospital, the doctor told him he wasn't going to let him leave in such a sorry condition, and the nurses prepared a bed for him. The room wasn't terrible. If it were a hotel, it probably would be the nicest in town. He had his own bathroom and color TV. There was even a little minibar by the wall.

But a hospital bed, no matter how comfortable, was a long way from where he wanted to be. For weeks he'd been studying the reports that Marcelo and Altair had written from previous expeditions in search of the lone Indian, and he was planning to launch one of his own. He got to know the lay of the land around the interdicted area. He even put together a new team of explorers. He was itching for a real woodland adventure, but for now the closest thing to excitement he could muster was flipping through the pages of *The Da Vinci Code* between naps.

Orlando wasn't accustomed to inactivity, and normally he was the picture of rude health. He was toned and tanned, his dark hair fell in natural ringlets, his cheekbones were high-ridged, and his jaw was sharply chiseled. He wore a dark stud earring. His natural bashfulness charmed girls, and his romantic entanglements were already complicating his life, significantly. Before he left Brasília, he'd gotten a girl pregnant. He supported her decision to have the baby, and genuinely was excited about the prospect of being a father. But he had made it clear that he wasn't going to drop everything and become a full-time family man. He had a new career, one he practically had been raised for, and he knew very well that the job demanded one thing above all else: a willingness to cut yourself off from family and friends and spend time in a place that was a long, long way from home. His own father had taught him that this line of work could be rough on a person's love life, but good things don't come without a price. Orlando believed the rewards outweighed the drawbacks. He relished the idea of testing his skills against the jungle, and this was supposed to be his chance.

During the interim between Altair's departure and Orlando's arrival, Sydney had appointed a man named Moacir Cordeiro de Melo to serve as acting chief of the Protection Front. And in that time, the lone Indian's situation appeared to worsen. The congressional investigations into Marcelo's actions hadn't resulted in any change in the status of the state's Indian territories, but it had emboldened the local ranchers and politicians. In 2003, the governor of Rondônia flatly stated to a Spanish television station that no isolated Indians existed in his state. If anyone found isolated tribes in Rondônia, he said it was because "they had been taken from Bolivia and planted here by FUNAI's own agents." Illegal logging on Indian territories increased. Even Celso de Sordi—the owner of the Socel Ranch who'd made the pact with Altair when threatened by the squatters from the MST—had started grumbling about the idea of curbing development to protect the lone Indian. His relatives had spoken with FUNAI agents to complain about the Indian, saying they were eager to convert the forest to farmland. Now that the squatting threat had passed, so had the rancher's enthusiasm for protecting the Indian, it seemed.

Moacir initially agreed with Sydney that contact should be made with the Indian before it was too late. He organized a couple of small trips into the forest, but they were unsuccessful.

After those expeditions, Moacir had a change of heart. Soon his official dispatches to FUNAI's headquarters in Brasília indicated that he was racked with doubts. His experience in Rondônia had led him to believe that Marcelo and Altair had arrived at the correct conclusion: forcing contact with the Indian wouldn't do any good. In 2004, just before Sydney sent Orlando to Rondônia, Moacir wrote Sydney a letter that he marked MAXIMUM URGENCY. He wrote that his two unsuccessful expeditions had caused the Indian to abandon yet another of his huts, and it appeared that he had fled to the southeastern edge of the temporarily interdicted area. If they continued to press for contact, Moacir feared that the Indian would flee the interdicted area altogether and end up in a territory that was totally unprotected. Not only had the Indian rejected the gifts they had laid out for him, but he had also gone out of his way to *destroy* them. Moacir wrote, "Clearly his message is one of warning. If we could understand these messages, always delivered through these communications of escape and rejection, wouldn't he probably be saying: LEAVE ME IN PEACE!?!"

However, Sydney remained convinced that contact was the only way to protect the Indian in the face of the threats from politicians and landowners. If FUNAI agents could somehow communicate with the Indian, they could inform him of the dangers he faced if he were to move out of the interdicted zone. A few weeks after he received Moacir's memo, Sydney sent Orlando to Rondônia to take over the efforts to contact the Indian.

The day Orlando was released from the hospital, he began to prepare for an extended expedition to try to contact the Indian. Orlando wanted to venture out, for however long it took, until they found the man.

When putting together an expedition team, Orlando started with Francisco Couto Lima Rosa, a twenty-two-year-old whom everyone called Chico. All of the FUNAI field assistants who had worked for Marcelo and Altair had either quit or transferred to other regions, and Chico had been one of the replacements hired by Moacir. Orlando felt comfortable around Chico, partly because of his age. Orlando knew that some of the older guys who worked for FUNAI didn't like his father, and he assumed they probably grumbled about nepotism behind his back. But he didn't pick up any of those negative vibes from Chico. Orlando turned to him as a planning partner in the same way that Marcelo had always turned to Altair.

Two other assistants rounded out Orlando's new team. One was Francisco Moura, whom everyone called by the nickname Chiquinho ("Little Chico"). He was in his midtwenties and didn't have much experience in the woods, but Orlando liked his attitude. The other was Celso José dos Santos, who went by the nickname Tunio.

At thirty-four, Tunio was the oldest member of the new team. He'd grown up in the area, on a farm outside the same town where Altair's family lived. In fact, it had been Altair who had hired Tunio's cousin a few years before to help out at the Rio Omerê camp. When Moacir was looking for someone to assist with an expedition the previous year, his cousin recommended Tunio. With just one year under his belt with FUNAI, Tunio also had more seniority than anyone else on Orlando's expedition team.

Within a month after his release from the hospital, Orlando launched his first expedition with Chico, Chiquinho, and Tunio. Just before they left, the results from his blood tests came back. The doctors told Orlando that he had been infected with leishmaniasis, an insectborne disease that if left untreated can cause skin sores that resemble leprosy or can even kill a person by destroying his spleen, liver, or bone marrow.

Before he left for the jungle and the hunt for the lone Indian, Orlando packed the intravenous medicine the doctor prescribed for him. The hospitalization seemed like little more than another check mark on Orlando's résumé, one of the uncomfortable but necessary hurdles any self-respecting explorer has to get over to earn the title. Leishmaniasis wasn't malaria, but it was close.

* * *

The search wasn't going well. They had been in the forest for exactly a month, from March 12 to April 12 of 2005, and they had found nothing. Not a glimpse of the man, not a footprint, not a trace. They had found one old hut and spent several days camping beside it before they determined that it had been permanently abandoned.

Of all the members of the team, none was riddled with more uncertainty than Tunio. He respected Orlando's enthusiasm, but he didn't believe Orlando had enough experience to be the team leader. Tunio and some of the other FUNAI workers who'd been on Moacir's team sometimes poked fun at their new boss, chuckling at stories about how Orlando had flipped his canoe when he visited the Massaco Indian Reserve in another part of the state. Some of the guys had grumbled that all Orlando knew about jungle exploration was how to use a GPS. Tunio had grown up in a shack on the edge of the forest, the youngest of eight children, and he'd spent his whole life exploring the woods. He confessed to his colleagues that Orlando hadn't earned his respect yet.

But even more troubling than his doubts about his leader, Tunio wasn't convinced that the object of their search was real. With Moacir, he'd gone on a ten-day expedition the year before on the lone Indian's land, and they hadn't found a single trace of the man. Tunio had only heard stories about the Indian—he'd never seen the pictures Vincent had taken, or the actual artifacts his predecessors had collected. By the time he had spent a month with Orlando in the forest, Tunio had started to seriously doubt that the man actually existed. These expeditions had begun to seem like an Amazonian version of a wild goose chase.

He needed to see to believe. Within a week, he would get his chance.

Orlando and his team hiked all day, every day, and usually they camped wherever they happened to be when the daylight ran out. Each night they strung their hammocks and tarps in a different part of the forest. Food was short, and together they decided that if they ran out, two members of the team would leave to fetch more, and two would stay.

On the morning of April 12, 2005, the team decided that they liked the campsite they had found enough to stay there for one more night. They planned to walk all day, then return to the same spot late in the afternoon. They spent the entire day hiking, and on the way back, at about four o'clock in the afternoon, they spotted a gouge in the side of a tree trunk. It was a fresh slash, no more than a couple of days old. The honey oozing out of the tree's wound was fresh.

They searched the immediate area for tracks but didn't find any. Daylight was fading. They decided that they should head back to their camp before it got dark, and Chico suggested that they travel a different route than they had taken to get there: if the Indian perhaps had seen them at some point during the day and fled, they'd have a better chance of encountering him if they cut a new trail back instead of the one they'd used before.

Orlando marked the coordinates of the honey cut in his handheld GPS, and they began to walk back toward their camp. The slightly roundabout route they took led them across a stream. On the bank, they found a clear human footprint. A small amount of water had filled the print. The water in the print was muddy—it hadn't had time to settle, which meant the print was fresh. It probably was only hours old.

The footprint seemed small to Chico. "There are four of us and only one of him," he said. "If we find him, we could probably capture him if we wanted to."

The others weren't sure if he was being serious. But after a month of long hikes and no clues, they began to consider the idea that contact was a real possibility. Chico's suggestion of taking action after confronting him was a novel one. The idea hadn't occurred to Orlando. He simply thought that they'd try to confront the Indian, wait for him to react, and respond instinctively.

Orlando entered the site of the footprint in his GPS, and they walked back to their camp in silence, scanning for signs of life along the way.

For the next five days, they searched the area but returned to the camp each afternoon having found nothing. On the morning of April 18, they passed around a plastic thermos of instant coffee and some biscuits and agreed to make the most of the day. Instead of playing it safe and returning to the camp in the middle of the afternoon, they'd search until dusk. They packed some rice and farofa, figuring they'd hunt for meat if they needed to make a full meal. With a full day of hiking in front of them, they were careful not to weigh themselves down with anything but the bare necessities. Tunio brought along a tiny miner's headlamp that he could use if it started to get dark before they made it back.

They walked all morning, looking through the trees for signs but not finding any. At about noon they spotted a stand of manioc plants and some corn in the middle of the forest. Orlando was ecstatic.

They would wait for the Indian all afternoon if necessary. When they spotted a group of wild pigs nearby, they took advantage of the opportunity for a good meal. Chico quietly followed the animals a short distance through the woods until he got a clear shot. A few minutes later, he returned with the carcass of boar.

With plenty of food for a big evening meal, he suggested they spend the rest of the day right there, at the side of the plantation.

Orlando was supposed to be the leader of the group, but he felt as if he had been deferring to the older guys too much. He needed to try to assert some control.

"I can't," Orlando said. "I left my leishmaniasis medicine back at the camp."

Chico protested, arguing that they'd surely find him if they stayed, and Orlando let the matter drop. They would wait, and if Chico felt the same way by the end of the afternoon, they could debate the matter then.

In the meantime, they divided the meat from the pig into fourths. With nowhere to store it, each of them carried his portion spiked atop a stick. They searched around the plantation for more Indian tracks. They didn't have to search long. A short distance away they found a hut in a small clearing amid a tall stand of manioc plants.

They couldn't see if the Indian was inside the hut, so they split into groups of two to surround the structure. If he was inside, he couldn't slip out the other side of the hut unseen. They jammed their sticks into the ground and split up. Tunio and Chico walked around to the other side of the hut, while Orlando and Chiquinho approached from the near side.

Chico had some peanuts with him, and he wanted to place them inside the hut, to leave as a gift for the Indian. He inched closer to the hut, with Tunio right behind him. Orlando and Chiquinho stayed back, about thirty feet on the other side of the hut, watching Chico and Tunio approach. Orlando wasn't comfortable with how close they were getting.

"What if he's inside?" Orlando said to them.

Chico and Tunio ignored him. If the Indian was inside, they wanted to see him, not just sit back and give him the chance to slip away. All the cautionary tales they'd been told about Indians, and about this Indian in particular, were washed away by adrenaline. FUNAI officials often talked about the importance of sensitivity when protecting native cultures, but that, too, was lost in the moment. All that mattered was the exhilaration that drove them toward the hut—slowly, apprehensively, but with all the caution of a runaway train.

Chico dropped to his knees and crawled toward the hut's opening. Tunio silently followed in a tense crouch.

From his knees, Chico turned to Tunio, grabbed him by the shirt, and whispered, "I think he's inside! I heard something."

Everything happened at once: Chiquinho, from the other side of the hut, saw the Indian and yelled at them, "Get away from there!" Chico sprang up from his knees. Orlando heard the sickening twang of a bowstring. Tunio felt something hot in his chest and saw a spurt of his own blood splash against the wall of the hut.

Without thinking, Tunio yanked a five-foot-long bamboo arrow out of his chest, tossed it to the ground, and yelled, "Run!"

They tore off through the clearing in different directions, tripping over vines, slamming into manioc plants, dodging tree trunks. Tunio staggered after them. After a few frantic minutes, they stopped.

"What just happened?" Chico asked, panting. He was the only one who hadn't seen the arrow.

A dark stain bloomed above the left chest pocket of Tunio's work shirt. The color drained out of his face as Orlando helped him unbutton the shirt. Tunio's breaths were shallow. He lifted his bloodied hand from the place in his chest where he'd been hit. It was a crescent-shaped gash, about an inch long, and it belched wetly with every breath. They couldn't tell how deep it went.

They knew they had to get help quickly, and Chico suggested they check the GPS to see how far they were from the ranch. Only then did Orlando realize he'd set the GPS on the ground beside their stakes of pork. To get the GPS, they'd have to return to the hut. They all looked at each other for a moment. None of them wanted to be the one to approach the hut after seeing what had just happened.

"Come on," Tunio said with a groan, lying on the ground. "I'll go back there and get the damn GPS—I need to get out of here!" Chico slunk back toward the periphery of the clearing, scooting around toward the place where Orlando had dropped the GPS. Then he scooted right back as fast as he could, unscathed.

While Chico was getting the GPS, Orlando removed his belt and his T-shirt and asked the others to do the same. With the shirts and belts, he made a sling harness. They lifted Tunio into the contraption, each holding on as they began to walk through the forest toward the nearest ranch, which the GPS indicated was several miles away.

It was a rough ride, and Tunio groaned as he bumped and bounced on the lopsided stretcher. After a while Orlando fashioned another kind of harness and carried Tunio as if he were hoisting a very heavy backpack. Orlando and Chico took turns carrying Tunio, while Chiquinho led the way, trying to clear a path for them with his machete. When the light began to fail, Tunio's tiny headlamp did little to cut through the gathering darkness.

Sharp leaves of razor grass reached out of the darkness and raked scratches into their bare arms, shoulders, and sides. Tunio, bundled into the loose harness, was jostled with every step. He was convinced they were going to drop him, and he decided he'd be better off walking himself. With the support of the others, he trudged slowly toward the ranch.

Four hours after Tunio had been shot, they reached a fence near the edge of the ranch where they had left their truck a month earlier. Tunio dropped to the grass, unable to walk farther. Orlando stayed at his side while the others ran to try to find someone who could help them.

Orlando was scared. Tunio seemed to be drifting into and out of consciousness, tilting his head back and closing his eyes, collapsing into uncomfortably long silences. Tunio had tried to keep his hand pressed against the wound during the four-hour walk. The cotton fabric of his navy blue shirt was thick with blood and it stuck to the wound, keeping it closed. But when they peeled the shirt back to take a closer look, it burbled with his breath.

They tried to make small talk, but resentment had already begun to fester. Orlando wondered aloud if his girlfriend might have already given birth to his child. Tunio was unable to summon concern for Orlando, only annoyance. Before he'd been shot with the arrow, Tunio had worried that Orlando might have been too inexperienced to lead an expedition; after the shot, Tunio was convinced of it.

Chico and Chiquinho reached the ranch and drove back toward the fence where Tunio lay. They parked and ran toward him and Orlando with a satellite phone and a medical kit.

Orlando rifled through the contents of the medical kit, but the names on the bottles meant nothing to him. Because of his leishmaniasis, he had the number of a family doctor in Brasília, and he punched his number into the satellite phone. After Orlando recited the contents of his kit, the doctor told him to inject Tunio with a painkiller and tape a bandage over the top of the wound, leaving the bottom of the bandage unattached. The bandage sucked close to the wound when Tunio took a breath, and flapped outward when he exhaled.

They helped Tunio into the truck and drove to Vilhena. When they turned off the BR-364 toward the hospital in the center of the city, daylight had already arrived.

The emergency doctor who looked at Tunio's wound told him he'd need to stay in the hospital for about a week. The tip of the arrow had nicked the lung lining, but it would heal. Luck had been on his side. The arrow had struck a bone a couple of inches under his collarbone and deflected upward. Had it hit the bone just a fraction of a centimeter lower, it would have deflected downward, toward his heart.

For the next five days Tunio lay in a hospital bed. Any doubts he had harbored about the existence of the lone Indian had completely vanished. He had seen, and he believed.

After the expedition, Orlando flew to Brasília to meet his new son, and he stayed with Sydney for about three weeks. If Tunio's injury had discouraged Orlando, Sydney wiped out his son's self-doubt by reminding him at every turn that their cause was inviolate. If Orlando was to be faulted for pressing too hard to contact the Indian, then Sydney—as his hands-on adviser—would have to shoulder some of the blame, too. He wasn't prepared to do so. In those weeks after the shooting, when Sydney described the incident with Tunio and Orlando, it was clear he relished the telling: it was a rip-roaring adventure undertaken for a noble cause, with more than a little danger involved. The fact that father and son could now share such stories seemed to fill Sydney with pride. Orlando had become more than a son; he was becoming a colleague, and amassing the hard-won experience necessary to eventually earn the title of a sertanista.

"Contacting him is a last resort for us," Sydney said, sitting next to Orlando at his kitchen table that May, explaining the lone Indian's predicament to a reporter. "I hate to do it. I hate it. It's never good. They lose everything. But when a tribe gets to be so small, it's sometimes the only way to save them."

And when contacting isolated Indians, people get hurt. A Korubo tribesman who slaughtered one of Sydney's colleagues in 1996 later explained to Sydney why he had killed the FUNAI worker: "We didn't know you then." Sydney accepted it as a perfectly reasonable explanation. Similary, in 2003, Sydney wasn't fazed when the same tribesman ordered the slaughter of three white men who'd been cutting trees near his tribe's protected area in the state of Amazonas. Even though Sydney, who had been staying at a nearby base at the time, had found the men's bodies hacked in pieces in their canoe, he extended them no sympathy. When news of the killing spread to other riverside settlements in the area, he seemed pleased. "I prefer them to be violent," Sydney later explained to a reporter from *Smithsonian* magazine, "because it frightens off intruders."

In that context, Tunio's brush with death seemed a comparatively mild example of the kinds of hazards that traditionally accompany the work of a sertanista. At every turn, Sydney underscored the importance of maintaining the courage to face such dangers, and he lamented the fact that fewer explorers within FUNAI seemed to share his passion for the jungle. His rants against his own agency grew sharper, and he cast himself and Orlando as the last of a dying breed upholding a sacred mission. When he spoke about the lone Indian, he spoke as if the stakes couldn't be higher, as if his four decades working with tribes had spiraled down to this: a single Indian running through a forest that developers were threatening to turn into a postapocalyptic necropolis of charred stumps. He encouraged Orlando to bounce back from the incident and to be more careful next time.

Sparked by his father's fire, Orlando returned to Rondônia with a reinvigorated sense of purpose. He constucted a permanent campsite on the acreage that had been interdicted for the lone Indian. He picked a small and flat triangle of wooded land wedged between the waters of a forking stream. The site was about an hour's hike from the stables of the Socel Ranch. From there it was a short walk across the stream and into the Indian's territory. Orlando and a team of workers built a large wooden hut, kind of like the ones that Marcelo and Altair had erected for the Rio Omerê encampment. They strung lightbulbs from the rafters and powered them with an electrical generator. Orlando began to spend most of his time at the camp, launching day trips into the forest with Chico and a group of eight or nine Indians from the Massaco Reserve.

Orlando loved it out there. In his journal, he wrote that he'd grown so accustomed to camping out near the Indian's territory that during the few nights he spent in town, he had trouble sleeping in a bed. His spirits were held high by the optimism that he'd soon make significant contact, once and for all, with his elusive target.

"Here, out in the territory of the Indian of the Hole, I have a lot of hope that contact will be made very soon," Orlando scribbled in his journal in June. "Every day I wake up thinking that this might be the day it happens."

And every day, he was wrong. Sydney and Orlando's brother traveled to Rondônia in June to celebrate Orlando's twenty-first birthday, and they ventured into the Indian's territory. When they reached the area where Tunio had been shot, they saw that the Indian had abandoned the area. Over the next three months, Orlando found some more pitfalls, some hunting blinds, and other vestiges from the Indian—but it was clear that he was on the run again. He had abandoned the planting field, and he wasn't accepting the gifts they left for him. On the rare occasion when Orlando found the Indian's footprints on a patch of bare ground, those prints were impossible to follow—the Indian left other prints that led in five different directions, a trick to confuse anyone who might be trying to follow him.

By the end of the year, Orlando's hope for contact turned into something closer to despair and self-doubt. His enthusiasm left him, like air hissing out of a punctured tire. After launching his own expeditions and confronting the Indian, Orlando was reaching the exact same reluctant conclusion that each of his predecessors had eventually embraced: no matter how good their intentions might have been, trying to force contact wasn't helping the Indian. Every shred of evidence indicated that their attempts were making the Indian's situation more precarious.

The Indian's well-established plantation, his construction of sturdier huts, his acceptance of gifts—all of those signs that Altair years earlier had interpreted as steps of progress were gone. FUNAI was moving backward.

The reasons for the Indian's change of behavior could only be guessed at. During the years when Marcelo and Altair had been in charge, the Indian likely had learned to recognize the faces of the team members. When a new group of men began to follow him, maybe he had been scared back into a fugitive life of strict resistance. The Indian couldn't have known that Orlando and his new team were affiliated in any way with the other white men whose presence he seemed to cautiously accept.

Orlando concluded that he should put the expeditions on hold, and Sydney came to agree with him. They had given it their best shot, but every scrap of evidence indicated that the Indian had made a deliberate choice to avoid their advances. Even though this was the most extreme case of isolation Sydney had ever encountered, and even though the Indian was at great risk, he reversed his position, accepting the policy of noncontact as the best approach.

But within months, none of that would matter because the same agency for which Sydney had become a living symbol decided to fire him.

Mércio Pereira Gomes, who became president of FUNAI in 2003, was an anthropologist who had earned a reputation as a thoughtful advocate for indigenous rights in Brazil. But in early 2006, a Brazilian journalist asked him about the continual conflict his agency had with people who argued that too much of the country's land had been reserved for Indian tribes. Gomes said he respected the argument, stating, "It is a lot of land," and then suggested that the Supreme Court would have to set a limit at some point, defining how much land could end up as Indian territory.

The resulting headlines suggested that Gomes agreed with those who believed that Brazil's Indians had too much land. FUNAI contended that Gomes had been misunderstood and that he had intended to simply acknowledge the bare fact that 12 percent of Brazil's territory—the amount reserved for Indians—added up to a substantial chunk of real estate, and that a systematic approach to future preservation should be formulated.

But before he was able to clarify his statements, several journalists called Sydney to ask for his reaction to Gomes's comments. Sydney had plenty to say.

He was out in the field at the time, with a tribe of Zo'é Indians, and over the radio he blasted Gomes, holding nothing back. "I've heard this talk from ranchers, land speculators, prospectors and loggers," he told a reporter from the newspaper *O Estado de S. Paulo*. "I'm used to it. But from the president of FUNAI, it's the first time. This is scary." He told other reporters, "It's the equivalent of the environmental minister calling on people to cut down trees."

Days later, FUNAI fired Sydney for "growing incompatibility" with other specialists within the agency.

Sydney was defiant to the end. He refused to apologize. If his career with the government was going to go down in flames, he wanted the blaze to shed light on what he considered a sickening injustice toward the country's Indians. Orlando Villas Boas, he reminded people, was unceremoniously dismissed for no particular reason from his largely honorary position with FUNAI near the end of his life. Even Candido Rondôn had resigned his position as founding director of the Indian Protection Service in 1930 after conflicts with the country's president.

Sydney felt he was in good company. He had spent his career pushing back against the same government that employed him, and stopping now would have been the equivalent of a moral surrender.

Survival International and other international organizations promoting indigenous rights cast his firing as a tragedy for Brazil's native populations. He'd been fired for speaking his mind, they said, and there had been absolutely nothing wrong with what he had said. Without Sydney leading the Isolated Indians Division, some feared that the policy of noncontact might fly out the window and that ranchers and loggers might have free rein to slash the protected territories that Sydney had so publicly defended.

"There are people who can take over from Possuelo and do similar work but they won't do it as well," Gilberto Azanha, the executive coordinator of a charity called the Center for Indigenous Labor, told the *Christian Science Monitor* at the time of Sydney's dismissal. "No one else is at his level."

September 9, 2000

September 26, 2006

Normalized Difference Vegetation Index

0 0.2 0.4 0.6 0.8

Satellite photographs taken on September 9, 2000 (above), and on September 26, 2006 (below), show the extent of deforestation that occurred in the territory where the lone Indian lived.

CHAPTER FOURTEEN

A New Beginning

The institutional headquarters of FUNAI inspires no awe or reverence. The building itself looks like an urban school in an underfunded district. The elevator inside the lobby is an airless rattletrap that shakes violently on ascent, then shudders to a precarious halt, usually a few inches short of being perfectly aligned with the destination floor. Unsorted paperwork, broken chairs, outdated computers—everything about the place screams of bureaucratic paralysis.

The atmosphere of inefficiency is partly explained by the fact that few people within the institution's leadership stick around long enough to gain any traction. FUNAI has, on average, changed presidents at a rate of almost one per year throughout its history. The agents in the field have learned to regard their bosses in Brasília as if they were playing cards, shuffled and dealt to them at a furious pace—most of the new deals didn't change anything, but once in a great while, the agents got lucky.

Mércio Gomes had been leading the agency for nearly three years and thus had qualified as its longest-serving president since the military government fell in 1984. But when he fired Sydney, he called for a broad reorganization of leadership within the Isolated Indians Division. His first choice as Sydney's replacement had been José Carlos Meirelles, a sertanista in charge of FUNAI's operations in the state of Acre (and no relation to Apoena Meirelles). But Meirelles didn't want the job. The jungle post where he worked was one of the agency's most remote, and he didn't want to leave it for a desk job at headquarters. He declined the offer, but passed on a couple of names of other qualified sertanistas he thought might be interested.

One of the names on that list was Marcelo dos Santos. Gomes hired him. For Indian advocates in Rondônia, it was like being dealt an ace.

In the six years after the congressional inquiries into Marcelo's work, it had grown increasingly clear to everyone in FUNAI that he'd been the victim of a political hatchet job. Those familiar with Marcelo's work knew all along that the charges that he had planted Indians in Rondônia were patently ridiculous. But now the credibility of those who had testified against him had become all but impossible for anyone to defend.

In 2006, Carlos Antonio Siqueira—the supposedly impartial retired FUNAI anthropologist who had been the key witness against Marcelo at the Senate hearing—had been publicly exposed as a paid employee of ranchers, hired to contest indigenous claims on land. It was true Siqueira had been an anthropologist at FUNAI at one time, but by the time he had "investigated" Marcelo's track record, he was actually employed as a consultant for several agricultural advocacy groups. What's more, in 2006 Siqueira was jailed as one of eleven ringleaders of a band of loggers, ranchers, and businessmen accused of illegally extracting more than $100 million of hardwood from an Indian reserve in the state of Mato Grosso between 2000 and 2005. In a letter to a local newspaper following his arrest, Siqueira denied that he had committed any crimes, but admitted that he had been hired by agricultural organizations that had paid him to challenge the legitimacy of indigenous territories they hoped to develop.

Since the hearings, Marcelo had struggled to get used to life outside the jungle. He and Divina had bought a house and a couple of acres of land in Goiás. The only physical reminders of Rondônia were the two jungle landscape paintings that hung in their living room. His late father had painted them years earlier during a visit to the Nambiquara Reserve.

Like all of his neighbors, Marcelo hung a sign at the gate to his property that christened the land with a name, as if it were a ranch: he called it "The Divina." On land that had been cleared for pasture, he planted trees.

The life of a retiree, however comfortable, didn't sit right with

Marcelo. Soon after leaving FUNAI, he accepted a contract job with an NGO called the Instituto Socioambiental (Socio-Environmental Institute), which looked after the interests of the tribes in Mato Grosso's huge Xingu Reserve. The job required extensive travel, which took a much greater toll on fifty-year-old Marcelo than it had in his younger years. He had cultivated a complex set of abdominal complications during his years in the jungle, which meant that a single expedition might shave as many as twenty pounds off his already slim frame. Those weeks away from home also put a strain on his marriage to Divina—something he never had to worry about during his years in Rondônia. The job with the institute quickly became more than he could bear. He and Divina agreed that the travel was excessive, and he decided to break his contract three months before it was set to expire. But he wasn't sure what he was going to do next.

Marcelo hadn't held a grudge against FUNAI itself; his ire had been reserved for those who'd bad-mouthed him during the hearings. He observed the agency from a distance during his absence, and he'd heard all about Sydney's row with Mércio Gomes through the newspaper and television coverage. When he heard that the legendary Sydney Possuelo had been fired, the first thing that went through Marcelo's mind was, *My God, Mércio must have brass balls to do something like that.* It didn't occur to him that Sydney's job might end up in his lap. But when FUNAI welcomed him back with open arms, Marcelo and Divina decided that the move might be a good fit for them. It was a desk job, not fieldwork, so he wouldn't have to travel so much.

Accepting the offer also gave him the chance to address something that had felt like unfinished business: the lone Indian of the Guaporé Valley. When he moved to Brasília in 2006, it became an instant priority for him. Through periodic correspondence with other FUNAI workers, Marcelo knew the case essentially had been forgotten. After the incident with Tunio and the arrow, the Indian had disappeared. Most of the FUNAI workers in Rondônia feared that he had strayed out of the interdicted zone and into a patch of forest that was fair game for loggers. The danger of a run-in with an armed ranch hand was ever present. Some speculated that Marcelo's return to FUNAI might have come too late. They thought that the Indian might already be dead.

Marcelo knew he couldn't do much for the Indian from his desk in Brasília. He'd need someone on the ground in Rondônia with the knowledge necessary to work in the jungle and the experience required to manage the complex task that remained unfinished after more than a decade.

Altair Algayer was living in Minas Gerais, a couple of thousand miles east of the forests of Rondônia. After his controversial dismissal, he managed to stay on as a contract worker with FUNAI stationed near the town of Governador Valadares. His daily routine was nothing like it had been during the years he spent looking after the Kanoe and Akuntsu tribes and hunting for the lone Indian, but his bosses quickly learned to exploit Altair's uncanny ability to instantly get along with almost anyone.

The Maxakali, a group of acculturated Indians in his new area of responsibility, had lapsed deep into alcoholism. It was a common occurrence. When the gifts that lured the Indians into contact completely dried up and the Indians found themselves split between two worlds, neither of which was a perfect fit, addiction was an easy escape. In most local FUNAI offices you could find pamphlets taped to the walls reminding people that it was strictly prohibited to buy alcohol for Indians or to give them rides to bars. Those pamphlets had been posted too late to help the Maxakali, who often wandered into the nearby towns to buy liquor from sellers who catered to them. By the time Altair arrived, the Indians wanted nothing to do with FUNAI.

Altair cracked the standoff between the agency and the tribe. After about three months of patient and relaxed discussions with them, he became the first FUNAI agent in years they allowed to spend the night in their camp. Without lecturing, he tried to talk to them about opportunities that might give them something healthier to do with their lives than drink. He convinced some of the liquor dealers who had catered to the tribe to stop targeting them. He hadn't cured their addictions, but at least he'd gotten them to open up to the possibility of help.

Marcelo's first act as new director of the Isolated Indians Division was to call Altair and offer him the position as head of the Ethno-

Environmental Protection Front. It wasn't an easy choice for Altair, whose two daughters were too young to remember Rondônia. His wife, Jussara, had relatives in Governador Valadares, and they'd made good friends there. But the chance to return to a job and a place he had loved exerted too strong a pull. Like Marcelo, he believed he had unfinished business in the Guaporé Valley. Jussara backed the decision to return because it meant so much to Altair.

They moved back to Vilhena, and Altair established the Protection Front's new headquarters on the open-air back porch of his sun-washed ranch house. Within a couple weeks of his return, Altair had assembled—or, in a lot of cases, *re*assembled—his team. Paulo Pereira came back, effectively becoming Altair's number two. Together they convinced many of the contract workers who'd accompanied them on expeditions years earlier to rejoin the team. Even Vincent Carelli, who was living in Olinda, on Brazil's east coast, and who had spent the intervening years overseeing his Video in the Villages nonprofit project, dove back into the case. He began compiling the old video footage he'd taken during their expeditions from 1996 to 2000 to create a documentary he hoped would raise awareness within Brazil to the threats facing the lone Indian.

Before Altair launched any new expeditions, only one loose end of the original team remained: Purá Kanoe. A lot had happened to the Kanoe during Altair's absence, and not all of it was good. Both Purá's mother, Tatuá, and her grandson, the young Operá, developed severe cases of dysentery in 2002. They didn't recover. Both died, reducing the tribe to just Purá and his sister, Tiramantú. Purá's efforts to court the young Akuntsu tribeswoman continued to be blocked by her chief, Konibu, but the thawing of the conflict between the Kanoe and the Akuntsu had borne unexpected fruit. Tiramantú had a son. The father was Konibu. The boy was raised as a full member of the Kanoe. His birth restored the tribe's possibility of surviving, however feebly, for one more generation.

Shortly after Altair was reunited with the tribe, Purá accepted Altair's offer to accompany the new team on expeditions to try to determine whether the Indian of the Hole was still out there somewhere, surviving against all odds, or silenced by a death observed by no one.

So much had happened to the original members of the team since they first banded together a decade earlier: battles had been fought and lost, reputations attacked, families uprooted, and hopes shattered. But almost instantly, the slate had been wiped clean. In 2006, Altair faced a challenge remarkably similar to the one he and Marcelo had confronted with so much enthusiasm back in 1996: he needed to prove the existence of a shadowy man who may or may not be living, and—if successful—protect the man's shrinking habitat from destruction once and for all.

The lone Indian hadn't been seen since the Tunio shooting, and Orlando's final expeditions suggested that if the Indian was still alive, he had probably strayed out of the zone that had been temporarily interdicted. Even if he had stayed put, that interdiction had expired. They'd be lucky to find him alive. But in September 2006, Altair and his team embarked on a three-day hike to try to do exactly that.

They were in the middle of their trek inside the forest where the Indian was last seen by Orlando's crew when, near the Tanaru River, Altair found a series of broken twigs about shoulder high. The leaves on the broken ends of the twigs were still green. The slash wounds on the trunks of a pair of nearby trees, made to collect latex, were just as fresh. A little later he found a hut that had been built sometime in the past five months.

Altair couldn't wait to return to Vilhena and call Marcelo. Thinking how pleased his friend would be with the news, Altair's sense of déjà-vu was replaced by the electric realization that things were not exactly the same as they had been a decade before. They might be *better*. The Guaporé Ethno-Environmental Protection Front finally had a real chance to provide long-term protection for a man who had spent at least a decade alone and on the run from near-constant threats. During previous years, their attempts to establish anything more than a temporary ban on logging—one that constantly needed to be renewed and that was easily ignored by landowners—always seemed to stall inside FUNAI's headquarters. But now Marcelo was perfectly positioned to shepherd any proposal through the bureaucratic maze in Brasília. With Altair in the field and Marcelo in the office, they formed a formidable duo who could fight on behalf of the lone Indian.

If Altair could more firmly establish that the Indian was alive and well, Marcelo could dedicate himself in Brasília to putting all of FUNAI's resources behind an effort to protect him. The circumstances were perfect—as if after years of bad luck, they'd been dealt a royal flush.

But given how quickly things could change within FUNAI, they had to act fast to take advantage of their best, and perhaps last, chance ever to create the world's only one-man indigenous reserve.

While Marcelo collected a decade's worth of paperwork, Altair and his team amassed more fresh evidence in the jungle. They found huts and pitfalls, tracks and planted cornstalks. The Indian was living in a small clearing close to a supply of fresh water and a good supply of edible nuts and fruits. He appeared to be in good health, able to chop deep into trees with an ax, which presumably was one of the gifts he'd picked up from Altair about five or six years earlier.

The temporary interdictions that FUNAI previously had secured comprised an area of a little more than twenty square miles, though about half of that area had been deforested, mostly by the Dalafini brothers of the Modelo Ranch. When Marcelo and Altair spread their maps out and plotted the points of his recently discovered huts, they saw that his current habitat appeared to be contained within a slightly larger zone of forest that bordered numerous properties.

In October 2006 they went to FUNAI president Mércio Gomes with a formal proposal for the creation of the thirty-one-square-mile Tanaru Indigenous Territory, which they named for the river that ran through it. They suggested that if the reserve was approved, the Guaporé Ethno-Environmental Protection Front would establish an encampment on the border of the territory and conduct monthly surveys to make sure the Indian was alive and well. Under no circumstances would they attempt to directly interact with the Indian, they wrote, unless the Indian himself initiated contact. The reserve would be meaningless if they didn't establish conditions not only to protect his land but also to give him peace.

In Brasília, the government agency's leadership didn't have to debate their pitch too long. Though Sydney had taken a special interest in the case of the lone Indian before he was fired, Marcelo's intimate knowledge of the situation better equipped him to present a convincing argument that the man was endangered and in need of protection. The shooting of Tunio—a well-known incident within the agency—had also raised the case's profile. Marcelo met no resistance when he identified protecting the lone Indian as a priority; the only question was whether the Indian represented a "tribe" that FUNAI could legally protect. After reviewing the case, the agency's attorney general issued his opinion in the final weeks of 2006.

"A single individual can be considered a 'people' if he is the only remnant of his culture and ethnic group, and is distinct from the national collective in his customs and traditions," declared Luiz Fernando Villares.

To quash the temptation for anyone to simply kill the Indian to open up the land for development, the agency's director of agrarian affairs prepared an explanation for local ranchers.

"The land is property of the Union, and it must remain so until the end of the Indian's life," said Nadja Bindá. "In the case of his death, the area will continue to be property of the Union."

With Marcelo's prodding, the customary bureaucratic delay of a year or more for the declaration of new indigenous territories was avoided. In January 2007, less than a month after Altair had made his request, the Brazilian government made it official. The borders of the Tanaru Indigenous Territory were demarcated.

After more than a decade of work, it had happened so fast. The territory would be open to review in a few years, but Marcelo and Altair finally had succeeded in establishing a zone of protection for a man they had never really met.

The suddenness of the resolution almost felt anticlimactic, and perhaps that was appropriate. It was a victory, but what had the Indian won? Protection, certainly, but no matter how much land they reserved for him, there was no bringing back the rest of his tribe. All they could do was respect the right that Marcelo had identified years before: the right to die alone.

As long as the Indian stayed within the thirty-one-square-mile zone, they believed he would be safe. For their part, they resolved to do nothing to chase him away.

In cities such as Seoul and Tokyo, more than 1 million people live in the average thirty-one-square-mile plot of land. In Manhattan and its immediate surroundings, that same area houses about 2.5 million people. If a thirty-one-square-mile area were populated at the same levels as the most crowded parts of Hong Kong, about 6.1 million people would live there.

The Tanaru Indigenous Territory has a population of 1.

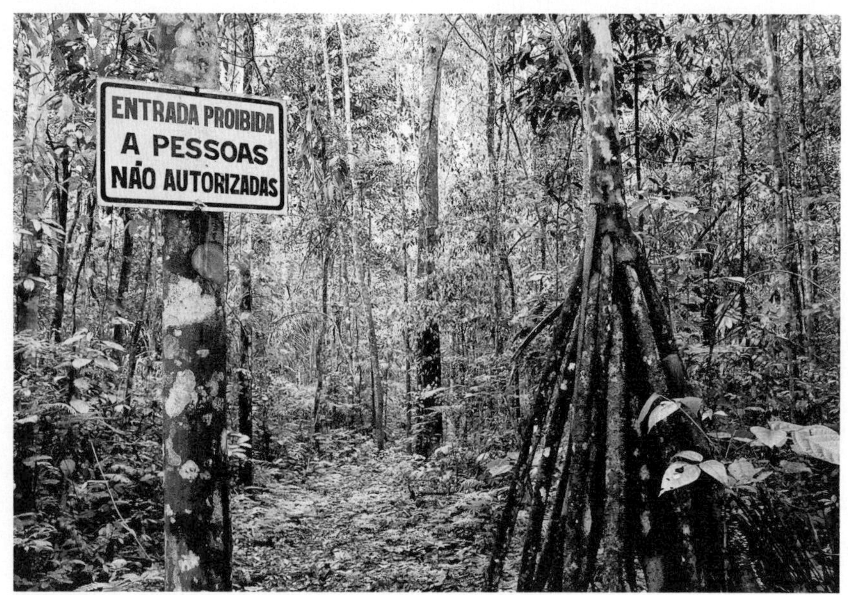

A sign posted in the Tanaru Indigenous Territory warns that entrance to the land is prohibited to unauthorized persons.

CHAPTER FIFTEEN

A Nation of One

On May 29, 2008, FUNAI released several aerial photographs of a clan of isolated Indians in the state of Acre, near Brazil's border with Peru, taken by José Carlos Meirelles—the sertanista who two years before had turned down the job Marcelo had assumed. The photographs showed the Indians standing outside their huts, wearing bright red war paint and aiming their bows and arrows at the airplane that carried Meirelles. After FUNAI distributed the pictures and a press release to Brazilian media outlets and several international NGOs, the London-based organization Survival International circulated the photos to media outlets all over the world with its own press release.

At the time the photos were taken, Peru was debating whether to expand oil exploration and logging close to its border with Brazil. Some people were arguing that it would jeopardize the livelihoods of isolated Indian tribes believed to be living nearby. Others, including Peruvian president Alan García, questioned the very existence of the tribes.

"It is like the Loch Ness monster," said Cecilia Quiroz, legal counsel for Perupetro, the Peruvian state agency responsible for doling out prospecting rights to energy companies. "Everyone seems to have seen or heard about uncontacted peoples, but there is no evidence."

Meirelles decided to give them proof. As FUNAI's agent in charge of isolated tribes in Acre, he had cataloged four different tribes living near the border area. Their lands had already been interdicted, but the territories were so remote and so inaccessible that even Meirelles had little idea exactly where the tribes might be living within those zones.

He rented a Cessna airplane for three days and began flying over the region, first trying to find the unmarked boundaries of the protected territories within the larger tract of unbroken forest, and then trying to find any trace of tribal activity within those areas. On the third day of overflights, he found a small village of thatched huts. The Indians' reaction to his plane—drawn bows pointed skyward—was understandable: planes almost never fly over that part of the jungle. Meirelles said he believed it was possible that those Indians had never seen an airplane before.

"We did the overflight to show their houses, to show they are there, to show they exist," Meirelles was quoted as saying in the Survival International press release. "This is very important because there are some who doubt their existence."

Overnight the photos beamed around the globe. Newspapers everywhere published the shots of the "Lost Tribe of the Amazon," and many of the most-watched television news programs in the world dedicated segments to the images. Most of the reports included almost no context about the clan of Indians itself, whose existence had been known to the Brazilian government since 1910. Many of the reports confused the concept of an "isolated" or "uncontacted" tribe—one that doesn't maintain contact with outsiders—with an "undiscovered" tribe that has never before been seen.

Meirelles lived at a FUNAI encampment seven hours by boat from the nearest small village, and no reporter was able to interview him until about a month later. Al-Jazeera television traveled to Acre and sat down with him. Meirelles repeated much of the same information that was included in the press releases, including the fact that he and other indigenists had known of the tribe's existence for years.

After that report, the *Observer* newspaper in London ran a story with this headline: "Secret of the Lost Tribe That Wasn't." Using the Al-Jazeera report as its source material, the *Observer* described the "revelation" that Meirelles "admitted" that the tribe's existence had already been known. Survival International "conceded" the same thing, the article stated.

The fact that neither Meirelles nor Survival International ever had claimed otherwise wasn't mentioned.

Almost instantly, international wire services, television stations, and newspapers ran with the *Observer*'s premise without doing additional reporting, and some took it a step further. The Associated Press released a story that repeated the *Observer*'s suggestion that the Meirelles photos were part of a hoax. The Chinese national news agency, Xinhua, distributed its own report under the headline "Photos of Lost Amazon Tribe Are Fakes." Countless internet sites, from the Drudge Report ("New Amazon Tribe a Hoax") to the Huffington Post ("HOAX: The Lost Amazon Tribe That Wasn't") questioned the credibility of Meirelles and, as a result, exacerbated the misconception he had been trying to correct.

It took another month for the *Observer* to apologize in print, when its ombudsman wrote that the paper in this case had "failed in its duty" to avoid publishing inaccurate, misleading, or distorted information. By that time the hoax angle had already been widely aired, and few news outlets were eager to return to the matter a third time to clarify a story they had already "corrected" a month earlier.

Meirelles and the handful of other sertanistas in Brazil found themselves in a familiar defensive crouch, accused of populating a forest with figments of their own imaginations.

In the middle of the controversy, two weeks after the initial *Observer* story had cast doubt on FUNAI's story, Odair Flauzino sat behind his desk in his office in downtown Vilhena. He shrugged off the story as yet another example of a conspiracy by what he called "the green mafia" against the landowners of Brazil. FUNAI did this all the time, he said. It was the agency's modus operandi.

"In other countries they respect property rights, but here, there's no respect for property," Flauzino said. "Property rights don't matter here. Indian rights come first. Then it's social rights. Those things come *before* property rights."

Elsewhere, a monumental legal battle over the borders of the existing Raposa Serra do Sol Indian territory in the state of Roraima was taking shape. After years of opposition from opponents such as Antonio Feijão, the ex-miner and legislator who led the congressional inquiry targeting Marcelo, Brazil's Supreme Court announced it would issue a ruling to decide whether the territory's borders could be altered to allow ranching, mining, and other commercial enterprises. Critics of the reserve argued that because farmers had titles to land inside the reserve before it had been demarcated, they had the constitutional right to develop it. If the Supreme Court ruled in their favor, it would set a legal precedent. More than a hundred pending indigenous reserves in Brazil—including the lone Indian's Tanaru territory—would be vulnerable to similar challenges.

All of the sertanistas who had spent years in the jungle mounting the expeditions that led to the protection of the territory anxiously awaited the ruling.

Finally, in December 2008, after postponing their verdict for further study, the justices ruled in favor of maintaining the existing borders of the reservation.

"With this decision, Brazil will be able to look at itself in the mirror of history and not blush with embarrassment" said Carlos Ayres Britto, one of the justices.

At night in FUNAI's Tanaru camp, the moon struggles to cast the foliage in a weak silver glow, and the leaves shine as if they are stamped

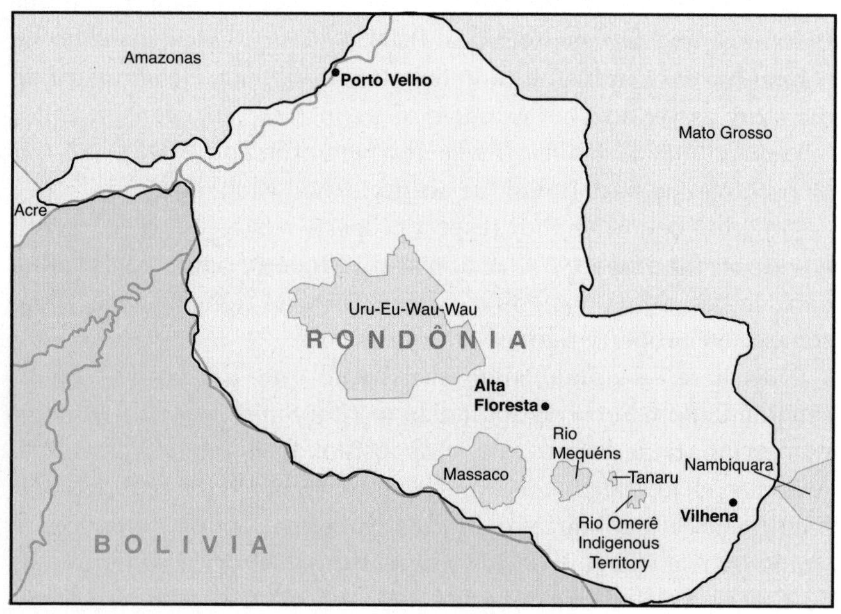

Indigenous Territories in Rondônia

in a thin foil. Every now and then, the croak of a bullfrog comes from the streams that flank the encampment. If the moon is full, sickle-winged nightjars sing a call-and-answer in the trees. But as the night stretches on, their voices hush, and what's left is a deep silence. During the rainy season, when the clouds blot out the moon, the darkness under the roof of the hut can seem suffocating. The nightjars are quiet. Moisture penetrates even the most expertly woven palm thatch. Droplets form among the spiderwebs that line the undersides of the weave, gathering weight. Time is measured in irregular drips. Within a darkness so complete, it is easy to imagine oneself as perfectly isolated, to forget that someone else is sleeping in another hammock just a few feet away.

The hut has no walls, only the roof, which rests on wooden supports that were cut and erected in 2005 by Orlando Possuelo, who now works with his father as cohead of a nonprofit advocacy group called the Instituto Brasileiro Indigenista. But the many others who had a hand in the reserve's creation can claim partnership in the hut's construction. It is slight, it is precarious, and vulnerable to shifting winds—but to everyone involved, it represents much more than a modest assemblage of wood and thatch. Each takes a sort of pride in it, and they periodically place calls to the Guaporé Ethno-Environmental Protection Front to make sure it is still standing, literally and figuratively.

Marcelo retired from FUNAI in 2007 because of recurrent abdominal problems, and he moved with Divina back to their house in Goiás. A few months after he retired, his health bounced back nicely, and he rediscovered that he was not built for a life of leisure. He called FUNAI once again and volunteered his services on an as-needed, contractual basis.

If he or anyone else wants to keep tabs on the lone Indian in Rondônia, the point of contact is Altair Algayer, who is in charge of monitoring the Indian's protected territory. Vincent, from his home in Olinda, maintains regular contact with Marcelo and Altair, and in 2009 he debuted a film called *Corumbiara* at a festival in São Paulo. That documentary used footage from the team's expeditions to highlight the persistent threats to Rondônia's Indians, including the Indian of the Hole.

About once a month, Altair and the new members of the Ethno-Environmental Protection Front sleep at the camp and make day hikes into the forest to look for evidence suggesting the Indian is alive and well within the Tanaru Indigenous Territory. Often Altair stops at the Rio Omerê encampment to pick up Purá Kanoe, who rarely passes on the chance to explore the land.

While the Supreme Court was deliberating their decision concerning the viability of the reserve in Roraima, Purá buttoned his collared shirt, zipped his jeans, pulled on his ankle-high cowboy boots, and hopped into Altair's Toyota to accompany him on a trip to the Tanaru encampment. After spending the night in the FUNAI hut, they and two other agents hiked through the forest and found a honey cut about a mile away from the FUNAI encampment. Fungus had already begun to grow in the slash; it wasn't recent. Altair scanned the ground for footprints and didn't find any, though he found some broken twigs and followed them for a while, walking slowly and quietly with the others behind him. After walking for several minutes, he lifted his gaze and saw the lone Indian standing about forty feet in front of him.

The Indian's back was turned to them, and he hadn't heard them approach. Altair turned to the others and put his finger to his lips. They watched the Indian gather wind-fallen fruits. He bent, took several bites out of a piece of fruit, cast it away, then bent to pick up another. He collected the fruits one by one, taking bites from each, then taking a couple of steps to grab another.

Altair pulled his camera from his case and took a few pictures, but the autofocus kept latching onto vegetation in the foreground. He walked around the perimeter of the fruit clearing to get a clearer shot, and the Indian saw him.

Altair put his camera down and they stood for a moment, facing one another. The Indian wore nothing but a breechcloth covering his groin. In the rope that encircled his waist, he had hung his machete. Altair recognized the machete's handle, which had a wooden base and an aluminum tip. It was the same machete he'd left outside one of the Indian's huts more than seven years before.

As they stood watching one another, the Indian turned and noticed Purá, who had been careful to stay behind, cautious as always, as

Altair walked around the clearing. The Indian looked at Purá, then back at Altair. The Indian didn't run. He walked a few feet to where he had stuck another machete into the ground, and pulled it out. Then he turned his back to them again and walked away.

They stood in silence, and watched him disappear.

Instead of following, they chose to leave.

Altair marked the spot in his GPS, and he mapped a direct course back to the FUNAI hut. As they followed the trail, they stumbled upon a tiny hut that appeared to have been abandoned. About a hundred yards from it lay a small plantation that had been burned clear about two or three weeks before. Within the clearing stood another hut that was larger and sturdier than the first. Altair recognized the pattern: the Indian had built the first hut as a provisional dwelling, where he lived while he built the sturdier one. Freshly discarded papaya skins lay outside the entrance to the hut, and close by was a fire for cooking meat and a charred armadillo shell.

They didn't stick around. Altair left sweet potatoes and corn, and they hiked back to their camp. They had done what they needed to do: verify that the Indian was alive inside the reserve's boundaries.

Afterward, Mario Canaá, one of the other two agents who accompanied Altair and Purá, shook his head in amazement at what they'd just experienced.

"He was right there!" he said. "Right in front of us!"

He fell silent for a moment, then he said, "If we would have run after him, I think we could have caught him. He didn't have a bow or an arrow with him."

Altair recognized something familiar in his words, the same suspicion that, sooner or later, tugged at everybody who'd ever gotten involved in this long and twisted tale. It was the irresistible urge to solve the mystery, to reach out and—by force, if necessary—grasp the answers, consequences be damned.

Like everyone else who'd spent enough time on that Indian's trail, Altair had determined that in a world of disappearing frontiers, the mystery itself was worth more than the solution.

There would always be newcomers, new generations of legislators and lawmen, ranchers and loggers, bureaucrats and field agents, all of whom would have to immerse themselves in the story and arrive at their own conclusions. Every decision was temporary, and every decree could be overruled in an instant.

The debate would never be over as long as one man, for reasons no one could fully articulate, continued to make a choice that seemed entirely honorable and quintessentially human. He had chosen to survive.

Acknowledgments

This book could not have been written without the help of many of the people who appear in its pages. I am grateful to everyone who generously gave their time for interviews and patiently endured my questions.

A special thanks goes out to Vincent Carelli, who allowed me access to his studio and vast archive of unedited videotapes. Those many hours of tapes proved invaluable, allowing me to describe expeditions in far greater detail than would have been possible through reconstructive interviews alone.

I also consulted dozens of field reports prepared by FUNAI and the members of the Guaporé Contact Front (later renamed the Guaporé Ethno-Environmental Protection Front). Those reports provided more details of expeditions, from basic routes and weather conditions to—in some cases—the thoughts and speculations of the explorers at the time of their journeys.

Other descriptions in the book are based on my own visits to the towns and forests of Rondônia. I would have been lost without Fred Alves, who during the course of three years accompanied me all over Brazil and helped me arrange and conduct many of the interviews that went into this book. Raquel Sacheto's assistance in Brasília also proved invaluable.

Among the people interviewed for the book, I would like to specifically thank the following for their insight and cooperation: Marcelo dos Santos and his wife, Divina; Altair Algayer and his family; Sydney and Orlando Possuelo; Wellington Gomes Figueiredo; Paulo Pereira; Adriano Soares Camargo; Reginaldo Aikna; all of the members of the Kanoe and Akuntsu tribes, particularly Purá Kanoe; Laercio Nora

Bacelar; Ines Hargreaves; Newton Pandolpho; Franciso Marinho; Odair Flauzino; Jaime Bagattoli; Fiona Watson; Nicholas Epley; and Andrea Tonacci.

I first heard of the lone Indian in 2005 when I met Sydney and Orlando Possuelo while working as South America correspondent for the *Washington Post*. I'm grateful for the support of several editors at the newspaper who encouraged my interest in the story, particularly Phil Bennett, David Hoffman, Jason Ukman, and Sydney Trent. My agent, Larry Weissman, championed this book from the beginning, and I'll forever be grateful for the enthusiasm and feedback of him and his wife, Sascha Alper. In Buenos Aires, Eric Eason read an early version and offered valuable suggestions. At Scribner, Samantha Martin's sharp editing pencil and insightful suggestions made this a much better book than it otherwise would have been. A big thanks also goes to copyeditor William D. Drennan, whose meticulousness saved me a lot of mistakes.

My heartiest thanks go to my wife, Mei-Ling Hopgood, and the rest of my family—my parents, brothers, and daughter—all of whom deserve much more gratitude from me than I could ever provide here.

Notes

PROLOGUE

1 *Behind a ragged green curtain*: The scenery and details in the prologue were compiled from unedited video footage shot by an assistant of Vincent Carelli during a Guaporé Contact Front expedition in December 1996.

CHAPTER ONE: THE HUT

3 *His small team of field agents was called*: The Isolated Indians Division of FUNAI was officially created in 1987. In the hierarchy of Brazil's federal government, FUNAI falls under the umbrella of the Justice Ministry.

4 *The new national charter specified*: Article 231 of Brazil's 1988 constitution states: "Indians shall have their social organization, customs, languages, creeds and traditions recognized, as well as their original rights to the lands they traditionally occupy, it being incumbent upon the Union to demarcate them, protect and ensure respect for all of their property. Lands traditionally occupied by Indians are those on which they live on a permanent basis, those used for their productive activities, those indispensable to the preservation of the environmental resources necessary for their well-being and for their physical and cultural reproduction, according to their uses, customs and traditions. The lands traditionally occupied by Indians are intended for their permanent possession and they shall have the exclusive usufruct of the riches of the soil, the rivers and the lakes existing therein." The constitution goes on to state: "The removal of Indian groups from their lands is forbidden, except ad referendum of the National Congress, in case of a catastrophe or an epidemic which represents a risk to their population, or in the interest of the sovereignty of the country, after decision by the National Congress, it being guaranteed that, under any circumstances, the return shall be immediate as soon as the risk ceases."

4 *Brazil's massive portion of the Amazon*: The Amazon rain forest stretches across parts of nine countries: Brazil, Peru, Colombia, Venezuela, Ecuador, Bolivia, Guyana, Suriname, and French Guiana. Different organizations and entities define its borders differently. Size estimates customarily range from about 2.5 million square miles (a figure used in many sources, including in Mark London and Brian Kelly's book *The Last Forest: The Amazon in the Age of Globalization*, New York: Random House, 2007, p. 21), to 3.17 million square miles (a figure used by Mongabay.com, an Internet compendium of rain-forest–related information, which can be found at www.rainforests.mongabay.com), to 3.6 million square miles (a figure used by Andrew Revkin in his book *The Burning Season: The Murder of Chico Mendes and the Fight for the Amazon Rain Forest*, Boston: Houghton Mifflin, 1990, p. 7).

Regardless of which size estimate is used, sources agree that the majority of the Amazon rain forest (about 60 percent) exists within Brazil.

5 *FUNAI was working to legally declare the newly demarcated territories*: After obtaining the necessary bureaucratic approval, the 193-square-mile tract of land was officially named an indigenous territory in July 1996.

5 *five hundred years after outsiders began exploring its depths*: Obviously native populations had been exploring the region's depths a long time before the first Europeans set foot in the Amazon. The first extended European exploration of the Amazon region was launched in 1541, when Francisco de Orellana and his crew journeyed the Amazon River to the Atlantic Ocean.

5 *Marcelo sat behind the wheel*: Many of the details of this drive were gleaned from hours of unedited videotape footage shot by Vincent Carelli, who accompanied Marcelo and Altair on this 1996 road trip, as well as each of their impressions of the drive.

6 *Scientists and environmental activists liked to say*: There's little consensus on this figure. Media reports that cite various scientific and ecological organizations generally peg the number somewhere between "at least 30 percent" (Associated Press newswire, August 10, 2007), to "more than a third" (*Smithsonian* magazine, January 1, 2008, p. 78), to "nearly half" (*Baltimore Sun*, April 23, 1998, p. 2A).

6 *This part of Amazonia long ago had earned itself the nickname*: The nickname has been around for years, and was used as the title of a 1940 film about Amazon adventurers directed by James Whale and starring Douglas Fairbanks Jr. Later, on April 22, 1966, *Time* magazine ran an article titled "Progress in the Green Hell" and described the Amazon as "a forgotten and forlorn land of jungle and despair." The article saw a rosy future for the region in the form of road-building and industrial progress "that is washing over the Amazon like a spring flood. Brazil's Green Hell is snapping out of its centuries-old snooze. New roads are slashing into the interior, buildings are sprouting up, and new schools and hospitals are throwing open their doors to the impoverished caboclo (Amazon peasant)."

7 *Rondônia was still less than twenty years old*: Before it was declared a state in 1981, the area that now includes Rondônia was part of the state of Mato Grosso. Some called the region "the Guaporé," for the Guaporé River Valley that stretches across the state.

7 *this part of Amazonia was experiencing a rural migration*: See chapter three for details of that influx.

7 *Chupinguaia's population was anyone's guess*: In the years since 1996, the town has established itself as a permanent fixture on Rondônia's Highway 391. According to the Brazilian Institute of Geography and Statistics, the town's population as of July 1, 2008, was 7,633 people.

8 *Ranchers in the area had been known to fly over the trees*: The information about the spraying and the scavenged drums of the chemical comes from David Price's book *Before the Bulldozer: The Nambiquara Indians and the World Bank* (Cabin John, Md.: Seven Locks Press, 1989), p. 120.

8 *Even before Marcelo and Altair decided to drive*: The previous September, a group of landowners with property in the area near the Kanoe and Akuntsu villages had hired Odair Flauzino to represent them and to dispute the demarcation of the territory. Flauzino vocally criticized the work of the Contact Front in numerous news articles published in 1995, including a September 13, 1995, piece in the newspaper *O Estado de S. Paulo* titled, "Lawyer Contests Presence of Indians in Rondônia."

9 *On September 3, 1995, Marcelo and Altair*: Many details in the description of the encounter between the Contact Front and the Kanoe—both visual and aural, including all of the dialogue included—were captured by Carelli on video, which I consulted.

9 *In Rondônia in the early 1980s, the Uru-Eu-Wau-Wau Indians attacked*: A detailed recounting of this attack can be found in Adrian Cowell's book *Decade of Destruction* (New York: Henry Holt, 1990), p. 115.

10 *Wildcat miners in Rondônia*: This is one of many such stories of confrontations between Indians and other segments of Brazil's population recounted in John Hemming's book *Die If You Must: Brazilian Indians in the Twentieth Century* (London: Pan Macmillan, 2004), p. 577. Hemming's book is the third of a trilogy of books about Brazil's Indians; the previous titles include *Red Gold* and *Amazon Frontier*. Anyone searching for information about Brazilian Indians in English should start with Hemming.

10 *Since the 1970s, 120 FUNAI workers*: The figure comes from a profile of Sydney Possuelo written by Paul Raffaele that appeared in the April 2005 edition of *Smithsonian* magazine.

12 *About a month later, scholars studied their language*: After determining that the language was Kanoe, FUNAI found an elderly man named Monunzinho living on an Indian reserve in another part of Rondônia. Monunzinho spoke both Portuguese and a form of the Kanoe dialect, and he had

been among the Kanoe chased out of the region by rubber tappers more than fifty years before.

12 Time *magazine's piece was titled*: Michael S. Serill, "An Amazon Discovery: Indian Workers Find a Couple in the Rain Forest Who Speak No Known Language—Are They a New People?," *Time*, vol. 146, October 2, 1995.

12 *In time, the explorers would learn that both of the tribes had been thinned out by pistolero raids*: This information came to them gradually as FUNAI sent various translators to the two groups to collect testimony. I verified the information by looking over transcripts of the translators' conversations with the members of the tribes.

13 *Marcelo and Altair were finding that more of the wooden gates*: When they confronted a locked gate, the Contact Front had to ask for a warrant from federal prosecutors in Porto Velho. Dozens of reports filed by Marcelo to the Justice Ministry in those years confirm that the experience was frustratingly common for the Contact Front's members.

13 *But nothing blocked*: The detailed description of the lumberyard and the interview with Gilson come from Carelli's tapes.

13 *Like most of the wood that was trucked out of Rondônia*: The wood industry remains Rondônia's dominant link to the international marketplace. Lumber accounts for more than 80 percent of the state's exports, according to the Brazilian Institute of Geography and Statistics.

14 *They followed Gilson to the sharply defined*: All dialogue, either quoted or paraphrased, comes from Carelli tapes, and physical descriptions of the discovery of the hut come from the tapes and from interviews of those who were present.

CHAPTER TWO: GOING NATIVE

18 *His father, Francisco "Chico" Meirelles, had led many of Brazil's expeditions*: The physical description of Apoena and the details about Francisco come from John Hemming's book *Die If You Must: Brazilian Indians in the Twentieth Century* (London: Pan Macmillan, 2004).

19 *The* Cultural Survival Newsletter *in 1980 tried to translate this grim incongruity*: "FUNAI's Subcontracted Research," *Cultural Survival Newsletter* 4:4 (Fall 1980), pp. 5-6.

19 *A 5,115-page government inquiry had found that of the IPS's*: This inquiry is summarized in Shelton H. Davis's *Victims of the Miracle: Development and the Indians of Brazil* (Cambridge, U.K.: Cambridge University Press, 1977), p. 10.

19 *"It's not only through the embezzlement of funds"*: Ibid.

20 *In 1971, a doctor visiting the Parakanan Indian village*: Ibid.

20 *"I am tired of being a grave-digger of the Indians"*: Ibid.

21 *As recently as the 1960s, the Nambiquara was considered one of the most primitive*: David Price, *Before the Bulldozer: The Nambiquara Indians and the World Bank* (Cabin John, Md.: Seven Locks Press, 1989).

21 *The French anthropologist Claude Lévi-Strauss had spent almost a year*: Claude Lévi-Strauss. "South American Indians," *Handbook of South American Indians,* Vol. 3: *The Tropical Forest Tribes* (New York: Cooper Square Publishers, 1963).

21 *"They think of nothing but their paychecks"*: Letter from Marcelo dos Santos to Louis Fernanelez, April 17, 1983, as quoted in Price, p. 202.

24 *By the early 1990s, pressure on the Negarote to sell timber*: An overview of the situation the tribe—and Marcelo—found itself in can be found in "The Indigenous Peoples of Brazil": Hearing before the Subcommittee on Western Hemisphere Affairs of the Committee on Foreign Affairs, House of Representatives, 103rd Cong., 1st sess., July 14, 1993.

25 *On a morning in August, the four of them gathered*: Some descriptions of the trip come from the official FUNAI expedition reports provided by Brazil's Ministry of Justice office in Porto Velho.

26 *Situated on the banks of a murmuring brook*: The detailed descriptions of the camp, and the actions of those present, come from footage of the events taped by Carelli. I also camped at the Rio Omerê site multiple times during visits in 2007 and 2008.

27 *"He cleared the land by hand"*: VC footage.

27 *"There was a guy at the gate"*: Ibid.

27 *Before setting out on the expedition the next morning*: The descriptions at the Kanoe camp come from a combination of Carelli's video footage and the official expedition reports obtained from the Justice Ministry. All of the dialogue included between pages 28 and 32 is taken directly from audio tracks recorded by Carelli.

31 *On their way to explore a small plot of forest next to a property called the Cachoeira Ranch*: From FUNAI expedition report.

33 *Clean forest, high, rich and exuberant:* The excerpt quoted on page 33 comes from the expedition reports authored by Marcelo dos Santos.

CHAPTER THREE: A LAND WITHOUT MEN

35 *Brazil's military government began actively encouraging people to migrate to the region in the early 1970s:* Descriptions of the campaign to populate Rondô-

nia can be found in numerous sources. My descriptions on pages 35–36 rely on Hemming's *Die If You Must: Brazilian Indians in the Twentieth Century* (London: Pan Macmillan, 2004) and Davis's *Victims of the Miracle: Development and the Indians of Brazil* (Cambridge, U.K.: Cambridge University Press, 1977).

35 *Brazil's president in the early 1970s, General Emílio Garrastazú Médici, had launched an ambitious road-building program*: The program is detailed in Gabriel A. Ondetti's book *Land, Protest, and Politics: The Landless Movement and the Struggle for Agrarian Reform in Brazil* (University Park: Pennsylvania State University Press, 2008), p. 63. In describing the colonization campaign I also consulted Riordan Roett's book *Brazil: Politics in a Patrimonial Society* (Westport, Conn.: Praeger Publishers, 1999), p. 190.

35 *After a dirt road was cleared through*: The effect of the road improvements on travel comes from Michael Williams's book *Deforesting the Earth: From Prehistory to Global Crisis* (Chicago: University of Chicago Press, 2002), p. 470.

36 *"You used to hear that slogan—*Integrar para não entregrar*—all the time"*: The quote comes from an interview with Bagattoli by the author.

36 *In 1980 alone, more than 70,000 people*: Hemming, p. 306.

36 *"BR-364 has sparked a land rush into Rondônia unmatched in speed and ferocity"*: Jonathan Krandall, *Passage Through El Dorado* (London: William Morrow, 1984), p. 132.

36 *In 1978, about 420,000 cumulative hectares of forest were cut*: From a progress report published by the World Bank, 1997, Planafloro Project. Additional reports detailing the rapidity of deforestation that were consulted included "Cutting Down Deforestation in the Brazilian Amazon," prepared by the Brazilian Ministry of Environment for the Thirteenth Conference of the Parties to the United Nations Framework Convention on Climate Change, December 2007; Daniel Nepstad, "The Costs and Benefits of Reducing Carbon Emissions from Deforestation and Forest Degradation in the Brazilian Amazon," Woods Hole Research Center, prepared for United Nations Framework Convention on Climate Change, December 2007.

37 *Amazonian soil is notoriously nutrient-poor, and Rondônia's is just slightly better*: The business of agricultural loans in Rondônia is addressed by Williams, p. 470.

37 *"At the time, the government was pressuring people to clear land"*: Author interview.

38 *Even if they showed him artifacts, he wasn't swayed*: I met with Flauzino in 2008, and he voiced this argument to me when countering FUNAI's findings.

38 *Francisco de Orellana, the Spanish conquistador*: Charles C. Mann, *1491: New Revelations of the Americas Before Columbus* (New York: Vintage, 2006), p. 317.

39 *Centuries later, latter-day Carvajals*: An overview of this discovery can be found in the magazine article "Women's Lib, Amazon Style," *Time*, December 27, 1971.

39 *The Dalafinis' Modelo Ranch spreads across more than*: The physical descriptions included here were collected by the author during visits to the ranch.

40 *Hercules and Denes Dalafini began locking their swinging wooden gates*: The members of the Contact Front reported encountering locked gates at the Modelo Ranch in several FUNAI reports between 1996 and 2000, provided by the Justice Ministry.

40 *When Hercules Dalafini stepped onto the porch of the ranch house one morning*: Descriptions of this incident were culled from Carelli's tapes. When encountering Dalafini in this instance, Vincent carried in his shirt pocket a tiny camera that recorded the encounter through a hole in the fabric.

40 *In Rondônia, ranchers occasionally hired gunmen to rid their undeveloped property of Indians or squatters*: An account of the Corumbiara massacre can be found in Ondetti, *Land, Protest, and Politics*, p. 64. Amnesty International also issued a report on it called, "Brazil: Corumbiara and Eldorado de Carajás: Rural Violence, Police Brutality and Impunity," January 19, 1998.

41 *"I heard something about that happening at the Modelo Ranch"*: From Carelli tapes.

42 *In Flauzino's opinion, FUNAI's local office in Rondônia went off the rails sometime back in the 1980s*: Author interview.

42 *João Carlos Nobre da Veiga was forced to surrender his leadership of the agency for allegedly accepting personal kickbacks*: In his book *Indigenous Struggle at the Heart of Brazil* (Durham, N.C,: Duke University Press, 2001), Seth Garfield describes Nobre da Veiga's attempts to bribe tribes to ensure that they remained dependent on his agency. On p. 200, Garfield writes of Nobre da Veiga's reign, "For the FUNAI directorate, the importance of defusing indigenous land claims and securing state power far outweighed eliminating dependency."

42 *"He issued outright anti-Indian statements"*: Schmink and Wood, p. 92.

42 *"Good Lord, they seem to be bringing more Indians"*: David Price, *Before the Bulldozer: The Nambiquara Indians and the World Bank* (Cabin John, Md.: Seven Locks Press, 1989), p. 142.

43 *With a group of tribesmen, Marcelo searched the area and uncovered clay pots*: Carelli first shot video of Marcelo at this time. In his archive, he has footage of the first time that Marcelo and Flauzino laid eyes on each other, alongside that dirt road in 1986—a meeting described in this section.

44 *"There's no doubt that Indians once lived there," Possuelo told the ranchers*: Carelli taped Sydney's meeting with the locals in 1986.

44 *"Sydney Possuelo—this guy is a serious sertanista"*: Ibid.

45 *"How, how, how?" Flauzino said*: Ibid.

45 *When then senator Al Gore said*: Luiz Bitencourt, "The Importance of the Amazon Basin in Brazil's Evolving Security Agenda," in Tulchin and Golding, eds., *Environment and Security in the Amazon Basin* (Washington, D.C.: Woodrow Wilson Center Reports on the Americas, no. 4), p. 71.

45 *"The settler and pioneer have at bottom"*: Roosevelt's quote is cited in Jared Diamond's *The Rise and Fall of the Third Chimpanzee* (New York: Vintage, 2002), p. 278.

46 *"The country along this river"*: Theodore Roosevelt, *Through the Brazilian Wilderness* (Teddington, U.K.: Echo Library, 2007), p. 80.

46 *About three out of five Brazilians surveyed by the country's largest polling firm*: The results of the poll were reported by Larry Rohter in the *New York Times* in "In the Amazon: Conservation or Colonialism?," July 27, 2007, p. 4.

46 *During debates over how much autonomy*: Alcida Rita Ramos writes about the controversy surrounding the newspaper series in her book *Indigenism: Ethnic Politics in Brazil* (Madison: University of Wisconsin Press, 1998), p. 177.

47 *"I'm sure Marcelo planted those Indians there"*: Author interview.

CHAPTER FOUR: THE VILLAGE

50 *"You can't protect what you don't understand"*: The quotation is written as remembered by both Francisco Marinho and Marcelo dos Santos during interviews with the author.

51 *"So what happened after that?"*: The dialogue comes from tapes recorded during a meeting that Marcelo and Vincent had with Luiz Claudio in Porto Velho.

51 *"We guessed it might have been either some fugitive . . . Denes and Hercules"*: Carelli tapes.

53 *It was hot, and the sun burned straight overhead as Marcelo hiked . . . "was an entire village"*: Descriptions and dialogue in this section come from Carelli tapes; some descriptions of weather and background were taken from FUNAI expedition reports provided by the Justice Ministry.

54 *Later that same day . . . "My head hurts"*: Carelli tapes.

56 *Laborers employed by the Modelo Ranch were bulldozing*: Ibid.

59 *such as the time a rubber tapper infected with measles encountered the Tupari tribe in 1954*: John Hemming, *Die If You Must: Brazilian Indians in the Twentieth Century* (London: Pan Macmillan, 2004), p. 63.

60 *Chupinguaia was an imperfect grid of pitted dirt roads*: The town has changed considerably since the mid-1990s. The descriptions provided here come from a blend of archival video footage and photographs, recollections of visitors to the town in the mid-1990s, and my own travels in the city a decade later.

61 *She invited him in, and they talked for an hour*: Carelli videotapes.

61 *"I didn't sleep at all last night because of this" . . . as soon as he saw them, she said*: Ibid.

62 *Many of the regional justice officials and politicians had come to Rondônia to start ranches*: Even today, the vast majority of political officials—including the state's governor and national senators—are ranch owners who first came to Rondônia as agricultural entrepreneurs.

CHAPTER FIVE: THE ACCIDENTAL ENVIRONMENTALIST

65 *Between 1980 and 2000, the number of Brazilians*: This comes from Brazilian census figures I quoted in an article for the *Washington Post*, "Evangelicals Eyed in Brazil," February 3, 2007.

67 *"Eat it on the bus"*: The quote is written as recollected by Altair Algayer.

67 *Most of the route was unpaved*: David Price, *Before the Bulldozer: The Nambiquara Indians and the World Bank* (Cabin John, Md.: Seven Locks Press, 1989), p. 21.

69 *The most common malarial parasite in the region*: Carol J. Pierce Colfer, Douglas Sheil, and Misa Kishi, *Forests and Human Health: Assessing the Evidence* (Jakarta: Center for International Forestry Research, 2006), p. 50.

71 *"These barbarians, who think only of robbing us or attacking us in ambush"*: John Hemming, *Die If You Must: Brazilian Indians in the Twentieth Centurty* (London: Pan Macmillan, 2004), p. 33.

71 *"Why would you want to do that?"*: As recollected by Altair Algayer.

71 *"Marcelo? Do you read me?"*: All dialogue in this section comes from Carelli tapes, and the physical descriptions come from the video and expedition reports.

73 *Anthropologists believe that when Europe*: Hein Van der Voort, *A Grammar of Kwaza* (Ossining, N.Y.: Mouton de Gruyter, 2004), p. 2.

74 *most lived independently of the others*: The anthropological history of the region was compiled by multiple sources, including Van der Voort's book and two different anthropological reports: Denise Maldi Meireles's "Populaçãoes Indigenas e a Ocupação Historica de Rondônia" (1996), and

Virginia Valdão's "Laudo Antropologocio—Indios Isolados do Igarape Omerê," Centro de Trabalho Indigenista (December 1996).

74 *Dutch linguist Hein Van der Voort, who has spent years working with the tribes*: Author interview with Van der Voort.

75 *Brazilian linguist Laércio Nora Bacela traveled to Rondônia*: The story of the Kanoe comes from author interviews with Bacela and the online *Encyclopedia of Indigenous Peoples in Brazil,* published by the Instituto Socioambiental.

76 *"He isn't good with the flute"*: The quotation is written as recalled by Algayer and Bacela.

77 *Altair revisited the site of the destroyed village*: All dialogue and descriptions of the December 6, 1996, encounter come from tapes shot by Carelli's assistant, FUNAI expedition reports authored by Altair and Marcelo, and interviews with those present.

CHAPTER SIX: WINDOWS TO HIS WORLD

85 *Purá sat on the wooden edge*: The descriptions of Purá crafting arrows were gathered from my own observations during visits to the Kanoe village.

87 *"That's big enough for a lion!"*: As recollected by Algayer.

89 *Since colonial times, whites had used gifts of tools and other energy-saving products to buy goodwill*: John Hemming, *Die If You Must: Brazilian Indians in the Twentieth Centurty* (London: Pan Macmillan, 2004).

89 *whole tribes had been wiped out by people who laced . . . firebombed them*: Hemming, p. 229.

90 *Purá scaled the forty-five-degree incline of a fallen tree*: Some of the detail in this section was gathered during my own honey-gathering trip with Purá in 2007.

91 *Researchers at the American Museum of Natural History found that*: Charles C. Mann, *1491: New Revelations of the Americas Before Columbus* (New York: Vintage, 2006), p. 335.

92 *Over the next several months, they continued to invite Purá and Owaimoro*: Expedition reports.

93 *"When I saw it get hit with the arrows"*: Carelli tapes.

94 *"I'm scared of them"*: All of the dialogue included in these sections through the end of the chapter detailing Kanoe and Akuntsu relations was preserved either by Carelli's tapes or by transcripts of interviews with the tribes conducted by FUNAI-employed translators. The descriptions come from the videotapes, expedition reports, and recollections of those present.

CHAPTER SEVEN: SAVAGES

105 *In the first half of 1997, Brazil's environmental protection agency temporarily*: FUNAI expedition reports.

105 *Throughout the second half of 1997, Marcelo:* Ibid.

106 *During a four-day trek in September*: Carelli tapes and expedition reports.

107 *a mode of thought called positivism*: To describe positivism and its influence on Brazil's indigenous policy, I consulted numerous sources, particularly Hemming and Ramos.

108 *"It may seem strange that among the first-fruits of the efforts of a Positivist"*: Theodore Roosevelt, *Through the Brazilian Wilderness* (Teddington, U.K.: Echo Library, 2007), p. 29.

108 *Freud suggested that primitive Indians*: Mércio P. Gomes, *The Indians of Brazil* (Gainesville: University Press of Florida, 2000), p. 127.

108 *Jean Piaget, a Swiss philosopher*: Ibid., p. 126.

109 *In the country's civil code of 1916*: Gomes, p. 84.

110 *a jury in Rondônia found a man guilty of genocide*: Hemming, p. 299.

110 *Brazil's permanent representative to the United Nations*: As reported in UN Human Rights Communication no. 478, September 29, 1969.

110 *"get out of the swamp of underdevelopment and backwardness"*: From an article by James Brooke in the *New York Times*, April 12, 1992, p. 17.

110 *"There will be no more Indians in the twenty-first century":* Ramos, p. 46.

111 *One afternoon in 1997, Altair was staying in the Rio Omerê camp*: Descriptions of the massacre of Owaimoro come from Altair's memory and from a description filed in a 1997 FUNAI memorandum received by the Justice Ministry.

CHAPTER EIGHT: LETTING GO

116 *In the second half of 1997 and the early part of 1998, Marcelo and Altair found several additional huts*: Expedition reports.

117 *In July 1998, workers on Jaime Bagattoli's property*: Ibid.

118 *In the early 1900s, observers believed the Sirionós' culture*: William Balée, "The Sirionó of the Llanos de Mojos, Bolivia," in *The Cambridge Encyclopedia of Hunters and Gatherers* (Cambridge, U.K.: Cambridge University Press, 1999), p. 105.

118 *Early Jesuits in Bolivia*: Charles Erasmus, *Man Takes Control: Cultural Development and American Aid* (Indianapolis: Bobbs-Merrill, 1961), p. 365.

119 *Possuelo believed that in this case the lone Indian's death was inevitable; ranchers or loggers would kill him*: Author interview.

119 *FUNAI gives its sertanistas an* Operational Manual: Ramos, p. 153.

122 *"Symptomatically, the manual is almost silent"*: Ibid.

122 *Purá finished packing for the expedition on the morning of August 1, digging around . . . and his right to be left alone*: Physical descriptions and all dialogue come from Carelli tapes; additional details of the expedition and encounter were found in the FUNAI expedition reports authored at the time of the encounter by Marcelo and Altair.

CHAPTER NINE: BATTLE LINES

133 *In one of the oldest neighborhoods in the city lived a doctor named Newton Pandolpho*: Author interview.

134 *"They're going to fight it hard"*: The quotation is written as remembered by Pandolpho and Marcelo.

135 *"It's incredible"*: Armando Antenore, "Justica interdita 60 km2 por um indio," *Folha de S. Paulo,* March 7, 1999, p. 13.

136 *The project had been authorized by the international lending institution to assist the Brazilian government*: The phrasing is taken from a progress report published by the World Bank, 1997, Planafloro Project.

137 *to James Fenimore Cooper's*: James Fenimore Cooper, *The Last of the Mohicans* (New York: Penguin Popular Classics, 1994), p. 32.

138 *Even within FUNAI, people were asking such questions*: Leonardo Sakamoto and João Marcos Rainho, "The Last Survivor," *Problemas Brasileiros,* March–April 2000.

139 *Moral psychologists call it the Trolley Problem*: To provide the overview of the Trolley Problem concept, I consulted Fiery Cushman, Liane Young, and Marc Hauser, "The Psychology of Justice," in *Analyse & Kritik* (Stuttgart: Lucius & Lucius, 2006), p. 95.

140 *In Brazil, the indigenous population makes up about 2 percent*: Anthony Stocks, "Too Much for Too Few: Problems of Indigenous Land Rights in Latin America," *Reviews in Advance,* May 20, 2005, p. 85.

141 *Eventually the Supreme Court would be saddled with*: Ibid.

141 *Among the most powerful politicians in the state of Rondônia*: The background about Lando—and his responses to FUNAI's allegations—come from

official FUNAI reports from 1999 and 2000, interviews with Julio Olivar Benedito, editor of the *Folha do Sul* newspaper, and articles in the April 29, 2000, edition of the *Expressão* newspaper.

CHAPTER TEN: THE CORRIDORS OF POWER

145 *On the morning of October, 10, 2000, Congressman Antonio Feijão*: Information in this section comes from the official congressional report of the congressional hearing, published by Brazil's federal government and titled *Relatório da comissão parlamentar de inquérito destinada a investigar a ocupação de terras públicas na região amazônica* (Brasília, 2001).

145 *The congressman had become one of Brazil's most vocal critics of Indian reserves*: "Estatuto do Índio agrada mineradoras," *Jornal da Tarde*, April 20, 2000.

145 *He had denounced several international*: "Anthropological Work Threatened," American Association for the Advancement of Science's Human Rights Program e-mail alert, January 26, 1998.

146 *Feijão also had proposed a law*: "Congressmen Want 'Acculturation Diploma' of the Indigenous Peoples of Roraima," *Indigenist Missionary Council Newsletter*, October 7, 1999.

146 *A year earlier, in 1999, Feijão also had sponsored a bill*: "Punishment for Environmental Crimes by Indians," *Gazeta Mercantil*, February 25, 1998.

146 *The tensions between the tribes*: James Brooke, "Boa Vista Journal; Gold Miners and Indians: Brazil's Frontier War," *New York Times*, September 7, 1993.

146 *Before entering politics, Feijão*: Tyler Bridges, "Amazon Gold Rush Leaves Behind Dross," *Christian Science Monitor*, September 27, 1988.

147 *The investigation seemed to be his way of keeping a promise*: "Parliamentary Inquiry Committee Will Investigate FUNAI," *Indigenous Missionary Council Newsletter* no. 362, May 27, 1999.

148 *"Indian trafficking is not something new in Marcelo's history"*: The dialogue and overview of testimony come from the congressional report of the hearing.

149 *Afterward, a separate Senate panel*: Information and all quoted testimony come from the official transcript of the Senate hearings, published in Brasília by the government's information service.

150 *Senator Valdir Raupp, who himself had worked*: Clarinha Glock, "A Crime with Many Suspects, No Arrests," from the Crimes Against Journalists Immunity Project website, December 1, 2000.

151 *said Botelho, who later would introduce legislation*: Isabella Kenfield, "Brazilian Agribusiness Boom's Dark Side: Violence and Plunder in the Amazon," *Brazzil Magazine*, October 16, 2008.

152 *"In the beginning of 1986, the farmers had made one clearing of ten thousand hectares"*: All quoted testimony comes from the congressional report.

CHAPTER ELEVEN: NEITHER BEAST NOR GOD

155 *By the end of 2000, approximately 80 percent of the "protected" land*: The deforestation figures are estimates included in a FUNAI archival report dated October 18, 2000.

155 *The peasants were part of the Movimento dos Trabalhadores*: Information regarding the MST comes from a variety of sources, including the group's own website: www.mstbrazil.org.

157 *The headquarters of the Socel Ranch was a humble grouping of stables and shacks*: The description of the area comes from Carelli's tapes and my own visits to the ranch; the encounter between Sordi and Altair, including all of the dialogue included here, was recorded by Carelli.

158 *At six o'clock on a wet November morning in 2000*: All dialogue comes from Carelli tapes, and descriptions come from the tapes and expedition reports.

162 *We are hardwired for company*: The descriptions of the physiological changes caused by isolation are described in Joe Robinson's article "Marooned," *Los Angeles Times*, June 15, 2004.

162 *Rousseau claimed that only when alone*: The quote is from Jean-Jacques Rousseau's *The Reveries of the Solitary Walker* (New York: New York University Press, 1979), p. 12.

162 *Thomas Merton praised solitude*: The quote appears in the essay "Notes for a Philosophy of Solitude" in Merton's *Disputed Questions* (San Diego: Harcourt Brace Jovanovich, 1985), p. 194.

162 *"But he who is unable to live in society"*: Aristotle's *Politics* (Charleston, S.C.: Forgotten Books, 1972), p. 3.

163 *"Man* lives *perhaps first of all in his skin"*: Tzvetan Todorov, *Life in Common: An Essay in General Anthropology* (Lincoln: University of Nebraska Press, 2001), p. 54.

163 *In 1932, a girl dubbed "Isabelle" by University of California researchers*: For the story of Isabelle I consulted Kingsley Davis's journal article "Extreme Isolation," which was collected in *Down to Earth Sociology: Introductory Readings*, edited by James M. Henslin, (New York: Simon & Schuster, 2007), p. 153.

164 *In the 1950s, the U.S. government's intelligence agencies*: The information comes from a memorandum from the FBI directorate dated April 25, 1956, and titled, "A Report on Communist Brainwashing."

164 *A 1963 clinical study that examined*: N. Burns and D. Kimura: "Isolation and Sensory Deprivation," *Unusual Environments and Human Behavior*, edited by N. Burns, R. Chambers, and E. Hendler (New York: Macmillan, 1963), p. 167.

165 *Researchers in Norway found that*: More information on the study can be found in *Man in Isolation & Confinement*, edited by John Rasmussen (Piscataway, N.J.: Aldine Transaction, 2007), p. 101.

165 *"Case studies of people undergoing extreme"*: Nicholas Epley, et al., "Creating Social Connection Through Inferential Reproduction: Loneliness and Perceived Agency in Gadgets, Gods, and Greyhounds," *Journal of the Association for Psychological Science* 19, no. 2 (2008).

165 *"The mind is a terrific device and it can generate"*: Author interview.

166 *Some of the region's tribes say that two brothers were the creators*: For the overview of the beliefs of the region's tribes, I consulted the work of several anthropologists, principally Lévi-Strauss and Betty Mindlin.

166 *The Nambiquara said that agriculture sprang*: Price, 13.

166 *He discovered that many of them believed*: Lévi-Strauss, p. 301.

167 *The Aruá tribe of Rondônia told the story*: Betty Mindlin, *Barbecued Husbands and Other Stories from the Amazon* (New York: Verso, 2002), p. 244.

170 *For example, the Nambiquara Indians didn't have a name*: Price, p. 13.

170 *One evening in early 2000, a storm*: Expedition reports.

172 *The Spix's macaw is a long-tailed*: "Species Factsheet: *Cyanopsitta spixii*," *Birdlife International*, retrieved July 24, 2008.

173 *The news of the lone macaw's existence*: "Rare Bird Feared Dead in Brazil," *Associated Press Online*, November 30, 2000.

173 *The bird had tried to mate*: Michael McCarthy, "Tragic Tale of the Loneliest Bird on Earth," *Independent*, June 7, 2000.

173 *"The bird had clung on grimly despite all odds"*: Ibid.

174 *He'd slyly smile at her, then stroke her hair*: Purá's physical advances toward the Akuntsu girl were captured by Marisol Soto, who filmed a documentary called *Indios* that was broadcast on Spanish television in 2002. Five years later I observed Purá's attempted courtship of the girl while accompanying him on a visit to the Akuntsu village; again, his advances were to no avail.

CHAPTER TWELVE: LARGER THAN LIFE

179 *In 1959, Sydney Possuelo was eighteen years old*: The anecdotes about Sydney's background as a sertanista come from numerous interviews with the author unless otherwise noted below.

181 *Before Orlando Villas Boas died at age eighty-eight*: From an obituary appearing in *Independent*, December 14, 2002.

181 *"the tick on Orlando's neck"*: Author interview.

181 *"You know, Orlando had malaria more than 200 times"*: The quote comes from an author interview, but the tally of Villas Boas's malarial bouts also can be found in Hemming's *Die If You Must*.

181 *Back in the 1970s, during a run-in with a colonist, five of his teeth*: This anecdote is included in John Hemming's profile of Possuelo, "Last Explorer of the Amazon," which appeared in *Geographical* magazine, February 2005.

182 *Some of his colleagues in FUNAI rolled their eyes*: Possuelo's reputation within the agency is complex: he is afforded tremendous respect for his dedication and passion for his work, but numerous former coworkers of his told me that they considered him egotistical and difficult to work with. The image of colleagues rolling their eyes is a literal one—more than one did exactly that while speaking of his personality quirks.

183 *a philosophy that more than one writer had labeled "quixotic"*: Sydney encouraged such comparisons. In 2005, when the city of Toledo, Spain, celebrated the four hundredth anniversary of Cervantes's epic, Sydney was invited to the ceremony and received a banner—which he keeps in his office in his apartment—dubbing him the "Don Quixote of the Jungle." It's one of his most prized possessions. "I've received many honors in my life," he told me, "but the Don Quixote one is the most emotional for me."

183 *In the early 1800s, the Indians of the Island*: For the story of the lone woman of San Nicolas, I relied on Joe Robinson's article "Marooned" in the *Los Angeles Times*, June 15, 2004.

184 *Fifty-eight years later . . . in Deer Creek Canyon in August 2000*: The story of Ishi is recounted in Theodora Kroeber's *Ishi in Two Worlds: A Biography of the Last Wild Indian in North America* (Berkeley: University of California Press, 1961). Some of the details, including those about the discovery of Ishi's brain in the National Museum of Natural History's storage facility, come from Orin Starn's book *Ishi's Brain: In Search of America's Last "Wild" Indian* (New York: W. W. Norton, 2004).

187 *A San Francisco newspaper published*: The poem was written by Ernest J. Hopkins and appeared in the *Bulletin*, April 1, 1916.

187 *His name was Carapiru*: In recounting the story of Carapiru, I consulted Andrea Tonacci's *The Hills of Disorder*, a 2006 Brazilian film that mixes documentary footage and dramatic reconstructions and features appearances by Carapiru, Sydney Possuelo, and others who were involved in the events described. Additional details included come from author interviews with Sydney and Orlando Possuelo, Tonacci, and Wellington Gomes Figueiredo. Two news articles written at the time of Carapiru's discovery also proved helpful: "An Indian Comes in from the Heat," by Brian Nicholson, the *Chicago Tribune*, November 27, 1988, and "Primitive

Survivor Finds His Lost Son," by Richard House, the *Independent*, November 10, 1988. All dialogue included in this section is transcribed from Tonacci's film, where the dialogue was reproduced using archival television footage from 1988 and reenactments.

189 *prompted Australian art critic Robert Hughes*: The quotation is cited in Benjamin Schwartz's "A Vision in Concrete," *Atlantic Monthly*, July–August 2008.

192 *The movie* Amazon, *shown worldwide in IMAX theaters*: The 1997 film was directed by Kieth Merrill and was nominated for an Academy Award.

192 National Geographic *had run a cover story*: The article appears in the 195 2003 edition of the magazine.

193 *But for all his savvy, Possuelo stands practically alone*: Diane Schemo, "The Last Tribal Battle," *New York Times Magazine*, October 31, 1999.

CHAPTER THIRTEEN: ONE MORE SHOT

197 *His temperature had started to climb*: The descriptions of Orlando's physical maladies come from his diary entries written at the time, which he provided to the author.

198 *In 2003, the governor of Rondônia flatly stated*: From Soto's documentary *Indios*.

199 *His relatives had spoken with FUNAI agents*: This information comes from interviews with FUNAI's Celso José dos Santos, who was among the agents who spoke with Sordi's family.

201 *Tunio and some of the other FUNAI workers*: Author interviews.

202 *On the morning of April 12, 2005*: The account of the expedition was compiled with the help of interviews with those present, Orlando's diary, and photographs taken by members of the team during the expedition. All dialogue is based on the recollections of those present.

207 *"Contacting him is a last resort for us"*: This quote comes from an interview I conducted with Sydney and Orlando in Brasília in 2005, days after Orlando had returned from the expedition.

207 *"We didn't know you then"*: The information about Sydney's reactions to the Korubo killings can be found in *Smithsonian*, "Out of Time," by Paul Raffaele, April 2005, p. 62.

209 *Mércio Pereira Gomes, who became president of FUNAI*: "Land Wars; Brazil's Indians," *Economist*, February 4, 2006.

210 *"I've heard this talk from ranchers, land speculators, prospectors and loggers"*: Sydney's remarks appeared in *O Estado de S. Paulo* on January 14, 2006.

211 *"There are people who can take over from Possuelo"*: Andrew Downie, "Champion for Brazil's Indigenous Gets Fired," *Christian Science Monitor,* January 26, 2006.

CHAPTER FOURTEEN: A NEW BEGINNING

213 *FUNAI has, on average, changed presidents at a rate of almost one per year*: From a list obtained from the agency.

214 *Carlos Antonio Siqueira—the supposedly impartial*: Details about Siqueira's efforts to discredit Indian reserve boundaries on behalf of agricultural and logging interests, as well as the criminal charges of lumber theft, were outlined in a release by Mato Grosso prosecutors and posted on the state's official website on November 29, 2006.

214 *In a letter to a local newspaper*: The letter was titled, "Celula 'Elite'?" and published in *Diario de Cuiabá* on December 5, 2006.

218 *They were in the middle of their trek inside the forest*: Expedition reports.

220 *"A single individual can be considered a 'people'"*: The quotation comes from an article by Felipe Milanez in FUNAI's magazine *Brasil Indigena,* July–September 2006.

220 *"The land is property of the Union"*: Ibid.

220 *In cities such as Seoul and Tokyo*: The population comparisons come from the report "Population Density: Selected International Urban Areas and Components" compiled by Demographia: The Wendell Cox Consultancy, Belleville, Illinois.

CHAPTER FIFTEEN: A NATION OF ONE

223 *After FUNAI distributed the pictures*: "Uncontacted Tribe Photographed Near Brazil-Peru Border," Survival International news release, www.survival-international.org, May 28, 2008.

223 *"It is like the Loch Ness Monster"*: The quote comes from my article, "In Amazonia, Defending Hidden Tribes," *Washington Post,* July 8, 2007.

223 *Meirelles decided to give them proof*: Gabriel\ Elizondo, "Finding Brazil's Isolated Tribes," Al-Jazeera.net, June 2008.

224 *After that report, the* Observer *newspaper*: Peter Beaumont, "Secret of the 'Lost' Tribe That Wasn't," *Observer,* June 22, 2008.

225 *The Chinese national news agency*: "Photos of Lost Amazon Tribe Are Fakes," Xinhuanet (http://news.xinhuanet.com), June 24, 2008.

225 *It took another month for the* Observer: Stephen Pritchard, "Comment: The Readers' Editor on How a Tribal People's Charity Was Misrepresented," the *Observer,* August 31, 2008.

225 *"In other countries they respect property rights"*: Author interview.

225 *Elsewhere, a monumental legal battle*: Adriana Brasileiro, "Brazil Supreme Court Rejects Challenge to Indian Land," Bloomberg News, December 10, 2008.

226 *"With this decision"*: Ibid.

Index

Page numbers in *italics* refer to illustrations.

INDEX

INDEX

INDEX

INDEX

About the Author

Monte Reel lives in Buenos Aires with his wife and daughter. He was the South America correspondent for the *Washington Post* from 2004 to 2008 and previously worked for the paper in Washington and Iraq.